AF411747

Strategy Management

Strategy Management

How to Plan, Execute, and Control Strategic Plans for Your Business

Kevin W. Tourangeau

McGraw-Hill Book Company

New York □ St. Louis □ San Francisco □ Auckland
Bogotá □ Hamburg □ Johannesburg □ London □ Madrid
Mexico □ Montreal □ New Delhi □ Panama □ Paris
São Paulo □ Singapore □ Sydney □ Tokyo □ Toronto

Library of Congress Cataloging in Publication Data
Tourangeau, Kevin W
   Strategy management.

   Bibliography: p.
   Includes index.
   1. Management.   2. Planning.   I. Title.
HD30.28.T67   658.4'012   80-18717
ISBN   0-07-065043-8

1234567890   DODO   8987654321

Printed and bound by R. R. Donnelley & Sons Company.

Contents

Preface

As we enter the 1980's, it is becoming clear that management is beginning an era of unprecedented attention to strategic planning. Developments of the previous decade significantly enhanced many of the key management functions but left strategic planning relatively untouched. Many of these developments were in the realm of budgeting and resource allocation. Consequently, the focus of a good number of organizations became restricted to short-term considerations. It was only in the late 1970's that organizations renewed their interest in strategic planning, and it is only now that new developments in this area have become popular.

These improvements in long-range planning involve a concept that is commonly called strategic business planning. The element which makes this concept unique and distinguishes it as a new development is the use of strategic business units as the primary vehicle of strategy formulation. Strategic business planning entails both rigorous attention to the environment within which the organization performs and the expression of a strategic position in some form of business portfolio matrix. A number of leading corporations and consulting firms have pioneered in refining various components of this concept. Today, strategic business planning is gaining momentum, and its effectiveness is being heralded by a large number of organizations.

Improvements in the strategic planning process are certainly overdue and most welcome by all. But they should not be expected to cure all that ails an organization. Recent developments are directed towards a specific area — long-range planning. They cannot be expected to address other shortcomings of the management process. Because of this, strategic business planning can best be seen as a partial solution to management problems. In order to significantly and permanently assist an organization, a more comprehensive form of treatment is required.

The current state of management practice is similar to that of data processing systems in the 1960's. Each component is a closed, self-sustaining entity representing an independent and sometimes conflicting endeavour. There is a need to unify and rationalize each of these independent management techniques. The similar situation in data processing ultimately resulted in the development of management information systems.

The intention of this book is not merely to recite the latest technology of strategic business planning. It goes beyond this to address the true challenge of management, which when met, can produce a continuous and powerful sense of direction in an organization, from the chief executive officer down to the lowest level employee. Strategic planning or any other management technique is of limited value by itself. Only a partnership with all parts of the management process – particularly execution, control and rewards can result in synergy and lead to substantial advancement. The philosophy and intent of this book are reflected in its subtitle, emphasizing a strategically managed environment through an integration of planning, execution and control.

In writing this book, I am exposing myself to criticism from my consulting colleagues as well as the academic community. Consultants will argue that each organization needs its own unique form of Strategy Management and that application of a "canned" approach is not feasible. Academics will argue that a "canned" approach is too simplistic and does not adequately address these complex issues. I believe that both criticisms are valid. Nevertheless, I have pursued the idea because I believe the benefits to be gained from employing such an exposition outweigh the shortcomings. Furthermore, I believe that readers will be able to tailor the thoughts presented in this book to their own management situations.

This book is oriented particularly in its examples, to private sector corporations. In no way am I suggesting that the concept cannot be applied to government institutions. It can, with slight modifications, while retaining the overall methodology. However, I have chosen not to cover government issues in this volume, for the attempt to deal with both the private sector and government institutions would do justice to neither. I believe that readers will derive most benefit from the book by being flexible in their approach to both types of situations.

Kevin W. Tourangeau

About the Author

Kevin W. Tourangeau is a senior management consultant in the Toronto office of Woods Gordon. He joined the firm after a number of years as head of his own management consulting organization. Previously he had been corporate cost accounting manager for the Bank of Montreal and worked as a member of the management staff in the systems division of Bell Canada. He also had extensive financial experience with Microsystems International Limited (a former subsidiary of Norther Telecom Limited).

Mr. Tourangeau received a Bachelor of Commerce degree from Loyola of Montreal (now Concordia University). He is a member of The Society of Management Accountants of Canada. The author of numerous books and magazine articles on planning and budgeting, he is also a popular lecturer.

1

The Concept of Strategy Management

The constant efforts of executives and academics to improve the management process have resulted in a steady flow of technological advances. Business and government institutions have received a series of new management tools. These tools are normally applicable to specific management functions rather than being comprehensive systems of management. Nevertheless, their areas of usefulness often overlap, and quite frequently they compete with one another. All have a number of strong points and a number of weak points. A list of some of the more famous management tools would include such names as management by objectives, time management, zero-base budgeting, strategic business planning, job enrichment, project management and program planning and budgeting. Each of these concepts has made a significant contribution to the art of management by bringing more sophistication, structure and discipline to the process.

The reaction of today's executive to these management techniques in many cases is one of confusion. Some executives see these techniques in conflict with one another and find it difficult to select any best one. Other executives see them all as natural complements within the management process and utilize all of them either in whole or in part. Exhibit 1-1 on the following page presents the scope of these management tools. The exhibit illustrates the focus of each as it relates to the management responsibilities of planning, execution and control.

The exhibit clearly suggest that there is a considerable duplication of focus with these tools. The result is a contest for the attention of management. More important, the exhibit points out that none of these management practices addresses the complete range of management concerns. Each has its limitations with respect to area of concentration and none is a final remedy to the challenges of management.

AN INTEGRATED APPROACH

The current state of management practice can best be viewed as a portfolio of powerful, individual and sometimes overlapping procedures. Recent developments have brought a wealth of publicity to these sophisticated tools. As such, they have been perceived individually and in opposition to one another. The immediate need of executives is to make some sense out of this array of management enhancement opportunities. There is a need to sort out and optimize the effectiveness of the different management techniques now soliciting attention from today's organizations. Strategy management has been developed to respond to these needs.

Strategy Management is a comprehensive rationalization of the full spectrum of issues confronting executives in their leadership of today's organizations. It is not a revolution in management philosophy. On the contrary, it is a natural evolution from the atmosphere created by many of the leading management tools. Strategy Management is most accurately perceived as an integration of the existing management philosophies into a unified and streamlined approach to the duties of organizational leadership. Inherent in this integration process is the elimination of duplication, redundancies and overlaps that the simple merger of existing management techniques would produce. Of critical importance is the fact that this integrated approach allows executives to address the entire scope of their obligations using only one natural process. Aside from being more efficient, this approach is a radical simplification in comparison to using multiple systems for each

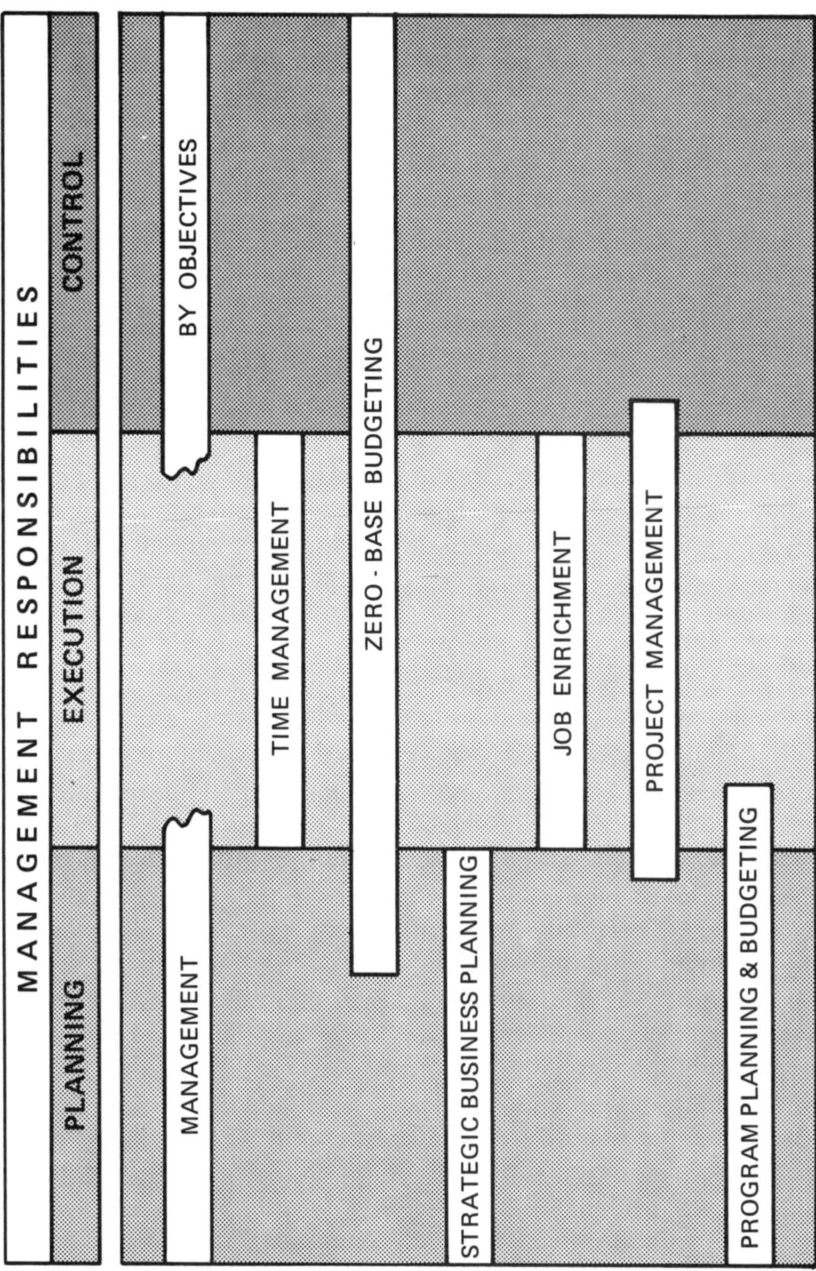

Exhibit 1-1 Management tools in relation to the responsibilities of management.

function of planning, execution and control. The importance of simplicity cannot be overemphasized in the increasingly more complex environments of which we are a part.

Exhibit 1-2 is an illustration of how Strategy Management relates to the major responsibilities of corporate and government stewardship. By itself, the exhibit is of limited value. It only becomes meaningful when compared to Exhibit 1-1. This comparison provides a visual display of the scope, simplicity and efficiency of Strategy Management versus the more traditional tools of management.

Presenting the idea of Strategy Management as an efficient merger of existing management techniques risks being an over simplification of the concept. In order to be both efficient and comprehensive, Strategy Management does introduce numerous fresh philosophies for consideration. These are required primarily to bridge the gaps between the traditional management tools. The vast majority of these original concepts are used to vitalize efforts centering around the function of long-range planning.

THE MANAGEMENT CHAIN

The simple consolidation of a number of the leading management techniques does not necessarily ensure that a comprehensive management program will evolve. The combined product may be lacking altogether in some areas of attention upon which none of the individual concepts focus. In addition, some of the areas may be addressed in an inadequate or incomplete fashion. These conditions certainly do exist with respect to the items of our concern. There are a number of such gaps in which Strategy Management is required to inject new and unique ideas to produce a continuous and complete flow of management thought. These gaps can be identified by comparing the major functions of management to the major techniques incorporated into the Strategy Management process. A matrix comparison of these two sets of variables is presented in Exhibit 1-3.

The exhibit illustrates that the primary focus of these major management tools is in the areas of short-range tactical planning, execution and control. In these areas, Strategy Management will be required to contribute only a limited number of additional

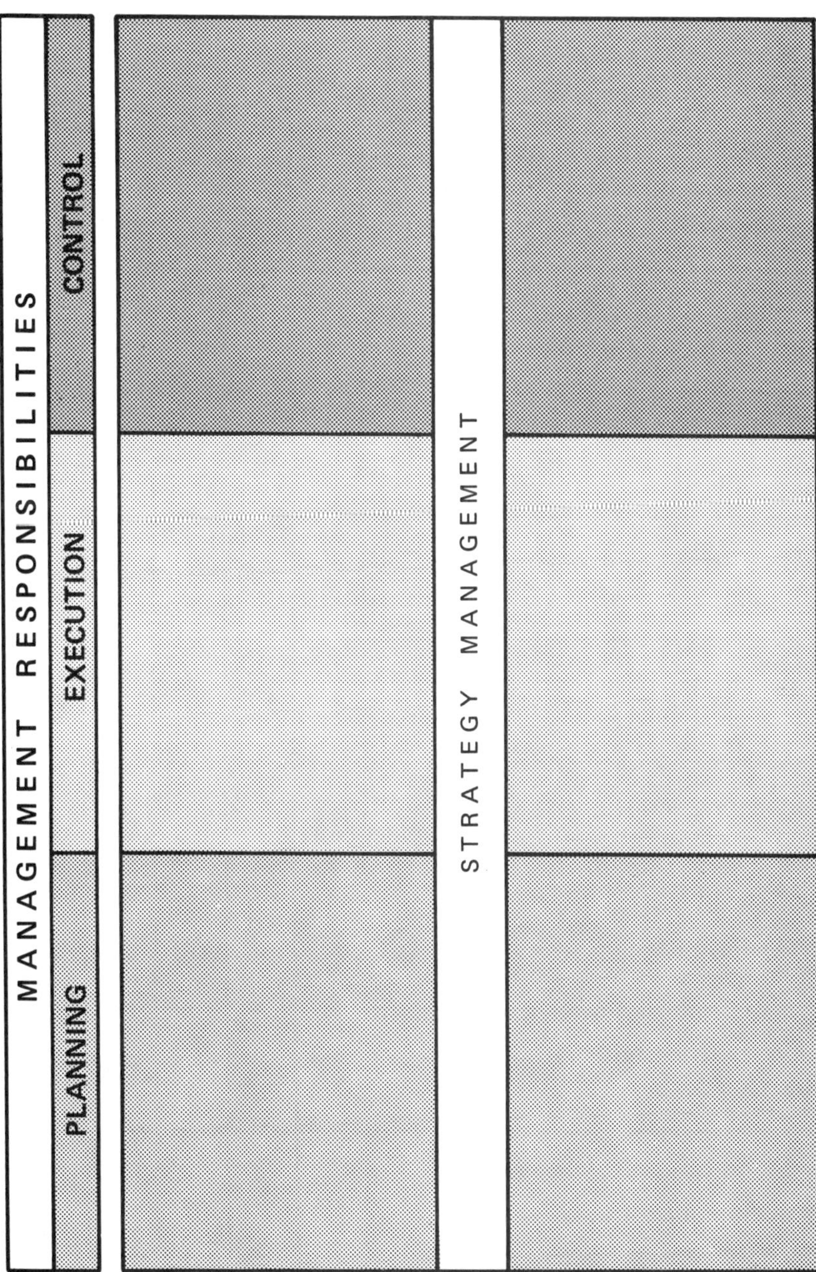

Exhibit 1-2 Strategy Management in relation to the responsibilities of management.

Major Management Functions \ Popular Management Tools	Management by objectives	Time management	Zero-base budgeting	Strategic business planning	Job enrichment	Project management	Program planning and budgeting
Evaluating the overall organizational purpose							
Selecting the primary businesses in which to be involved				●			●
Assessment of threats and opportunities				●			
Formulating patterns of strategic behaviour				●			●
Budgeting and short-term resource allocation	●		●			●	
Execution of plans		●	●		●	●	
Control of costs and results	●		●			●	
Rewards for realizing objectives	●						

Exhibit 1-3 Major management functions in relation to popular management tools.

thoughts to the process. This is the mature area of management behavior. The exhibit also illustrates that there are a number of areas which receive little or no attention from these major management techniques. It is in these areas where the majority of newly created ideas associated with Strategy Management will be unveiled.

The strength in the middle stages of the management process as depicted by Exhibit 1-3 indicates that there is something of an imbalance in the overall system. The stage of execution is the focal point. The pre-execution and post-execution stages receive little or no attention. This is comparable to a person owning a fine and sophisticated automobile but not knowing where to go with it and what to do on arrival. This imbalance is the major point of attack of Strategy Management.

Strategy Management approaches the management function as a chain of events. Each link is of equal importance and deserves equal attention. This is accomplished not by de-emphasizing the aspects pertaining to execution but by emphasizing the two extreme ends of the management cycle — namely planning and rewards. The aim is to equalize the strength of each link of the management chain by strengthening the weak points rather than

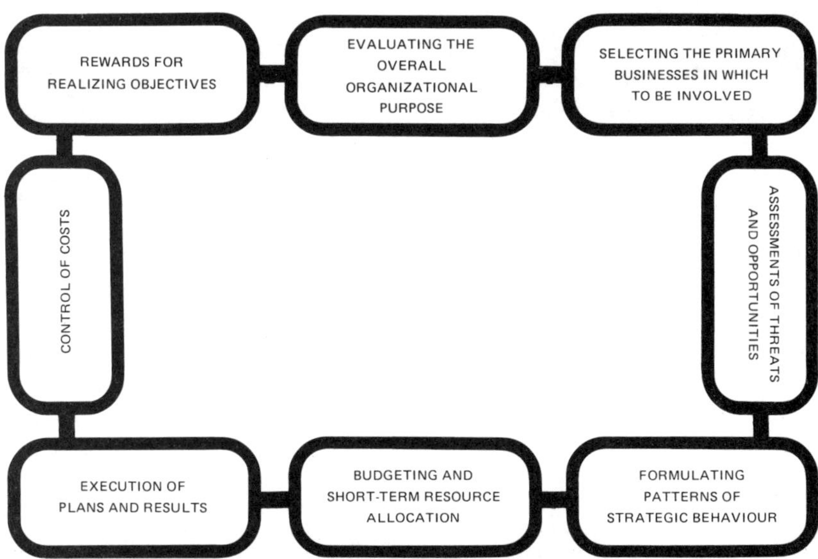

Exhibit 1-4 The management chain.

weakening the strong points. Needless to say, the overall effectiveness of the management process can be measured by the strength or weakness of its least capable component. The Strategy Management philosophy emphasizes balance and quality as they pertain to each segment of the management process.

CHARTER OF OBJECTIVES

The Strategy Management process is a cycle of events that deserves to be repeated. It is not a once in a lifetime undertaking designed to cope with a specific problem and then vanish upon solution. Although it has significant repercussions on the day to day management of an organization, it is not something that should be repeated constantly throughout the year. As a matter of good habit, the Strategy Management cycle is best repeated on an annual basis. This degree of frequency permits an organization to complete the cycle in a timely manner. It also allows an organization to build upon its existing data base rather than performing a complete reconstruction job as would be the case if the process was only repeated every two or three years. The contingency plans developed through the Strategy Management process eliminate any requirement to repeat the cycle more frequently than annually. Once a year is a happy and effective medium for embarking upon the Strategy Management process. The Strategy Management process begins with the charter of objectives. The charter of objectives is a concise statement of the central and fundamental concepts upon which an organization is based. It is the organization's "reason for being" from which all subsequent activity will flow. The charter of objectives describes the needs of society to which it is attempting to respond as well as the ability of the organization to meet those needs. This is a long-term statement of goals. As such, it is critically important that the charter of objectives be "right" or "sound" since it is the base upon which the organization will stand or fall. Conversely, the charter of objectives is not something that is likely to change on a regular basis. It can best be viewed as a fixed starting point for the Strategy Management process and should require little amendment from year to year.

Establishing a meaningful charter of objectives to initiate

the Strategy Management process may simply involve a dusting off or rejuvenation of the organization's existing statement of mission. The rejuvenation process would include a refinement and embellishment of the current perception of the organization's purpose to both improve and clarify a somewhat neglected issue. The importance of producing a superlative quality charter of objectives cannot be over emphasized. It is the cornerstone upon which the organization and its management philosophies are constructed.

The mere existence of a statement of the organization's reason for being, even of outstanding quality, can only be of limited value. This statement needs to be applied to the real world in order to take on a tangible sense of meaning. Such an application constitutes a communication and expansion of this organizational constitution into a concrete working philosophy. The working philosophy is a high level policy statement defining the organization's position with respect to a number of key ideological options. To name a few, the organization needs to explain its stance with respect to:

1. Desired market position.
2. Employment of technology.
3. Profitability.
4. Productivity.
5. Workforce development.
6. Public responsibility.

When an organization has identified its relationship with each of these issues, an operating base for the institution is created. A long-range sense of direction evolves as an extra dimension to the organization's reason for being. When included as part of the charter of objectives, it represents the first attempt to express the spirit of the institution in tangible terms.

CORPORATE STRATEGY

The task of developing the charter of objectives is reserved exclusively for the senior executive echelon of the organization. To maximize its impact, the charter must be introduced throughout the various levels of management. This introduction process is a progressive communication of the working philosophy to all levels of the institution. The ultimate goal is to enable all employees to see their role in the organization in the light of the charter of objectives. The first stage of this process is the development of corporate strategy. The corporate strategy flows from the charter of objectives and is expected to reflect a consistent direction for the organization. In essence, the corporate strategy commits the high-level goals of the organization to writing. What makes it different from the charter of objectives is that it relates these goals to key organizational units. These organizational units are called strategic business units (SBU's). Depending upon the current organizational structure of the institution, strategic business units may equate to already established entities. In other cases, strategic business units will represent artificial organizational creations.

Regardless of the formal organizational structure, a strategic business unit is best described as a natural segmentation of the overall organization into a discrete and independent business mission. Normally a strategic business unit describes a stand-alone undertaking with its own portfolio of markets, competitors and resources. Quite possibly, it is a module of the organization that could be divested or acquired as a unified operation.

The strategic business unit itself does not have an active role to play in the formulation of corporate strategy. Its opportunity to become involved begins during the next step of the Strategy Management process. Senior management is the author of corporate strategy. To fulfill that mandate, senior management must accomplish two things:

1. The identification of the appropriate businesses in which the organization ought to be involved. Inherently, this involves the actual identification of the strategic business units themselves.
2. The extrapolation of the charter of objectives into meaningful policy directions for each of these desired businesses as represented by strategic business units.

To accomplish these results, senior management embarks upon a two-part assessment of the suitability of the portfolio of business opportunities with which it is confronted. The first step is to assess the current and future attractiveness of the various industries of which the respective businesses are a part. Such an examination will produce an overall understanding of the appropriateness of each business in terms of the ambitions of the organization. Secondly, senior management reviews the competitive position that it enjoys within each of these industries. Again, this is done on both a current and projected basis. The result will yield an accurate understanding of the strategic position of each component of the organization. When the results of these studies are consolidated, the overall strategic status of the organization can be easily identified. Most important, senior management will be able to intelligently identify which businesses are appropriate to pursue.

There are two components to realizing the other objective of producing policy direction. One component is determining the desired strategic action. The other is blending it with the charter of objectives. In relation to the **current** strategic position of each business, senior management selects its **desired** strategic position consistent with its ability and external industry conditions. The **difference** between these two positions precisely identifies the strategic action required. These actions are expressed in terminology consistent with the charter of objectives to produce a definite sense of direction for each of the organization's businesses. The result is a meaningful corporate strategy illustrating the role each strategic business unit is expected to play in pursuit of the organization's fundamental reason for existence.

STRATEGIC BUSINESS UNIT ANALYSIS

The progression from the charter of objectives to an identification of the portfolio of businesses with which the organization should be involved is an expression of corporate strategy and is the first major coordination event of the Strategy Management process. It is the first of a long series of endeavours designed to align the goals of the individual with those of the organization. The formulation of corporate strategy responded to the basic question — what are the major operating functions in which we should engage? Now it is the strategic business unit's turn to occupy centre stage by addressing the question — how are we best to compete within these businesses? Strategic business unit managers respond to this question by breathing life into the corporate strategy. Their mandate is best explained by looking at the purpose of strategy itself: to determine a means of employing resources against one's competitors in the best possible way. The middle managers of the strategic business units are charged with the mission of discovering the optimum manner in which to compete. They must base their decisions upon an appreciation of the abilities of the strategic business unit and those of its competitors. This formidable task can be broken down into the following components:

1. Confirm that senior management's perception of the current strategic position is accurate.
2. Identify the strategic opportunities and impediments facing the strategic business unit.
3. Organize the strengths and weaknesses identified into an exploitable arrangement.
4. Recommend a course of strategic action in response to the analysis.

The management of an organization's various strategic business units is much closer to the threshold of operations than senior management. For this reason, it is prudent to ask these middle managers to apply their knowledge to making an independent assessment of the strategic position of their respective strategic business units. Using more detailed analysis, the strategic business unit will either confirm or suggest amendments to senior management's perception of the situation. In any case, the objective is to reach agreement upon the current and desired status of the strategic business unit so that the appropriate analysis may continue.

The major thrust of the strategic business unit's efforts is to document the opportunities and threats that are likely to be encountered. Such a documentation results from a rigourous examination of the strategic business unit's own strengths and weaknesses as well as those of each of its major competitors. This examination is conducted by preparing a small series of profiles that will enable the strategic business unit to evaluate itself in relation to the other major industry participants. The profiles will focus on key areas of resources such as:

1. Financial resources.

2. Human resources.
3. Physical resources.
4. Organizational resources.

A thorough examination of each of these topics will provide valuable insight into the strategic business unit itself. Equally important, this examination will provide comparable insight into each of the major competitors. This knowledge is a sound foundation upon which to determine the optimum course of action.

Before a strategic business unit can make use of its analyses, the information collected needs to be assembled into an intelligible format. Strengths and weaknesses should be separated and their potential impact on the strategic business unit should be evaluated. This will provide an understanding of the leverage that can be applied when addressing any one particular strength or weakness. By arranging its various strengths and weaknesses according to the magnitude of potential impact on competitive position, a strategic business unit is in a position to confidently select an appropriate course of strategic action.

THE STRATEGY RECOMMENDATION

The culmination of the strategic business unit's effort is the presentation of its strategy recommendation. It is the pivotal point, where theory is translated into practice. Strategic business units are the places where management assertively expresses the manner in which it will pursue the realization of its objectives. The decisions flowing from the strategic business units have an absolute impact on the degree of an organization's success. It is imperative that all possible precautions be taken to ensure that optimum strategy evolves. This is the reason why the strategy recommendation is preceded by a comprehensive analysis performed by the strategic business unit.

The strategy recommendation proposes the precise course of strategic action as dictated by the unit's portfolio of strengths and weaknesses. The appropriate action will also be influenced by the unit's current strategic position consisting of both industry attractiveness and competitive position. Combined, all of these factors will produce a strategy recommendation that can be broadly classified into one of the following four categories:

1. Build strategies.
2. Maintain strategies.
3. Harvest strategies.
4. Divestiture strategies.

Each of these strategies has unique characteristics and requires different employments of resources and action. However, neither the choice nor the name of the strategy is important by itself. It is the manner in which the strategic business unit intends to carry out the strategy that is crucial. This is the heart of the strategy recommendation. By answering the question of how it proposes to pursue its objectives, the strategic business unit establishes a definite direction that will be followed to reach the desired goals.

THE TACTICAL PROGRAM

The major contribution of senior management to the Strategy Management process is the charter of objectives and its derivative of corporate strategy. Similarly, the major contribution of middle management is the strategic business unit analysis and the formal strategy recommendation. For any planning exercise to be complete and effective, it must involve all persons within the organization. Ultimately, the lower level or first line managers need to be initiated into the process. Strategy Management enlists the efforts of first line managers in a very serious way. Their responsibility is to prepare the tactical program of the organization.

The goal of the tactical program is to translate the strategy recommendations of the strategic business units into specific, day to day action plans for each employee. Accordingly, the tactical program completes the planning phase of the Strategy Management process. Tactics differ from strategy in the point of focus. Tactics are more immediate and have a significantly more restricted time span. The tactical program attempts to retain consistency and meaning as it defines the role of each employee in support of the organizational objectives.

The tactical program is comprised of variable components and discretionary components. The variable components can be further categorized into a revenue program and a direct cost program. These components are the traditional budgeting vehicles of an organization. Their role in the Strategy Management process is significantly more pronounced than in traditional management situations. Consistent with the Strategy Management philosophy of upgrading the weak links in the management chain, the tactical program will perform a revitalized role in communicating and coordinating the objectives of the organization.

EXECUTION AND CONTROL

Long-range and short-range planning can have a deep and valuable impression upon an organization. Opportunities for managers to communicate with one another are uncovered. People can explain their problems, pose solutions and offer comments about topics of concern to the organization. The result is an increased sense of awareness that aids a manager in the understanding of his organization's operations. A better team approach cannot help but emerge.

Planning exercises do not yield immediate gains. Most advantages can only be gained through execution of the plan. This is the point where the investment matures and the gains can be tabulated. Execution is a vital link in the management chain. it must not be left to chance. The planning process requires a strong follow-through. Execution is a positive, high profile procedure. For proper execution, three ingredients are necessary:

1. A clear understanding of what is to be done.
2. A motivation to see that it happens.
3. A process to identify the degree of accomplishment.

The motivation to execute plans according to design can only be attained when managers are able to perceive some form of benefit that will accrue to them as the result of the prescribed action. On a short-term basis, this benefit may simply be the absence of a penalty for not performing according to plan. Regardless, a detection device is required that can fairly compare actual execution to plan and establish a basis upon which personal benefit can be distributed. This detection device is known as control. On a very short-term basis, control helps the manager himself to properly execute his program by providing him with feedback concerning the results obtained. On a more permanent basis, control provides an evaluation vehicle used as input to a reward scheme.

The Strategy Management concept places a strong emphasis on the aspect of control. It enjoys a significantly more comprehensive scope in comparison to traditional applications. Contrasting actual costs and revenues to those of the budget is only a small portion of the Strategy Management control facility. Other facets of control involve longer-term goal accomplishment, non-monetary goal accomplishment, achievement of results and simply the preparation of high quality plans. Strategy Management believes that control must operate over the full spectrum of planning issues. If any aspect of planning is ignored, managers may immediately begin to lose motivation. In this area, the design and existence of the control system can make a major contribution in ensuring proper execution.

REWARDS

A natural companion to any control system is a reward process. Rewards are part of the basic purpose for the existence of a control mechanism. The function of control acts as a means to determine when rewards are deserved — either negative or positive — and to what degree. This determination is extremely important when one considers that rewards are the "fuel" ingredients of the management process. Even the best plans and ideas need management action in order to become reality. Management activity is ignited when the rewards for doing so become known. This is a basic fact of human nature. Unfortunately, many of today's organizations address the reward issue in only an elementary fashion. A corresponding degree of employee motivation can be expected.

Strategy Management brings the function of rewarding into a strong and equal partnership with the other links of the management chain. Rewards are seen as the catalyst which bring vitality to each part of the management process. However, there is a characteristic of rewards which is unique to the Strategy Management process. Traditionally, an organization's control system describes the magnitude of the reward which each manager deserves. Magnitude is a value judgement. Strategy Management takes a novel approach to assigning value. Rather than value being measured only in terms of cost to the organization, it is correspondingly measured as gain to the employee. Strategy Management recognizes that these two approaches to measuring the value of rewards can produce significantly different results. By considering the degree of gain to the employee as well as the cost to the organization, rewards can be better understood and thus utilized in a more effective manner. The degree of gain available to an employee will be the creator of motivation. Harmony between a reward's gain to the employee and its cost to the organization is the only sound basis upon which to foster managerial motivation.

A further dimension of the Strategy Management reward process is its comprehensiveness. Preceding the reward function is a thorough planning exercise involving all levels of management and including a vast variety of issues and topics. For the reward process to be a partner to this planning effort, it too must be thorough and comprehensive. Consequently, rewards disbursed through the Strategy Management process will be triggered by a combination of both financial and non-financial as well as short-term and long-term issues. The employment of such a comprehensive reward scheme is the only way to adequately provide motivation to all segments of the employee's responsibilities.

AN ENTREPRENEURIAL ENVIRONMENT

Strategy Management attempts to be an integrated and efficient approach to managing an institution. It organizes a variety of existing management concepts into a sensible sequence of activities, supplements the deficiencies with new ideas and arrives at an effective process of managerial planning, execution and control.

Exhibit 1-5 is a summary of the communications flow associated with Strategy Management. It illustrates how the information developed with the organization's charter of objectives is refined, confirmed, expanded and transformed to arrive at a tactical program meaningful to first line managers and how it then proceeds through the stages of control and rewards. Each step of the Strategy Management process is associated with the

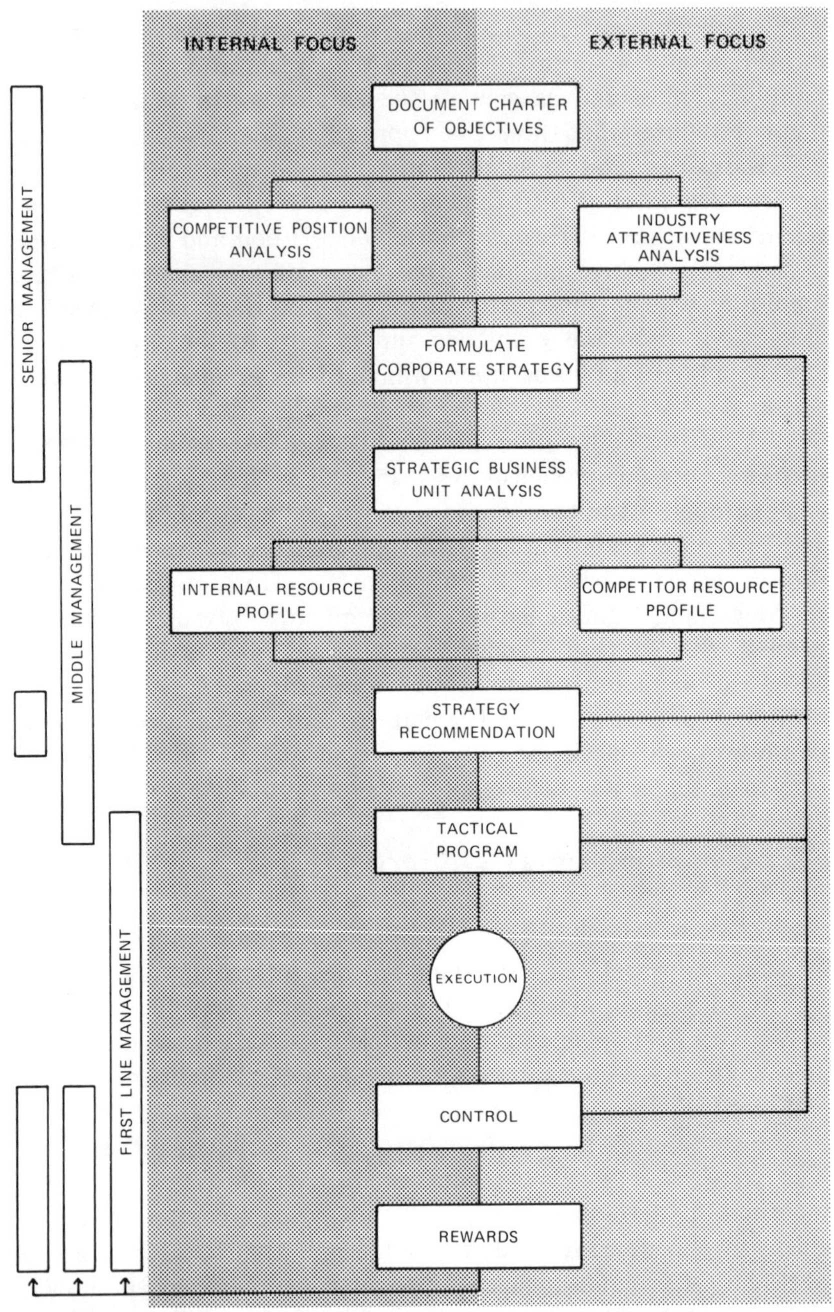

Exhibit 1-5 The Strategy Management communications flow.

level of management responsible for it. Finally, the process is divided between its internal focus and external focus to emphasize the foundation upon which it is created.

Although these mechanical arrangements tend to reduce the drama associated with the concept, and perhaps over-simplify it, there is actually a fundamental philosophical change inherent in the idea of Strategy Management. The change is illustrated by the responsibility awarded to the various levels of management.

The role of an organization's senior executive matures to a more policy minded, long-term oriented planning and reward function. This is consistent with contemporary developments in the art of management. Lower level managers are more intimately involved with the organization's communication process. They are awarded more trust and responsibility and as a consequence are expected to act as more dynamic individuals. However, the major philosophical change with Strategy Management involves middle management. Clearly, Strategy Management calls upon the talents of middle management as never before. Middle management is delegated the authority to take raw policy and to process it into refined plans of action. This monumental task is one of bringing an idea to a state of realization. In short, it is being an entrepreneur.

Traditionally, an organization had only one entrepreneur — its leader or chief executive officer. Recent times have seen such a strain put on this position that the leader can no longer effectively cope with the conditions of being the sole entrepreneur. Simultaneously, middle management has developed an appetite for more scope, responsibility and authority. Strategy Management solves this dilemma by lowering the entrepreneurial function to involve the middle management level. It satisfies the demand for "more" from middle management and rationalizes the leadership function as well. Making entrepreneurs out of middle managers enriches the culture of the organization to a degree enjoyed by only a small number of organizations.

2

The Scope of Strategy Management

As executives are confronted with new management tools or processes, one of their instinctive actions is to immediately search for an answer to the question of whether the concept is applicable to their organization. To find this answer, the executive will develop a basic appreciation for the major principles of the concept. With this knowledge, he will begin to test the characteristics unique to his organization against these principles in order to determine if there is a harmonious correlation. Should the outcome be positive, the new concept is deemed to be suitable to the organization.

To understand the applicability of Strategy Management to any given organization, the issue needs to be addressed from two points of view. One is theoretical. The other is practical. This dual approach is essential with Strategy Management because conflicting results are often possible.

Strategy Management is a logical approach to matching an organization's potential activities to both the needs of the society which it serves and the strengths and resources which it possesses. In a radically simplified description, Strategy Management is setting an objective and then proceeding to realize it. The question then remains — what type of organization is suited to this sequence of management action? In response to this question, it is immediately obvious that whether an organization manufactures one product or another has little bearing on the answer. Strategy Management is a behavioral philosophy unrestricted by the type of product which comes off the end of the assembly line. Similarly, the nature of the industry itself has little influence on the decision of whether Strategy Management is applicable. Service industries as well as manufacturing industries can readily identify with the concept. Perhaps the most significant question is whether non-profit institutions can suitably exploit the characteristics of Strategy Management. This question is popular because many people believe that without a profit incentive an organization has no sense of direction.

Non-profit institutions have a strong need for good management. Like any other organization, these institutions and their offspring have certain needs of society to fulfill and as such require a plan in which to do so. Since these two criteria are present, the non-profit environment can benefit to the fullest degree from the utilization of a Strategy Management process.

In summary, we may conclude that all organizations — because of their goal/execution relationship — can find Strategy Management to be a suitable operating endeavour. Only those organizations without goals or objectives would necessarily be deemed as unsuitable for the Strategy Management concept. However, is it possible for an organization to exist without goals or objectives? In many instances, we may conclude that a certain organization has no goals. At best the goals may be unclear or in conflict with one another. Such a situation can be only temporary at best.

By definition, all organizations have goals and objectives. Organizations are groupings of people and resources. A group exists simply because it shares a common purpose among its members. Without a common purpose, the group loses its cohesion and ceases to exist as an entity. For these reasons, all organizations must inherently have a set of goals and objectives. Granted, they may not be clearly documented and may be poorly explained, but every organization seeking more than a temporary existence is based upon goals and objectives. For this reason, there are no enterprises or institutions which are theoretically unsuitable to the concept of Strategy Management.

STRATEGY MANAGEMENT IN PRACTICE

The difference between theory and practice can be very alarming with respect to the applicability of Strategy Management to any given organization. There are significant obstacles which may render the use of Strategy Management impractical. What is of interest is the pattern which these obstacles form. The pattern of non-suitability does not follow the lines of a specific industry. Nor does it focus on government institutions. The pattern of situations where Strategy Management is not applicable to an organization follows a certain management style. This management style may reside in any type of organization and is not overly associated with any particular industry or sector. Before examining this management style, let us first explore what management styles **are** conducive to the Strategy Management concept. This will help clarify the subject.

Strategy Management has already been described as a simple and logical approach to planning, execution and control. What has yet to be sufficiently illustrated is the degree of physical and emotional effort that is required to make the process function. Regardless of its simplicity and logic, Strategy Management takes a lot of work. Issues are investigated and many hard decisions need to be made. Such activities require foresight and discipline. Management styles that display eagerness, confidence, discipline, creativity and a willingness to try something new are the best candidates for undertaking a Strategy Management program. In contrast, those organizations whose management teams do not possess these characteristics are poor risks for such adventures.

From these statements, one may conclude that Strategy Management is suitable for good managers and unsuitable for bad managers. However, the intention is not to label one style versus the other. The intention is to simply explain the practical limitations of the Strategy Management process. It takes a certain breed of management team to make it work. Before deciding whether the process is suitable to any particular organization, an understanding of the characteristics of this management breed is essential. It takes an executive who knows what he wants and is prepared to work for it.

The extent of this practical limitation concerning Strategy Management is often underestimated. Based upon the principle that senior executives are paid to operate in an eager and disciplined fashion, it would appear that this requirement would not be a great impediment. However, to blindly assume that the management of an organization does or will act in such a fashion is folly. More often than not, managements behave in the opposite manner. Protectionism and procrastination frequently overshadow the traits of eagerness and discipline. An organization — regardless of the nature of its operations — whose management team is not of this special breed will experience much discomfort when confronted with the idea of Strategy Management.

APPLICABILITY TO SMALLER ORGANIZATIONS

It has been asserted that the focus of an organization's operations, be it product or service oriented, has little effect upon its suitability to Strategy Management. The determining factor is the style or attitude of the organization's management. Before leaving the question of which organizations are suited to the concept of Strategy Management, one further factor should be considered. This is the size of the organization.

Again, there is a theoretical side and a practical side to the question of how an organization's size affects its suitability for Strategy Management. Like the nature of an institution, size has no theoretical limitation. The logic and universality of the process make this so. However, one must seriously question the practicality of using such a comprehensive and sometimes formal management philosophy in a small business. Although many small business persons will argue that they can utilize advanced management techniques just as well as larger organizations, there is often no apparent reason for them to do so.

Strategy Management projects its primary strengths in the areas of communication and coordination. Difficulties in these two areas normally increase in direct proportion to the size of the organization. As a corollary, small businesses often do not experience the same magnitude of communication and coordination problems as do their medium and larger size counterparts.

For this reason, it may not be a wise investment of resources to embark upon a Strategy Management program when only a relatively minor problem needs to be solved. Small businesses can apply the principles of Strategy Management in a drastically less formal manner and still reap maximum benefits. As a conclusion, it is best not to discourage small businesses from employing the concept. Such enterprises should be encouraged to use the process for purposes of providing direction and control. At the same time less rigid procedures need to be employed so that the cost/benefit characteristic is more favourable to a small business environment.

APPLICABILITY TO PARTS OF THE ORGANIZATION

Having seen that Strategy Management is applicable to organizations of all types and sizes, we now turn to the smaller parts of an organization. Are there certain areas unsuitable to the idea of Strategy Management within a given organization? The answer to this question is simple − no. All parts of an organization have a role to play in the fulfillment of its objectives; thus, all parts can participate in this management process designed to address the complete planning, execution and control needs of the institution. Nevertheless, there are some occasions when an organization would not use Strategy Management in one hundred percent of its operations.

While introducing Strategy Management, an organization may find it easier to do so in a sequential manner using different parts of its operations. Such a tactic could respond to a situation where to implement Strategy Management in total would simply be too large a task. Rather than delaying the implementation until the whole organization was completely prepared, a partial implementation will at least permit certain parts of the organization to begin realizing the benefits of a Strategy Management program. This type of approach also permits any fine tuning of the process to be made before engaging other parts of the organization.

The sequential approach to implementation may also seem to be an intelligent way in which to reduce the risk associated with the process. This is true but the degree of risk minimization

is of little significance — simply because there is little risk involved. The introduction of Strategy Management can do no harm.
It can only help to increase an organization's awareness of itself
and competitors. Should the worst case materialize, an organization can only be in a better informed and more confident position
than at the outset of the program.

3

Costs and Benefits of Strategy Management

The decision of whether or not to become involved with Strategy Management is likely to be strongly influenced by the amount of effort required to operate the process as compared to the results which are likely to be realized. As with any management adventure, costs and benefits are examined to determine whether the undertaking would be viable for the organization in question. Predicting the costs that an organization is likely to incur and the benefits which it will subsequently enjoy is a rather difficult task. Costs and benefits are determined by a series of variables which are both unique to the organization and perpetually changing. As such, no one can produce a formula which will permit an organization to exactly calculate its future cost/benefit position. However, we can describe the topics and framework which will allow an organization to assess the costs and benefits of Strategy Management within its own particular environment and according to its own analysis procedures. This is done by exposing the different components of both costs and benefits and by describing the relationship between each. Nevertheless, the magnitude of each component is something that can only be estimated in a meaningful fashion by the particular organization.

Before examining the different components of costs and the different components of benefits associated with Strategy Management, it is important to discuss some issues which will permit each component to be evaluated in its proper perspective. One issue is the difference between start-up costs and operating costs. Every new process requiring an application of skills has a certain break-in period. The first cycle of Strategy Management will include many activities which need not be repeated in subsequent cycles. These activities are only necessary for the initial implementation of Strategy Management. In addition, experience will reduce the effort needed in subsequent cycles of Strategy Management. It is quite feasible to anticipate a twenty percent reduction in effort between the first and second cycles. Therefore, management should not expect the effort required during the first session of Strategy Management to be necessary on a continuing basis. This reduced expectation of costs in subsequent years is a more realistic view of the Strategy Management concept and will obviously produce a more attractive cost/benefit relationship.

Another issue worthy of consideration is more a statement of caution. There is a tendency among a number of executives to determine the costs associated with a certain undertaking and based solely upon that understanding make a decision whether or not to proceed. Costs by themselves are only half of the story. Any decision concerning the adoption of Strategy Management should be delayed until an appreciation of the benefits can be formulated to round out the consideration. It is possible for an organization to conclude that it cannot afford the costs of Strategy Management and then after further investigation conclude that no price is too high to obtain the benefits which are likely to result. A premature judgement about Strategy Management based exclusively upon an understanding of costs runs a high risk of being faulty.

The last issue to be considered also involves the subject of costs. Rather than costs expended, these are costs saved. The introduction of Strategy Management will negate the need for numerous existing management exercises and activities based solely on the fact of redundancy. When tabulating the extent of costs associated with Strategy Management, the costs of activities which no longer will be performed should be subtracted to produce an equitable understanding of the incremental effort involved. The description and volume of activities being rendered redundant by Strategy Management will vary significantly from one organization to the next. Later chapters of this book will provide the knowledge necessary to identify these activities.

When comparing the costs and benefits of any organizational undertaking, it is normal practice to equate the incremental costs to the incremental benefits gained through efficiency improvement. This practice is somewhat misleading when it is applied to Strategy Management. Strategy Management is not merely an efficiency promotion tool. It has many concerns other than simply finding a better way in which to accomplish the same results. Strategy Management is more concerned with effectiveness than with efficiency. It is concerned with determining what to do, when to do it and why it should be done rather than simply how to do it. For these reasons it is important to view the benefits of Strategy Management in their full scope rather than limiting the consideration to savings derived from efficiency improvement. The majority of Strategy Management benefits will be overlooked if only efficiency is considered. Strategy Management brings a new dimension to an organization rather than restructuring it.

TIME COSTS

One of the most comprehensive measures of costs associated with any new management process is the amount of input time required to bring about its proper function. The time requirements of Strategy Management are significant and need to be thoroughly understood. Each of the primary steps involved with Strategy Management as outlined in the first chapter has a corresponding time demand. In addition to the unique time demands of each of these steps, the levels of management involved will also vary. As a further complexity, the overall size and nature of the organization in question will have its own personal influence on the situation. To sort these factors out and to produce a high-level examination of the time costs associated with Strategy Management, a matrix comparing its different steps to the degree of time required from various levels of management is presented. This matrix appears in Exhibit 3-1 on the following page.

The exhibit indicates that all levels of management are intimately involved in the process. As the Strategy Management focus shifts from planning and policy making to execution and control, a similar shift in attention from senior management to lower management is transpiring. This shift is consistent with the traditional roles of management whereby senior management devotes the majority of its attention to long-range issues and more junior management addresses the day to day concerns.

The description of the magnitude of time costs contained in Exhibit 3-1 is intentionally vague. Only four categories are used. A more accurate indication of these costs is not possible because of the significant variations in size and management talents among organizations. A comprehensive understanding of the expected time costs for a given organization can be developed after reviewing the mechanics of Strategy Management as presented in later chapters. In the interim, it is sufficient to know that the time costs of Strategy Management will be significant. Without question, Strategy Management is a major management chore. This, to a large degree, is what establishes the potential for deriving meaningful benefits from the process.

PAPER COSTS

Paperwork is used primarily for two reasons. The most important is to act as a medium of communication. The other is to act as an information storage device. Communication is often viewed as something good or positive for an organization. As a corollary, it stands to reason that paperwork is good as well since it is a reflection of the communication process. However, from a more practical point of view, paperwork is often a reflection of over communication or communication of frivolous information. For these reasons, managers often see any form of paper as an evil and as something that should be eliminated. Obviously, this is carrying the point to an extreme. By itself, paper is not evil. On the contrary, only excessive or meaningless paperwork should be a target of abuse. With this philosophy of paperwork, Strategy Management seeks to document information on paper for only the two basic purposes of effective information trans-

Major Steps of Strategy Management \ Levels of Management	Senior Management	Middle Management	Lower Management
Documenting the charter of objectives	VERY HIGH	MODERATE	LOW
Formulating corporate strategy	VERY HIGH	HIGH	LOW
Strategic business unit analysis	HIGH	VERY HIGH	MODERATE
Strategic business unit recommendation	HIGH	VERY HIGH	MODERATE
Tactical program preparation	MODERATE	HIGH	VERY HIGH
Execution	LOW	HIGH	VERY HIGH
Control	LOW	VERY HIGH	HIGH
Reward	MODERATE	HIGH	MODERATE

Exhibit 3-1 The time costs of Strategy Management.

mission and the storage of re-usable data.

Even with these honourable intentions, the generation of paper, and hence its cost, is extensive in the operation of a Strategy Management program. Paper costs are regularly being incurred throughout the process. The paperwork primarily involves communication of summarized information at formal checkpoints throughout the cycle. The precise number of forms involved in the Strategy Management process can be learned in the later chapters of this book. These chapters will explain that in most cases there are no "rigid" forms to be used universally by all organizations. Instead, personalized paperwork for the organization in question will be suggested in order to meet the unique needs involved. Depending on the informality of some organizations, it may be possible to avoid the preparation of certain forms as well. These sets of variables combine to form a wide range of possible paper costs in support of Strategy Management. As the mechanics of the process are unveiled beginning with the next chapter, the nature of each form, its style and its related preparation costs can be estimated. At this time, the intention is simply to create an awareness that paper costs are a major factor in the cost/benefit equation of Strategy Management.

MANAGEMENT COSTS

In terms of cash outlay, the time costs and paper costs associated with Strategy Management are most extensive. Should an organization decide that the cost/benefit equation of Strategy Management is not attractive enough for it to proceed with the process in its own environment, excessive time or paper is likely to be cited as the reason. However, citing excess time or paper as a justification for not proceeding with Strategy Management is most probably a rationalization of the organization's inability to cope with another issue inherent in the process. This issue is management costs.

The management cost requirements of Strategy Management are not something upon which the organization must expend funds. Management costs are something intangible. To be specific, management costs relate directly to the effort required to make the decisions brought forward during the process. To say that a large number of decisions need to be made during a Strategy Management cycle is an understatement. More importantly, these decisions are regularly of a very serious nature. The trauma of making these decisions can often cause such a degree of discomfort that it impedes the acceptance of Strategy Management.

The decisions constantly made throughout the process can be classified into three categories. The first category involves decisions required to define the objectives of the organization. This is not a task of simply issuing a statement to that effect. A rigourous examination of all potential objectives and then the selection of those which will optimize the organizational portfolio must be carried out. The second category of decisions pertains to the creation of action plans or programs designed to support the objectives. In effect, this addresses the issue of execution. The last category of decisions focuses on the area of control. Control involves monitoring as well as establishing corrective action and is followed by rewards. These three categories of decision requirements appear to reflect the normal demands placed upon management. One can claim that it is exactly for these reasons that management gets paid what it does. However, to blindly assume that the management of an organization is willing to make these hard decisions can be naive.

Managers, even senior managers, are no different than anyone else. It is always easier to let things continue as they have in the past than to make a strategic correction. Through the information uncovered during the Strategy Management process, a need to make a series of operating course corrections is likely to be identified. However, management will find it easier to follow the established path of inertia. As mentioned in the previous chapter, Strategy Management requires discipline, enthusiasm and a willingness to face hard decisions on behalf of **all** levels of management. Such a situation may represent a level of management costs which an organization may not be prepared to pay.

STRICT GOAL ORIENTATION

Switching from the cost side to the benefit side of the ledger, Strategy Management has a number of significant positive features. The various benefits of Strategy Management are difficult to assemble in their order of prominence. A certain benefit may be of high importance in one situation and may have little value in another simply because of the unique and situational needs of the particular organization. For this reason, it is important not to assign any comparative degree of importance to the benefits of Strategy Management based upon their sequence of presentation in the remainder of this chapter. The current opportunities and deficiencies facing your organization will determine the relative merit of each component of benefits.

Successful executives are usually goal oriented executives. They establish an objective for themselves and then conduct their activities in an appropriate manner to realize these goals. Goals provide a focus which helps optimize the effectiveness of subsequent activities. Strategy Management has many of these same characteristics. However, rather than yielding personal benefits, Strategy Management yields organizational benefits.

Strategy Management begins with attentiveness to the goals and objectives of the organization — both long-term and short-term. Throughout the process, the consideration of and the devotion to the goals of the organization never relent. The goals and objectives of the institution act as a permanent benchmark against which all supporting activities are measured. This strict goal orientation of the Strategy Management process produces a more results conscious organization. The importance of this characteristic can best be measured by its absence. With a lack of knowledge pertaining to where it wants to go, an organization will find that any activities it chances to engage in will take it there. Certainly all organizations have some room to improve their orientation towards the issues and needs they were created to fulfill.

OBJECTIVE ASSESSMENT OF ABILITIES

The Strategy Management process brings a significant degree of formality to the analysis of an organization's objectives and its ability to achieve them. The process follows a logical and natural sequence of events applicable to the different operating and support units of the enterprise. This structured formality permits an institution to more objectively assess itself both in terms of strengths and of weaknesses as they relate to the pre-established goals. In addition to objectivity, formality brings a sense of comprehension to the analysis. This structured environment of analysis results in a realistic and accurate perception of the organization's characteristics and abilities.

When analyzing its strengths and weaknesses, an organization is often so enthralled with itself that an unbiased assessment cannot immediately be made. Circumstances are viewed the way they ought to be viewed as opposed to how they are. What is needed is a device that will allow an organization to systematically examine each component of strength and each component of weakness. In this modular manner, an intelligent evaluation of the organization's position can be carried out with a minimum of subjectivity. An organization that truly and honestly knows itself is clearly in a position of advantage. This is one benefit of Strategy Management that can be exploited for significant gain.

In addition to creating an objective assessment of an organization, Strategy Management seeks to assess the organization's immediate competitors in order to develop ideas and philosophies to use for competitive advantage. Knowledge of an organization's capabilities, interests and shortcomings as well as those of its competitors gives an organization confidence and puts it in a position of power. It is precisely this position that makes for good strategy.

OPTIMUM RESOURCE ALLOCATION

One of the more tangible benefits of Strategy Management is an optimum allocation of the organization's resources — on both a strategic and tactical basis. The degree of optimization is determined by the proportion of resources utilized in a manner which contributes directly to the goals of the organization. Resources not making this type of contribution are somewhat misguided and result in a sub-optimization situation. For an optimum allocation of resources, an organization needs to possess the following characteristics.

1. A thorough understanding and communication of objectives as they pertain to all levels of management.
2. A process which provides an ability to measure the degree

of contribution towards the objectives for various resource allocation possibilities.

3. A disciplined management team that can bring the resource allocation decisions to fruition.

Strategy Management encompasses the first two requirements as different sub-functions to the overall process. A significant degree of emphasis is constantly directed towards the objectives of the organization. A mechanism to systematically and objectively evaluate potential resource allocation configurations is a basic premise of the Strategy Management concept. The process follows a philosophy that maximizes the contribution to the organization's objectives through a logical and natural selection of possible activities for execution. Strategy Management ensures that only the most suitable resource allocation decisions are made while remaining within the organization's level of affordability.

The third requirement of disciplined management action is something that no management process can guarantee. It is an organizational operating spirit that exists only after much nurturing and cultivation. The manner in which Strategy Management addresses this issue is by creating an environment which is conducive to this type of management behaviour. An atmosphere in which objectives are enthusiastically pursued takes time to develop.

DISCIPLINED EXECUTION OF PLANS

It has just been stated that no management process, regardless of its qualities, can force management to act. Action is the intermediary step between planning and results in which human desire and discipline are the fuels of motivation. Like all other processes, Strategy Management is not something that can act on behalf of management. However, this does not prevent the Strategy Management concept from addressing this issue and exerting influence within certain limitations.

Strategy Management brings discipline to the execution stage of the management process by placing an unusual emphasis on the events both immediately preceding and immediately following the activation point of execution. By bringing structure and understanding to the activities before and after this pinnacle of attention, the manager is relieved of as much concern as possible. His energies can be left to the only issue requiring resolution — namely the deed of execution. By organizing and concluding all of the peripheral matters, the distractions which managers often use as excuses for procrastination are eliminated. Strategy Management brings order and logic to the functions of planning and the functions of control so that a manager has little excuse for not facing his responsibility of execution. Obviously, the Strategy Management process cannot go further and force the manager to act. Nevertheless, by negating all of the surrounding opportunities to misdirect one's attention (both intentionally and unintentionally), a sense of discipline is instilled in the act of execution. This benefit of the Strategy Management process can be described in an elementary fashion as a simple act of "good management." Replacing management procrastination with discipline is always something deserving the utmost attention.

CONFIDENCE THROUGH COMMUNICATION

The Strategy Management process brings a degree of structure and formality to the determination of an organization's objectives, to the notification of the various levels of management and to the construction of action plans to ensure their achievement. These activities require a high degree of management communication if they are to be done properly. The formality of Strategy Management ensures that this communication becomes a reality.

The foundation of the process is a dialogue among all levels of management. This dialogue involves a discussion of what the objectives actually are, how they can be achieved, what obstacles are likely to be encountered, what role each individual plays and what type of contingencies are required. When addressing these issues, managers will share ideas, questions, concerns and suggestions. The exchange of this information broadens the individual's perception of the institution. The manager increases his awareness of the operations of other parts of the organization. He develops an appreciation of the restrictions and abilities inherent in the functions of other managers. The net result is a more accurate, comprehensive and objective understanding of the organization both in whole and in part. With this knowledge, a manager can develop a clear perception of both his role in the organization and how it relates to that of others. This situation represents a minimization of uncertainty. It provides fertile ground for a manager to identify his mandate and cultivate a feeling of confidence about his operations. These developments represent intangible but nevertheless valuable benefits to any institution. Confidence is a by-product of knowledge. An educated manager will distribute his knowledge throughout the full spectrum of the decisions he is called upon to make.

FLEXIBILITY IN THE FACE OF UNCERTAINTY

Strategy Management forces an organization to take a good, hard look at itself. An extensive assessment of its resources, abilities and competitive position is made. This is done with constant attention to the objectives of the organization. The result is an awareness of where the organization is, where it is going, why it is going that way, how it will get there, what strengths it can build upon, what impediments it is likely to encounter and what assumptions it used in formulating its plans. With this knowledge, an organization has control of itself. It is in a position to be assertive rather than reactive. It is purposeful and direct rather than being adrift. It follows its own path, disregarding distractions. The organization has control of its own destiny which inherently means that it has flexibility.

When opportunities confront an organization, it now has an ability to evaluate their merits in a timely and accurate fashion. Since the organization already knows what its goals and objectives are, the new opportunity can be examined from the point of view of how it contributes to the overall purpose of the institution. There is no need to question whether the results obtainable from the new opportunity represent acceptable or desirable goals for the organization. The issue of what the goals are has already been concluded. The net result is the creation of a capability to seize upon and exploit worthwhile opportunities as they present themselves.

The opposite of taking advantage of opportunities is coping with problems. An ability to do so in an effective manner is another benefit of the Strategy Management process. Problems can be broadly described as changes in the immediate environment, changes in the strength of a competitor or changes in an organization's own competence. The common link among all three is an impediment to the realization of the organization's goals. Strategy Management cannot eliminate this problem. However, it can help to find a solution for it or a way to avoid it. The process of formulating the action plans of the organization includes an evaluation of many alternative courses of action. This evaluation not only serves as the basis from which to select the optimum manner of performance, but it provides a series of substitute activities as well. An organization facing a problem can call upon this store of knowledge and ideas to aid in finding the appropriate remedial action. To a large degree, an organization can choose its solution rather than embarking upon a hasty exploratory mission.

EXECUTIVE BREEDING

What makes one organization better than another? Why is it that certain firms are always leaders in management behaviour? Why is it that certain organizations bring disaster to everything they touch? It is easy to respond to these questions by citing such things as financial resources or the good fortunes of technology. However, these types of responses are passive instruments by themselves. The active instruments — those that make things happen — are the true answers. Active instruments are people. People are an organization's instruments that display emotion, make decisions and cause things to happen. People are what makes an organization unique. Without question, the resourcefulness of an organization's people assets is what will establish its character and determine the degree of success it ultimately attains.

Attracting, developing and retaining human resources is one of the most critical functions that an organization undertakes. While Strategy Management does not directly attack this issue, it certainly does have a profound influence upon it. Strategy Management is a leading form of management technology which creates an extremely challenging environment. The presence of such an atmosphere will act as a magnet to attract and retain the type of people who can thrive in that form of situation. The factor which both attracts and retains people is the development they will enjoy. Strategy Management, through its intense communication facility, presents an unusual opportunity for managers to learn and mature from both a personal and professional point of view. Through a common strategic language, managers are able to develop a portfolio of good work habits dealing with the entire spectrum of planning, execution and control. Strategy Management helps to bring discipline to these key management responsibilities and widens the manager's understanding and appreciation of his organization all within a condensed time frame. This process is formally called executive breeding. It is a conscious effort to develop people who can contribute to the success and uniqueness of the organization. Since this is the life blood of any institution, executive breeding is a most serious matter.

COMPETITIVE SUPERIORITY

There is a wide variety of benefits that can accrue to an organization deciding to embark upon a Strategy Management program. Goal orientation, resource allocation, confidence and flexibility have all been discussed. These benefits can be seen as individual components of the overall advantage of Strategy Management. This overall advantage is known as competitive superiority.

Competitive superiority is a reflection of power. Power is something that is derived from knowledge. Organizations utilizing the Strategy Management concept acquire great knowledge concerning themselves. They undergo rigourous self-examination, searching for strengths and weaknesses associated with all categories of internal resources. To complement this, organizations apply the same analysis to their major competitors. This application results in a comprehensive understanding of the significant industry participants. In many cases, an organization can know more about a competitor than the competitor knows about itself. This is power. With a knowledge of this magnitude, an organization can clearly compete in a superior fashion. Conversely, an organization without this knowledge, facing a competitor that employs Strategy Management, can find itself in a struggle for survival.

4

The Charter of Objectives

From a chronological point of view, there is a question with respect to the relationship between objectives and strategy. Do objectives support or act as a refinement of strategy? Is the reverse case true? Where do goals fit into this relationship? To answer these questions, it is necessary to define each of these terms. Within our context, the words **purpose**, **objectives** and **goals** are considered synonymous and have been used as such to this point. They are most accurately defined as planned positions or results that one strives to attain or realize. The word **strategy** refers to the actions that one plans in order to achieve these objectives. In this sense, strategies are subsidiary to and more detailed than an organization's goals and objectives.

A further progression in the level of detail from objectives and strategy is the word **tactics**. Tactics refer to the more immediate and more concrete activities intended to support an organization's strategy and thus its objectives. Both the words strategy and tactics have military connotations. **Strategy** is derived from an ancient Greek word **strategia** meaning **the art of the general**. Using more contemporary terminology, the word strategy can be more vividly explained as **the science or art of planning large-scale military operations**. This is quite different from the word tactics which can best be described as **the science or art of maneuvering forces immediately prior to engagement with the enemy.** The relationship of the military expressions of objectives, strategy and tactics are parallelled in today's business world. Exhibit 4-1 below illustrates the connection among these three topics.

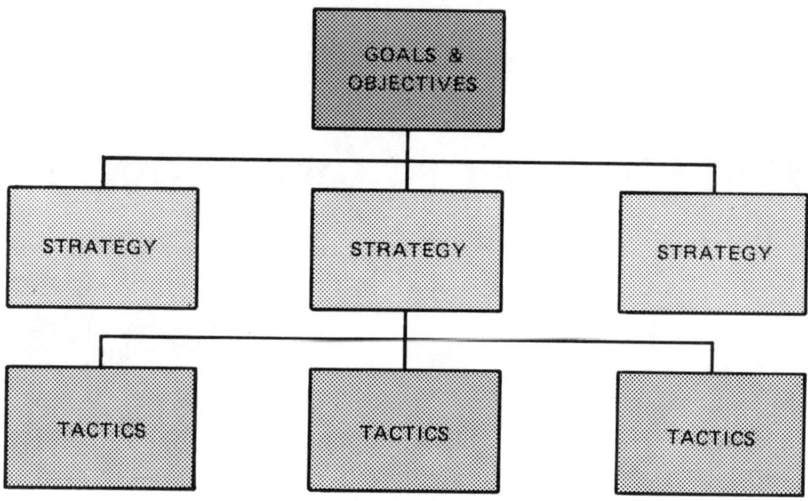

Exhibit 4-1   The relationship of objectives, strategy and tactics.

Although our distinction between objectives, strategy and tactics is described as a matter of detail, it is important to realize that these terms can be interpreted differently depending upon one's point of view. The top level of management may develop a series of strategies in response to the organization's objectives. When they are communicated to the next level of management, these strategies may be perceived as objectives themselves requiring a new set of strategies to be constructed in their support. This type of overlap can also cause confusion concerning the transition from strategy to tactics. As a result, the words objectives, strategy and tactics could possibly all refer to the same thing depending upon the level of management and its point of view. This can be seen in Exhibit 4-2 on the next page. The name given to any specific level of the overall plan is not of critical importance. The primary concern is understanding how the words relate to one another, particularly in regard to the level of planning detail.

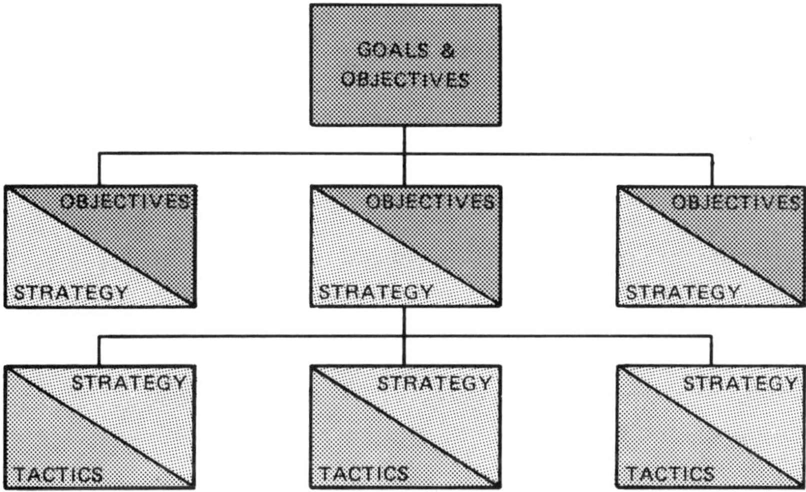

Exhibit 4-2 Objectives, strategy and tactics as a matter of interpretation.

Understanding this relationship is required in order to comprehend the communications flow of Strategy Management which is presented in later parts of this book.

THE NATURE OF GOALS

The goals and objective of an organization serve as a launching point for the mission of coordinating the activities within the institution. This mission is more traditionally known as planning. The purpose of planning is to align the goals of the individual with those of the organization and hence create co-ordination. However, there are some personal goals which will always be in opposition to those of the organization — at least to some degree. This makes the idea of perfect coordination within an organization something that can never be attained. Individuals will always seek to satisfy their own needs. The more these personal needs differ from those of the organization, the less desireable the situation. Although complete coordination cannot be realized, it does not follow that an organization's goals and objectives can never be realized. An organization will make allowances for this when it incorporates the factor of difficulty into the setting of objectives. This somewhat impure view of the goal setting process forms a basis for a further examination into the nature of goals.

Goals and objectives as they are expressed in their high-level form for an organization or in their more detailed forms of strategy and tactics can be classified into two separate categories. One is open-ended goals. The other is close-ended goals. Open-ended goals are described in general terms and are somewhat wishy-washy. "To have a happier work force" is an example of an open-ended goal for a particular organization. This type of goal can never be completely achieved because it is always possible to become happier. Such a goal is of limited value to management because it cannot be measured and because it is not known when or if it is achieved.

Close-ended goals are precise descriptions of intended results which management has an ability to achieve. They provide more character and substance than open-ended goals. "To improve work force morale so that staff turnover decreases four percent down to eighteen percent by the end of the year" is an example of a close-ended goal. This illustration demonstrates how the objective of happiness can be expressed in terms of expected end results that can later be measured.

For the purpose of management, only close-ended goals have true value. Open-ended goals present a sense of direction but lack a specific target. Expressing goals in terms of expected end results is critical to the Strategy Management process. For goals to adhere to this criterion, they must possess:

1. **Subject**: A topic matter identifying the nature of the position or result which is expected to be achieved (e.g. improve work force morale).
2. **Measurement**: A unit of measure that can be used to monitor the degree of accomplishment (e.g. staff turnover).
3. **Quantity**: A tangible description of the magnitude of results one intends to realize (e.g. decrease four percent down to eighteen percent).
4. **Time**: The time period in which the goal is to be fulfilled — a response to the question **when** (e.g. by the end of the year).

The presence of these characteristics will ensure that goals are both clear and specific. Opportunities for misinterpretation will be minimized and the probability of achievement will be maximized. Aside from these mechanical specifications, an organization also needs to adopt a philosophy for the degree of difficulty with respect to its goals and objectives. Some organizations believe that goals should be used to stretch the work force to its limit and set them so that they can never be achieved. Other organizations believe the opposite and set goals to represent normal expectations of behaviour. Extremely difficult goals with no chance of achievement run a high risk of being ignored. Soft goals of normal behaviour provide little incentive for improvement. The best philosophy for the degree of difficulty when establishing goals in an organization is to compromise between these two extreme positions. Achievable goals which entail significant difficulty will best serve the needs of the organization and its work force. They are progressive in nature as well as acceptable.

IDENTIFY THE ORGANIZATIONAL FOUNDATION

Now that the nature and relationship of objectives, strategy and tactics have been reviewed, it is appropriate to commence our examination of how the Strategy Management process functions. Beginning with this chapter, its operation will be presented in the order that the tasks of a Strategy Management cycle are actually carried out. This approach takes cognizance of the building block character of the concept. Consequently, the first area to be examined will be the organization's charter of objectives.

The Strategy Management process is a complete and comprehensive approach to planning, execution and control. Because of this full-scope philosophy, it is imperative that the process start at the conception point of the organization. This conception point pertains to the reasons why the institution was created and continues to exist. Only with a clear understanding of these motives can a sensible portfolio of objectives and strategies be developed.

The Strategy Management process is inaugurated by a review, questioning and examination of the fundamental mission or mandate of the organization. The ideas derived from this self-interrogation will represent the intrinsic purpose of the institution. These conceptions are formally documented and are referred to as the organization's charter of objectives. The charter acts as a form of constitution for the organization, taking precedence over all other means of direction.

The charter of objectives is a statement of the needs of society to which the organization intends to address itself but taking into consideration its own unique capabilities and resources. It is the grand vision of the organization stressing the principles and concepts upon which it is based. The charter of objectives, as indicated, is not likely to be something that will change from year to year. For an established organization, a change in its charter of objectives signals a very major alteration in its course of direction. It is tantamount to liquidating the existing operations and establishing a new basis of activity. As a result, the time and effort devoted to examining the charter of objectives will not be that significant – especially after the initial cycle of Strategy Management. Most organizations have a fairly good understanding of their charter of objectives to begin with even though it may not exist in written form. However, the degree of ease with which an organization can set down its charter of objectives should not detract from its importance. Should an organization make a mistake concerning the formulation of its charter, it can expect to pay the severest of penalties. It is similar to building a skyscraper on a faulty foundation.

CONCENTRATE ON THE SPECIFIC FUNCTION

The importance of the charter of objectives demands examination of the ingredients which will give it quality and usefulness. Comparison of some sample charter of objectives can serve to initiate this enquiry. A fictitious airline corporation, ABC Airlines, could choose to set forth its charter of objectives in a number of different ways. Listed below are four possible examples:

1. ABC Airlines will be a significant factor in the airline business and as such will concentrate on improving its position in the industry over the next five years.
2. ABC Airlines is a transportation corporation. Its business is to move anything, anywhere, by any means within

reason, and to do so in a profitable fashion.
3. ABC Airlines is strictly an airline business. Within this context, its primary focus is on servicing the needs of the businessman on short-haul trips.
4. ABC Airlines is a transportation corporation servicing the domestic needs of the country. It will concentrate on contemporary forms of transporation combining high price and high quality modes of service.

Although these examples of a charter of objectives are extremely brief they do provide a basis for analysis. Every charter of objectives inherently makes a selection between expressing itself in terms of either the products and services the organization will provide or the function it will perform. The airline business can be equated with a product or service. The transportation business can be equated with a function. In addition, each charter of objectives makes a selection between expressing itself in a specific or an unspecific manner. The airline business can be equated with an unspecific description. The short-haul, businessman oriented airline business can be equated with a specific description. Aside from the subject matter, the manner in which an organization makes these selections will have a profound influence on the quality of its charter of objectives.

An organization that describes its charter of objectives in specific product or service terminology is leaving itself open to the possibility of becoming obsolete due to quickly changing needs of society. The short-haul, businessman market of the airline industry could be severely eroded when the television conference services of the telephone companies become economically viable. An organization that describes its charter of objectives in unspecific functional terminology is undermining the quality of its direction by presenting an unrealistically broad target. Transporting anything, anywhere and by any means says a lot but means very little. An organization that describes its charter of objectives in unspecific product or service terminology runs the risk of both obsolesence and lack of direction. Being a significant factor in the airline business provides little insight as to what the organization will do and can be a risky proposition as well (remember the railway companies). The best charter of objectives will be expressed in specific functional language. This provides a strong sense of direction while acting as a hedge against the risk of obsolesence. The fourth charter of objectives example best exemplifies these characteristics.

A visual display[1] of these selections available to organizations when documenting their charters of objectives is presented in Exhibit 4-3. The unshaded, upper right-hand quadrant of the matrix represents the optimum format for the charter of objectives. Expressing the charter of objectives in this fashion will not turn an organization with a faulty purpose into a success. However, it can prevent an organization with a sound purpose from becoming a failure.

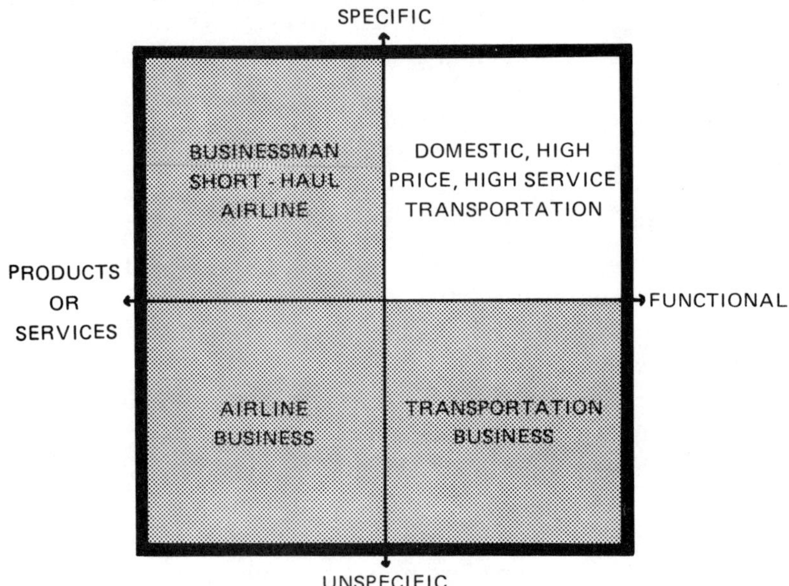

Exhibit 4-3 Criteria for selecting a meaningful charter of objectives.

THE OBJECTIVES IN HARMONY

The merits of a specific and functional charter of objectives have just been discussed. In doing so, the four examples presented were described as being "extremely brief." A logical question is: How extensive should the charter of objectives be? To arrive at

1 Hofer, Charles W. and Schendel, Dan, *Strategy Formulation: Analytical Concepts,* (St. Paul: West Publishing Company, 1978), page 43.

an answer, let us now examine the contents of the charter of objectives.

From a corporate point of view, one can argue that the embellishing of the charter of objectives is a simple task. Aside from being involved with a specific function, the goal of a corporation is to maximize return on investment. Traditionally, profitability has been said to be the number one goal in a capitalist society. From a public sector point of view, one can argue that the embellishing of the charter of objectives is an equally simple task. Rather than striving for profitability, public service could be used as a substitute. However, these two points of view are seriously over simplified and somewhat naive.

A corporation concerned solely with profitability can postpone investments and discretionary expenses such as advertising, research and development, maintenance and training. These actions would certainly give an immediate boost to profitability but could disable the corporation in the long-term. Governments concerned solely with public service could supply an unlimited number of programs without concern for cost and plunge the nation irreversably into debt. These actions would prove popular in the short-term but could eventually lead to devastation. From these descriptions it is clear that corporations and governments do not have a single objective but many objectives designed to maintain both the short-term and long-term health of the organization.

Peter Drucker was one of the pioneering management scientists to recognize the complexity of this issue.[2] He believed, and was later proven correct, that an organization must address itself to a number of different objectives at the same time. Should there be an area of deficiency, the organization is sure to suffer in terms of meeting its long-term purpose of growth and prosperity. To be specific, Drucker cited eight important topics with which the objectives of the organization should be concerned. These topics are best seen as **categories** of objectives that every organization, regardless of its nature, should seriously consider and to which it should positively react. These categories of objectives are as

---

[2] Drucker, Peter F., *The Practice of Management,* Harper and Row Publishers, Inc., New York, 1954, pp. 62-87.

follows:
1. Market standing.
2. Innovation.
3. Productivity.
4. Physical and financial resources.
5. Profitability.
6. Manager performance and development.
7. Public responsibility.
8. Worker performance and attitude.

Market Standing refers to the share of the overall market which a particular organization possesses. Market standing is of importance for two reasons. Should an organization have less than a certain share of the market, it becomes a marginal participant and is therefore highly dependent on the decisions of larger competitors. Secondly, a marginal participant cannot be expected to enjoy a favourably comparable cost structure for its products or services. Economies of scale dictate that lower costs can be achieved through greater market share.

Innovation is concerned with the degree of technology employment that an organization sets as an objective for itself. Innovation is most frequently seen in research and development efforts aimed at developing new products or services for the organization. Innovation also pertains to management techniques and organizational arrangements which every organization utilizes in the course of its actions.

Productivity is a measure of organizational competence. It is a relationship between the input of resources and the output of results in terms of products or services. Productivity measurements permit a comparison of production skills among various organizations as well as among different functional units of the same organization.

Physical and Financial Resources refer to assets such as plants, equipment, offices and liquid cash. The nature and magnitude of these resources will be dictated to a large extent by the type of organization in question. The acquisition and disposal of physical and financial resources is accomplished only with much forethought and effort. Consequently, decisions of this kind cannot be improvised and need to be made within an overall organizational context. In particular, physical and financial resource objectives should focus on providing the means to attain the goals set for market standing and innovation.

Profitability represents the reward which the organization has earned for its efforts and within the long-term, is the ultimate measure of performance. In this context, profits are remuneration for the risk undertaken by the business in its endeavours. If an organization does not produce a minimum level of profit, its existence will be in jeopardy. This level of profitability can best be determined by analyzing the steps that must be taken to insure a supply of future capital to the organization. Capital cannot be attracted unless the cost of its utilization can be afforded. In this respect, capital attraction is one of the basic premises of profitability.

Manager Performance and Development deals with the issues of defining managers' responsibilities, providing them with guidance and structuring the management function. Management spirit or morale and the propogation and enhancement of both today's and tomorrow's management talent are also considerations in this category of objectives.

Public Responsibility refers to addressing the needs of society as well as respecting its concerns and aspirations. In both instances, objectives of this nature are quite tangible. Addressing the needs of society requires an involvement with things that are productive, progressive and strengthening in terms of the society as a whole. Respect centers on environmental, energy and national concerns. In each case, objectives in this area should reflect the social and political realities facing the organization.

Worker Performance and Attitude is concerned with issues of employee relations. Goals in this area are designed to enhance performance and attitude by addressing such concerns as absenteeism, promotion procedures, staff turnover and safe working conditions. Within this category is something critical to many organizations — union relations. In each instance, an organization needs to have concrete objectives so that it can influence and guide events rather than reacting to worker initiatives.

Constructing a charter of objectives that considers each of these eight categories of objectives adds a significant amount of complexity to the goal setting process. To further complicate matters, some of these objectives will now be in conflict with one another. For example, the objectives of public responsibility and profitability could be in direct opposition. If public responsibility dictates expenditures for pollution control activities, this will affect profit adversely. The same type of conflict could be formulated for any of the remaining objectives as well. The result of these conflicts is suboptimization. The organization cannot do everything it wants at the same time.

There is a natural tendency to seek harmony among these different objectives. The easiest solution is to rank them in their order of importance and fulfill the most important completely before moving to the next. However, this practice will result in a number of issues being totally neglected. It is precisely this situation which must be avoided. The way to bring harmony to these objectives is to create a relationship among them. This relationship is best depicted using a pie chart diagram as presented in Exhibit 4-4 below.

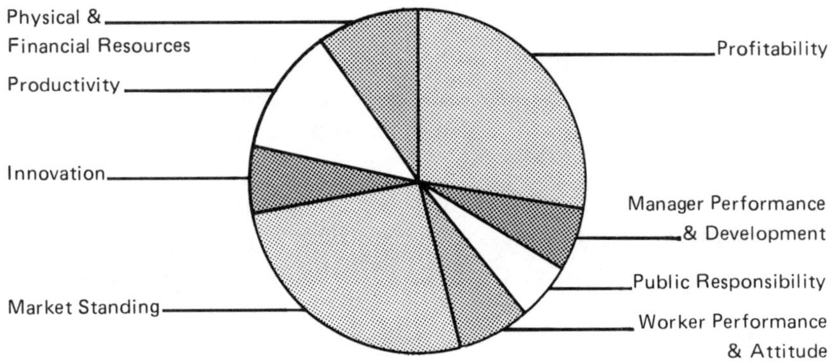

Exhibit 4-4 Harmony among the categories of objectives.

As the exhibit illustrates, each of the eight objectives of the organization shares some degree of the overall attention and thus they have a relationship among themselves. The proportion of importance that each individual objective is assigned will differ from organization to organization. It would be natural for corporations to have a large portion of the pie devoted to profitability. Similarly, public responsibility would likely occupy a prominent proportion for a non-profit institution. For these reasons one may conclude that **the process of setting goals requires an equal effort regardless of the type of organization**. It is all a matter of dividing up the pie to designate the relative importance of each category of objectives. As the pie expands, all factors share proportionately in the enlargement.

Before concluding the chapter, let us summarize our progress to this point. The formulation of the charter of objectives is the initiation point of the Strategy Management process and can be accomplished by adhering to the following steps:

1. Document the specific function of the organization.
2. Express this documentation in a manner that addresses all eight categories of objectives.
3. Bring harmony to the conflicting categories of objectives by formulating a relationship among them.

Exhibit 4-5 on the following page visually displays these first steps of the Strategy Management process. The key factors to appreciate in the preparation of the charter of objectives are that all eight categories of objectives must be addressed and that their proportion of importance will vary depending upon the individual organization.

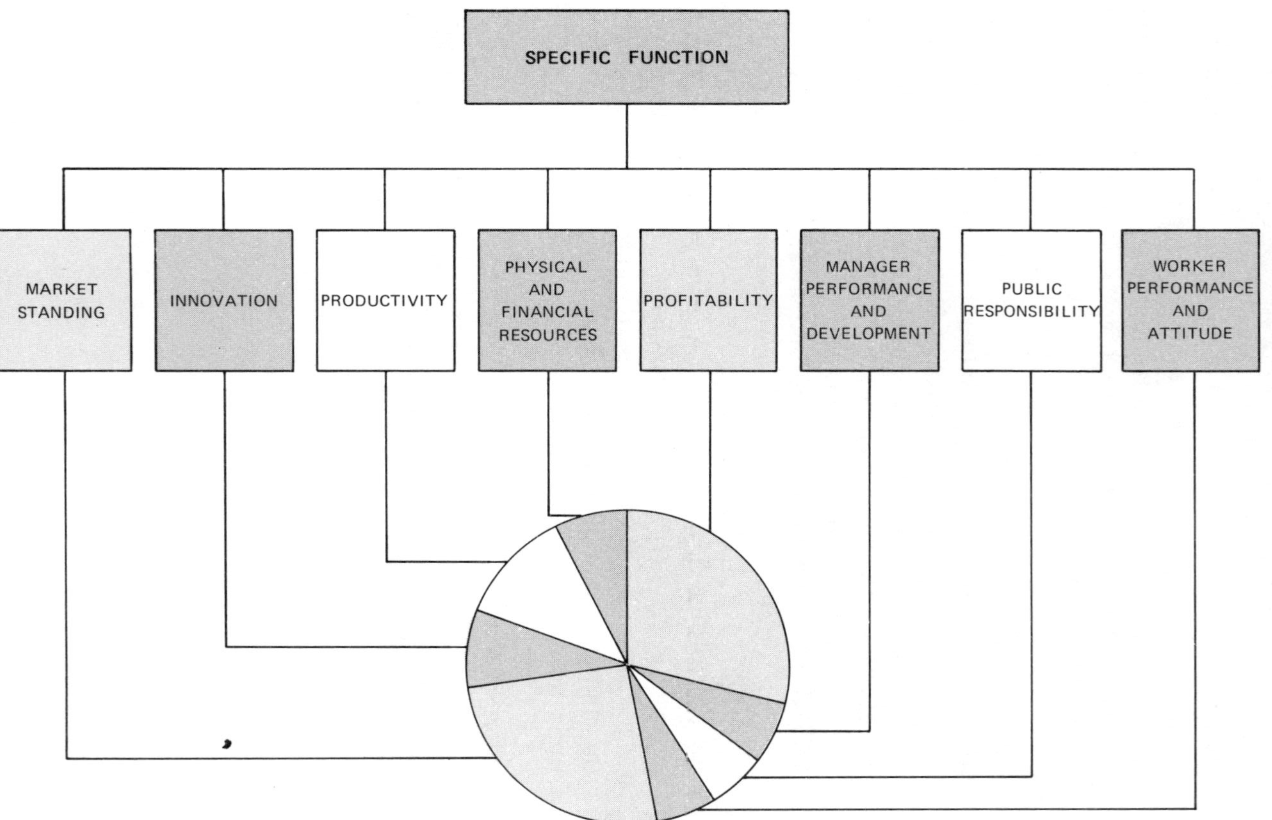

Exhibit 4-5 Considerations when preparing the charter of objectives.

5

Corporate Strategy Formulation

Following the establishment of a sound charter of objectives, the Strategy Management process enters the first of many stages designed to translate the charter into meaningful language for each employee. This requires that the charter of objectives be broadened in both substance and scope. It involves a progressive communication effort down through the various layers of management. At each lower level of management, the objectives are expanded into more precise detail commensurate with the authority of that level. This progressive step by step approach is essential to protect the integrity of the objectives as well as to bring discipline to the communication process. A gradual exposure of the organization's objectives is the only way to ensure that they will be well received by all concerned and at the same time retain the quality of the message.

The first stage of this communication process evolves from the charter of objectives and results in the development of a corporate strategy. Corporate strategy penetrates only to an intermediate level of the organization. The major thrust is to take the specific function of the organization as described in its charter of objectives and express it in terms of the particular businesses in which it ought to be involved. The formulation of corporate strategy entails deciding what key functions or overall businesses the organization should pursue in view of the direction outlined in its charter of objectives. The nature, scope, potential and resource requirements associated with these businesses need to be described. The identification of these businesses will result in the definition of the main organizational entities of the institution which are called strategic business units.[1] The strategic business unit level of the organization represents the lowest level to which corporate strategy penetrates.

STRATEGIC BUSINESS UNITS

Strategic business unit is the name given to that present or proposed part of the organization which has been distinguished as a separate and unique business venture because of its attractiveness to realizing the charter of objectives. Physically, the strategic business unit is that locality of the organization where most of the innovative ideas of Strategy Management are nurtured. However, the strategic business unit itself has a very limited role to play in the actual development of corporate strategy. Corporate strategy formulation is the fundamental responsibility of the chief executive officer and his senior executive committee. Although middle management will have an input into the process, they cannot be ultimately held accountable for the events. Developing corporate strategy is one task that does not lend itself to delegation. It is an extremely serious and complex matter which makes the chief executive officer worth his high-level of compensation.

Corporate strategy formulation, from an over simplified point of view, can be seen as a rationalization of the different businesses with which the organization intends to associate itself. It is not a plan outlining how the organization should effectively compete or function within these businesses. This latter issue will be addressed by the strategic business unit personnel themselves. It is an action which delineates the major functions in which the organization should engage. It provides a sense of direction for the strategic business units rather than constituting a detailed

[1] Other names are often used in place of the words strategic business unit such as strategy centre, business unit, strategy unit or business centre.

examination of them. With this in mind, let us now focus on the specific nature of a strategic business unit.

By definition, a strategic business unit is an organizational component representing an independent business mission. The word independent is of major importance in this definition. Each strategic business unit within the organization is a discrete operating entity with its own:

1. Market jurisdiction of customers, clients or beneficiaries.
2. Unique resource, technology or expertise requirements.
3. Set of competitors.
4. Ability to measure investment, operating expenditures and subsequent benefits.

Using these criteria, it seems logical to examine the organization chart in order to determine the boundaries of each strategic business unit. However, it is quite possible that a strategic business unit will not be found on the organization chart. It may very well be an artificial organizational entity that does not have a formal contingent of personnel. To illustrate this point, Exhibits 5-1 and 5-2 have been prepared to demonstrate how in one case a strategic business unit may conform to the layout of the organizational chart and how in another case it may not. As a further conclusion, one may expect that the employment of Strategy Management may very well result in an eventual reorganization of the institution. The purpose of such an action would be to streamline communication and authority in a manner that matches the process of strategic thinking.

THE ISSUES OF CORPORATE STRATEGY

Recognizing that the basic mandate of corporate strategy formulation is to determine the appropriate portfolio of businesses in which the organization should engage, it becomes obvious that these critical decisions require an enormous amount of preparation and advance investigation. Let us now direct our attention to the procedures for formulating corporate strategy so that the framework within which it is constructed can be appreciated. There are two main issues of concern when establishing corporate strategy. One is the assessment of industry

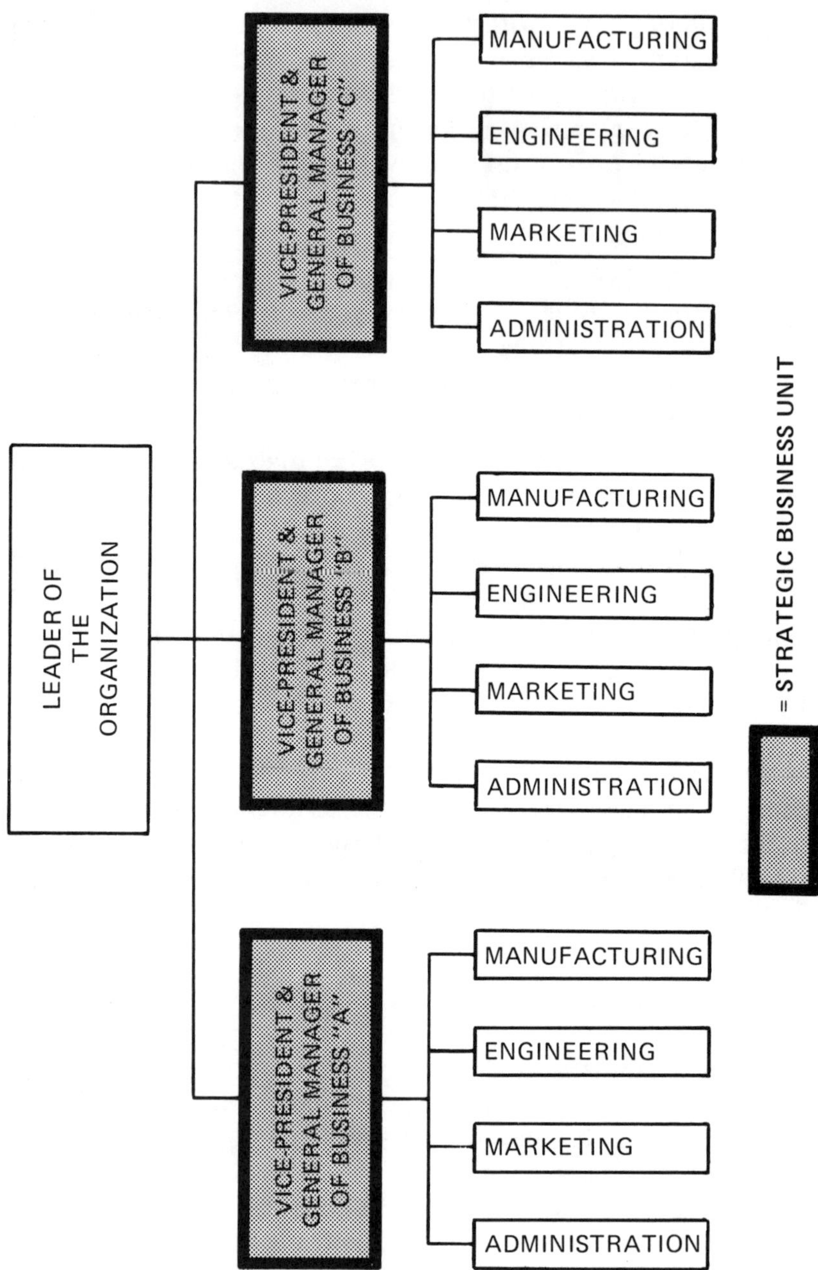

Exhibit 5-1   Strategic business units in synchronization with the organization chart.

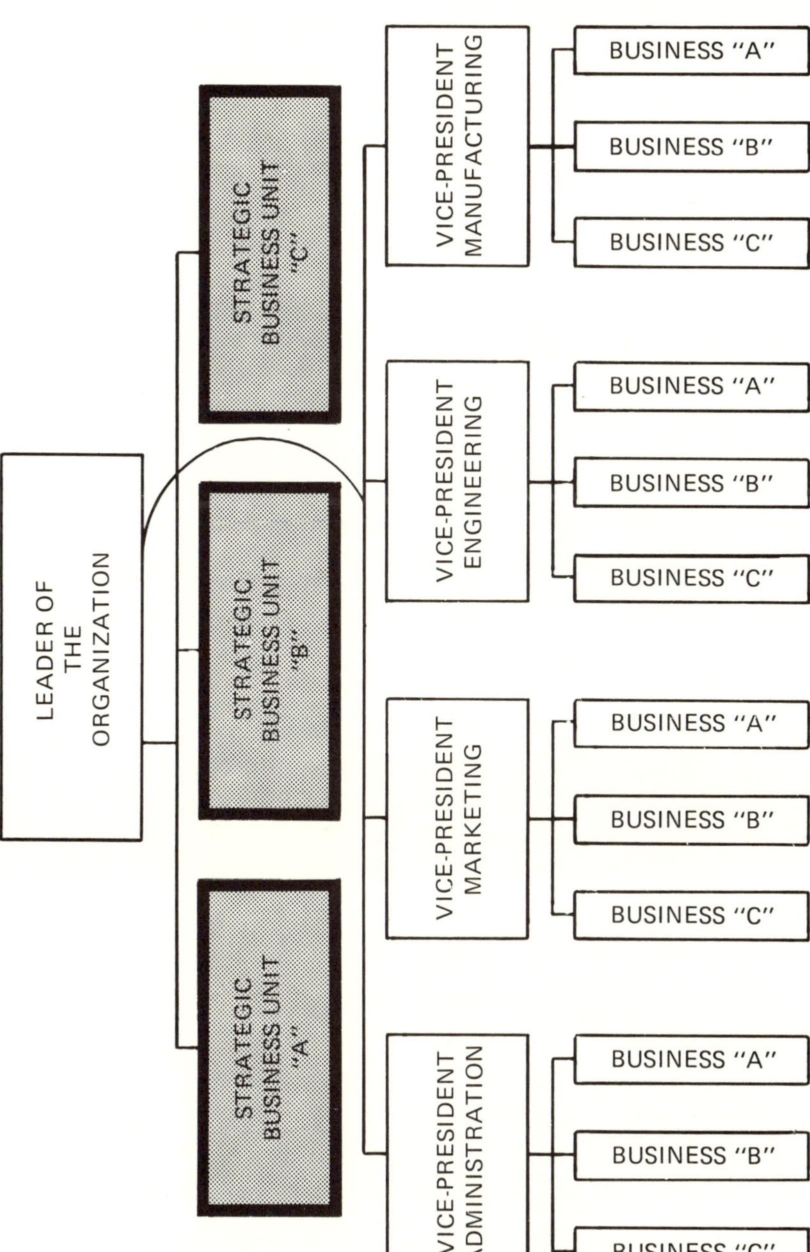

Exhibit 5-2 Strategic business units not in synchronization with the organization chart.

attractiveness. The other is the assessment of competitive position.

For each present or proposed business, corporate strategy begins with an evaluation of the general attractiveness of the industry of which it is a part. This results in an overall understanding of the opportunity facing the organization. Immediately following this, the competitive position of each business within the respective industries is examined. An appreciation of the business's unique place in relation to the aggregate industry is then gained. With this knowledge, an organization can appraise the viability of each of its major businesses and learn how each contributes to the realization of the charter of objectives. This identifies the businesses in which the organization ought to be involved and hence completes the corporate strategy formulation process. To emphasize, the examination of industry attractiveness and competitive position will result in:

1. An understanding of the current health of the organization as it relates to its existing portfolio of businesses and how each contributes to the realization of the charter of objectives.
2. An understanding of the organization's desired portfolio of businesses that would permit it to optimize the fulfillment of its charter of objectives.
3. An understanding of the discrepancies between the current status and desired status of the organization's portfolio of businesses and a determination of what must happen to achieve harmony between the two.

ASSESSING INDUSTRY ATTRACTIVENESS

An assessment of industry attractiveness is a logical starting point for corporate strategy because no business can be more attractive in the long-term than the industry of which it is a part. The industry evaluation will provide a global perception of the situation and determine the parameters within which the organization's particular business will reside. The absence of a thorough understanding of the industries in which it operates will almost certainly prevent an organization from reaching any meaningful perception of itself and therefore the opportunities and threats facing it.

Assessing industry attractiveness requires the consideration of a number of different factors. The two most prominent factors are growth rate and profitability. Growth rate has a strong influence on the potential of the industry and therefore the organizations which compete within it. The critical aspect of growth rate is its close relationship with the life cycle of the particular industry. The one characteristic that every industry has in common is a specific life cycle. The popular categories of industry life cycle can be described as follows:

1. Development.
2. Growth.
3. Competitive adjustment.
4. Maturity.
5. Decline.

As an industry progresses through its life cycle, it is natural to expect different rates of growth within each stage. The development stage will be a radical change from the decline stage of the industry life cycle. Obviously, it is more attractive for an organization to be involved with an industry that is still in its early stages of development. Nobody wants to become involved with a situation that is reaching extinction. Thus, growth rate as it relates to industry life cycle is a fundamental influence upon industry attractiveness.

Although growth rate is an extremely important consideration, it is by no means the complete story of industry attractiveness. It is quite possible that an organization can be enjoying participation in a very high growth industry and at the same time be in an extremely unattractive situation. The cause of such circumstances is likely to be insufficient profits. Without profits, growth rate has little value. The two are partners which must be combined to form a true sense of industry attractiveness. When a high growth rate of demand is outpaced by an even higher provision of supply, profitability will be adversely affected and the industry will lose its appeal. The assessment of industry attractiveness must take this into account.

Growth rate and profitability are the two most important factors in determining industry attractiveness. For a more accurate and comprehensive appraisal, a series of complementary issues should be incorporated into the assessment as well. The exact number and description of these issues will vary to a certain degree. These variations will reflect what the organization in question believes to be truly representative of industry attractiveness from its vantage point. A suggested list of supplementary issues of industry attractiveness is as follows:

1. Customer stature and stability.
2. Energy requirements (absence of).
3. Environmental damage (absence of).
4. Human resource skill availability.
5. Inflation potential (absence of).
6. Public acceptance and need.
7. Size of industry.
8. Technology accessibility.

An organization may wish to add to or delete from this list to arrive at what it views as an appropriate set of criteria to measure industry attractiveness. Nevertheless, these are the normal topics associated with industry attractiveness. They can form the groundwork for any particular organization's assessment.

Another factor which will vary in addition to the list of criteria is the weight of importance associated with each. Again, this is not a dramatic variation but one which will undoubtedly occur to reflect the unique opinion of the organization. Exhibit 5-3, a sample Industry Attractiveness Summary form, can serve to illustrate this point. After senior management has completed its investigation, the findings for each industry can be recorded according to the criteria of industry attractiveness. The form summarizes these evaluations, rating attractiveness on a scale from one to ten. A weighting factor is used to show the relative importance of each issue. This also allows the total attractiveness of the industry to be calculated mathematically. Choosing the weighting factors is a task which often causes many organizations significant discomfort. There is no right answer as to what makes an industry appealing. Accordingly, every organization must make its own judgement.

The task of selecting the weight of importance for each criterion is similar to bringing harmony to the eight categories of objectives included in the charter of objectives. As the form indicates, the weighting factors add up to a total of one hundred

THE ABC ORGANIZATION

INDUSTRY ATTRACTIVENESS SUMMARY

INDUSTRY NAME: ....DATE: ....

ATTRACTIVENESS ISSUE	CIRCLE DEGREE OF ATTRACTIVENESS HIGH .... LOW	WEIGHT FACTOR	TOTAL VALUE
CUSTOMER STATURE AND STABILITY	10 9 8 7 6 5 4 3 2 1	5%	
ENERGY REQUIREMENTS (ABSENCE OF)	10 9 8 7 6 5 4 3 2 1	6%	
ENVIRONMENTAL DAMAGE (ABSENCE OF)........	10 9 8 7 6 5 4 3 2 1	3%	
GROWTH RATE OF INDUSTRY	10 9 8 7 6 5 4 3 2 1	17%	
HUMAN RESOURCE SKILL AVAILABILITY.........	10 9 8 7 6 5 4 3 2 1	10%	
INFLATION POTENTIAL (ABSENCE OF)...........	10 9 8 7 6 5 4 3 2 1	8%	
PROFITABILITY OF INDUSTRY.................	10 9 8 7 6 5 4 3 2 1	22%	
PUBLIC ACCEPTANCE AND NEED	10 9 8 7 6 5 4 3 2 1	4%	
SIZE OF INDUSTRY..........................	10 9 8 7 6 5 4 3 2 1	15%	
TECHNOLOGY ACCESSIBILITY	10 9 8 7 6 5 4 3 2 1	10%	
TOTAL INDUSTRY ATTRACTIVENESS:		100%	

Exhibit 5-3 Example of an Industry Attractiveness Summary form.

percent. Because of this constraint, an organization must develop a relationship among the various criteria as it determines the meaning of attractiveness. Incorporating this type of thought and preparation into the exercise is the only way for an organization to be confident that it has properly assessed the attractiveness of each of the industries in which it is engaged.

ASSESSING COMPETITIVE POSITION

The second issue of corporate strategy formulation is an assessment of competitive position. This evaluation of competitive position provides an organization with a more accurate and personalized description of the long-term growth and profit probabilities of its potential businesses in comparison to an overall industry assessment. Competitive position analysis identifies the relationship between an organization's particular business and the totality of the industry of which it is a part.

As with the assessment of industry attractiveness, determining competitive position requires the consideration of a variety of factors. The most prominent factor is market share. Market share is equivalent to power, flexibility and superior profitability. Consequently, it will be the most influential factor in competitive position. The prominence of market share as a competitive criterion is followed closely by both marketing capability and product or service quality. These two criteria are often seen as instruments through which an organization can affect market share.

Market share is a key determinant of competitive position because of its strong relationship with productivity. It is a critical consideration because of a very simple premise: **The larger a market share that a particular business enjoys, the lower will be its overall cost structure.** To demonstrate the validity of this premise, a focus on "production line" costs and the learning curve effect is required. As a business experiences a larger volume of work, it can expect to progress further down the learning curve either because of increased knowledge or economies of scale. As a rule of thumb, each time the volume of work is doubled, a fifteen to twenty percent reduction in unit costs can be expected. In conclusion, those businesses with larger market shares of an overall industry can expect to enjoy a cost advantage over their competitors. Cost advantages will have a direct impact upon profitability. The economic effects of market share strength can allow a business to enhance its competitive position in other areas as well. Generating funds to improve product or service quality or to upgrade marketing competence are two such examples. Viewing the issues of competitive position within this context, it is easy to see the synergy among them as well as how they can be an accurate reflection of the business's competitive status.

Casting marketing capability and product or service quality as by-products of market share is not always a wise proposition. In many cases, marketing and quality may well be the causes of subsequent market share. For this reason, it is best to approach each of these topics as independent criteria for evaluating competitive position. In the early stages of industry life cycle, marketing capability and product or service quality can be unusually important factors of competition. This emphasizes their need for individual evaluation while recognizing the manner in which they complement each other.

Factors other than market share, marketing capability and product or service quality are considered in the assessment of competitive position to produce a more precise and confident appreciation of the situation. Like the issues of industry attractiveness, the exact number and description of these issues are something resulting from a unique decision of the organization. A suggested list of supplementary issues of competitive position is as follows:

1. Distribution ability for products/services.
2. Labour unrest (absence of).
3. Managerial competence and depth.
4. Market rapport and understanding.
5. Physical resource quality and availability.
6. Productivity of work force.
7. Technological ability and employment.

The weight of importance associated with each of these criteria will have a profound effect upon the overall assessment of competitive position. The specific importance of each issue should be decided upon only after careful consideration. This will produce the best possible evaluation for the organization. Exhibit

5-4 is an example of a Competitive Position Summary form containing a possible set of weighting factors. The mechanics of the form are identical to that of the Industry Attractiveness Summary form. Senior management can use it to summarize the results of their competitive position analysis for each industry in which the organization participates. The form permits a mathematical calculation of total competitive strength which is particularly useful when comparing positions in different industries.

The summary forms for assessing industry attractiveness and competitive position are equally primitive. This simplicity belies the seriousness and complexity of corporate strategy formulation. A careful examination of each issue listed on these forms can help in understanding the effort and diligence required to perform this task properly.

THE BUSINESS PORTFOLIO MATRIX

After an organization has evaluated the industry attractiveness and competitive position of each of its current and potential businesses, it must confirm their contribution to the realization of the charter of objectives and assess the integrity of these businesses as a unified whole. An organization must determine how (if at all) these businesses complement each other and how they collectively add strength to the institution.

One manner in which to accomplish this is through the use of a business portfolio matrix.[2] The basic purpose of a business portfolio matrix is to present the industry attractiveness and competitive position data for all of the organization's businesses. Exhibit 5-5 is an example of a business portfolio matrix. The matrix indicates the industry attractiveness and competitive position for five different businesses (A through E) within the organization. The size of the particular circle corresponds to the size of the industry while the darkened portion of the circle reflects the corresponding market share. The numbers below each circle, such as 2 of 7 or 1 of 12, refer to the market position enjoyed by each business in relation to the total number of

---

[2] The concept of employing business portfolio matrices was originally developed by the Boston Consulting Group.

THE ABC ORGANIZATION

COMPETITIVE POSITION SUMMARY

INDUSTRY NAME: ....DATE: ....

COMPETITIVE ISSUE	CIRCLE DEGREE OF STRENGTH STRONG........WEAK	WEIGHT FACTOR	TOTAL VALUE
DISTRIBUTION ABILITY FOR PRODUCTS/SERVICES .	10 9 8 7 6 5 4 3 2 1	4%	
LABOUR UNREST (ABSENCE OF)................	10 9 8 7 6 5 4 3 2 1	8%	
MANAGERIAL COMPETENCE AND DEPTH	10 9 8 7 6 5 4 3 2 1	6%	
MARKETING AND SALES ABILITY...............	10 9 8 7 6 5 4 3 2 1	18%	
MARKET RAPPORT AND UNDERSTANDING........	10 9 8 7 6 5 4 3 2 1	7%	
MARKET SHARE............................	10 9 8 7 6 5 4 3 2 1	25%	
PHYSICAL RESOURCE QUALITY AND AVAILABILITY	10 9 8 7 6 5 4 3 2 1	4%	
PRODUCTIVITY OF WORK FORCE...............	10 9 8 7 6 5 4 3 2 1	8%	
QUALITY OF PRODUCTS/SERVICES..............	10 9 8 7 6 5 4 3 2 1	11%	
TECHNOLOGY AVAILABILITY AND EMPLOYMENT ..	10 9 8 7 6 5 4 3 2 1	9%	
TOTAL COMPETITIVE STRENGTH:		100%	

Exhibit 5-4 Example of a Competitive Position Summary form.

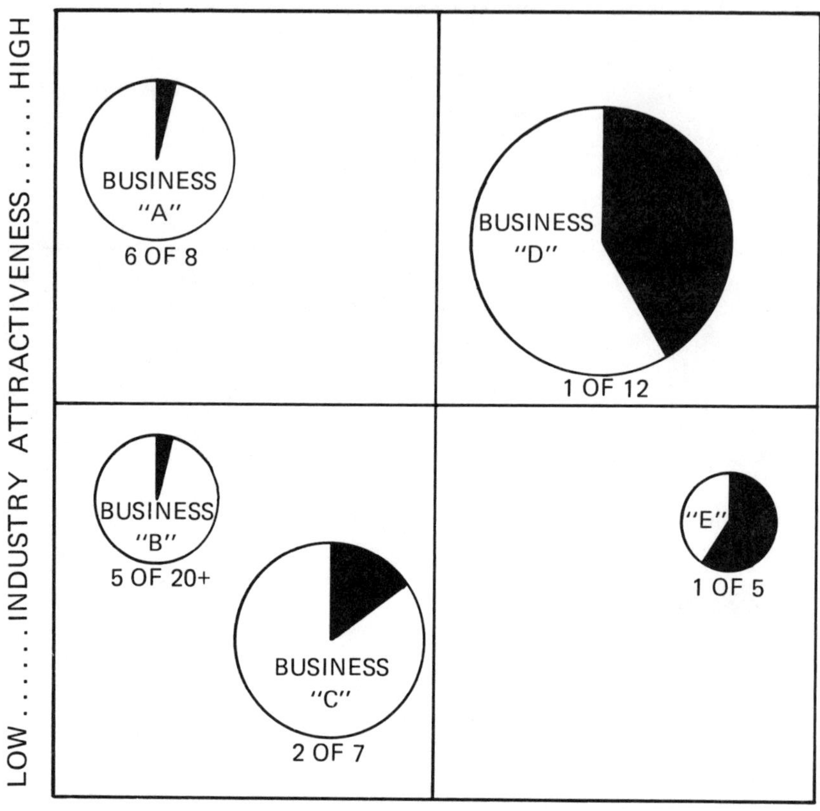

Exhibit 5-5 Example of a Business Portfolio Matrix.

competitors. The matrix can illustrate at a glance which businesses are more viable than others. In the case of this particular example, Business D represents a significantly more attractive venture than does Business B.

Businesses occupying a position in the upper right-hand quadrant of the matrix hold a strong competitive position within a highly attractive industry. Most likely, this means that the business has a large market share of a high growth industry. Businesses in this category are extremely valuable to an organization. Although they are likely to consume cash for plant and working capital expenditures, they are seeds which the organization will soon harvest into an attractive crop of benefits.

Businesses occupying a position in the lower right-hand quadrant of the matrix hold a favourable competitive position within a less attractive industry. Businesses in this category are again extremely valuable to an organization. Typically, such a business would be quite profitable due to its dominant low cost structure. This situation would generate surplus cash that could be employed to finance some of the other businesses of the organization, probably those in the upper right-hand quadrant of the matrix. Businesses in the lower right-hand quadrant are mature in nature and are in the vintage period of their life cycle.

Businesses occupying a position in the upper left-hand quadrant of the matrix hold a weak competitive position within a highly attractive industry. A low market share position is likely the cause of this situation. This type of business would not be attractive to an organization. Such a business is likely to consume cash and produce unacceptable benefits. An organization will attempt to either improve its competitive position or discharge the business rather than have it continue in this quadrant of the matrix.

Businesses occupying a position in the lower left-hand quadrant of the matrix are normally key problems for an organization. Their poor competitive position within an unattractive industry means unacceptable profitability and perhaps even losses. There is little hope of changing this situation due to the mature state of the industry life cycle. An organization would be fortunate to have no businesses occupying a position in this quadrant of the matrix.

An ideal portfolio of businesses for a given organization would have all of its undertakings crowded into the right-hand portion of the matrix. This would demonstrate that all businesses hold a strong competitive position within their industries. By balancing these businesses between the upper and lower right-hand quadrants, an organization can continuously renew the vitality of its operations by developing new businesses as its mature citizens decline in effectiveness. This is an ideal situation which very few organizations have managed to achieve. However, the first step towards achievement is always the recognition of such a situation as a desirable objective.

STRATEGIC ACTION

Business portfolio matrices can be used to collectively describe the competitive position and industry attractiveness pertaining to each of the organization's businesses. A business portfolio matrix representing the current state of affairs and one representing an ideal situation have already been discussed. In total, it is recommended that four business portfolio matrices be prepared. They are as follows:

1. An historical business portfolio matrix (perhaps 3-5 years in age).
2. The current business portfolio matrix.
3. A projected business portfolio matrix (assuming no changes in strategic policy).
4. A desired business portfolio matrix.

Aside from indicating the past position of the organization, the historical business portfolio matrix can be used to identify progress to date. This will isolate both the direction and momentum currently enjoyed by the organization. The projected business portfolio matrix will forecast the future position of the organization assuming all factors remain constant. This matrix is constructed using the historic sense and momentum of direction. The preparation of a desired business portfolio matrix is of extreme value to an organization. Discrepancies between this desired position and the current business portfolio matrix represent the strategic courses of action that the organization wishes to undertake. Before proceeding from one point to another, an organization must first determine the difference between the two. It is this value that a desired business portfolio matrix bestows upon an organization.

The difference between the current business portfolio matrix and the desired portfolio matrix describes the major operational objectives that an organization sets for itself. These objectives are consistent with the organization's charter of objectives and are the goals around which all subsequent activity will be coordinated. This is the essence of corporate strategy. In effect, the specific function of the charter of objectives is now being expressed in terms of the individual businesses which the organization should pursue. Furthermore, it incorporates all of the strategic actions necessary to make this expression a reality.

Conceptually, the progression from a charter of objectives to corporate strategy is an easy process to follow. Nevertheless, an indepth analysis and investigation is essential to ensure that the proper decisions result. As mentioned at the outset of this chapter, the development of corporate strategy is something that the chief executive officer and his executive committee cannot delegate. Only the organization's top people can be entrusted with the responsibility of determining such a fundamental course for the institution.

To add further complexity to the development of corporate strategy, the progression from the charter of objectives to the strategic business unit level also requires continued attention to the eight categories of objectives outlined in the previous chapter (market standing, innovation, productivity, physical and financial resources, profitability, public responsibility, worker performance and attitude and manager performance development). The strategic action planned for each business of the organization, regardless of whether it is a change or not, must address each of these eight topics. This will allow the full scope of needs to be considered in every business of the organization and protect against a situation where one or more of the long-term success factors is ignored.

The importance which each business of the organization places upon the individual categories of objectives will be largely determined by the harmony already created within the charter of objectives. Slight variations in harmony can be expected at the business level. However, any radical deviations should not be permitted. In summary, corporate strategy — representing the difference between the current and the desired business portfolio matrices — needs to be stated in such a fashion that all eight categories of objectives are considered and that harmony among them is created.

Exhibit 5-6 on the following page visually displays the relationship between corporate strategy and the charter of objectives. The strategy pertaining to each business addresses the full complement of objective categories. Finally, a new harmony among the categories of objectives is brought to each business. As the nature of the business flows from the specific function de-

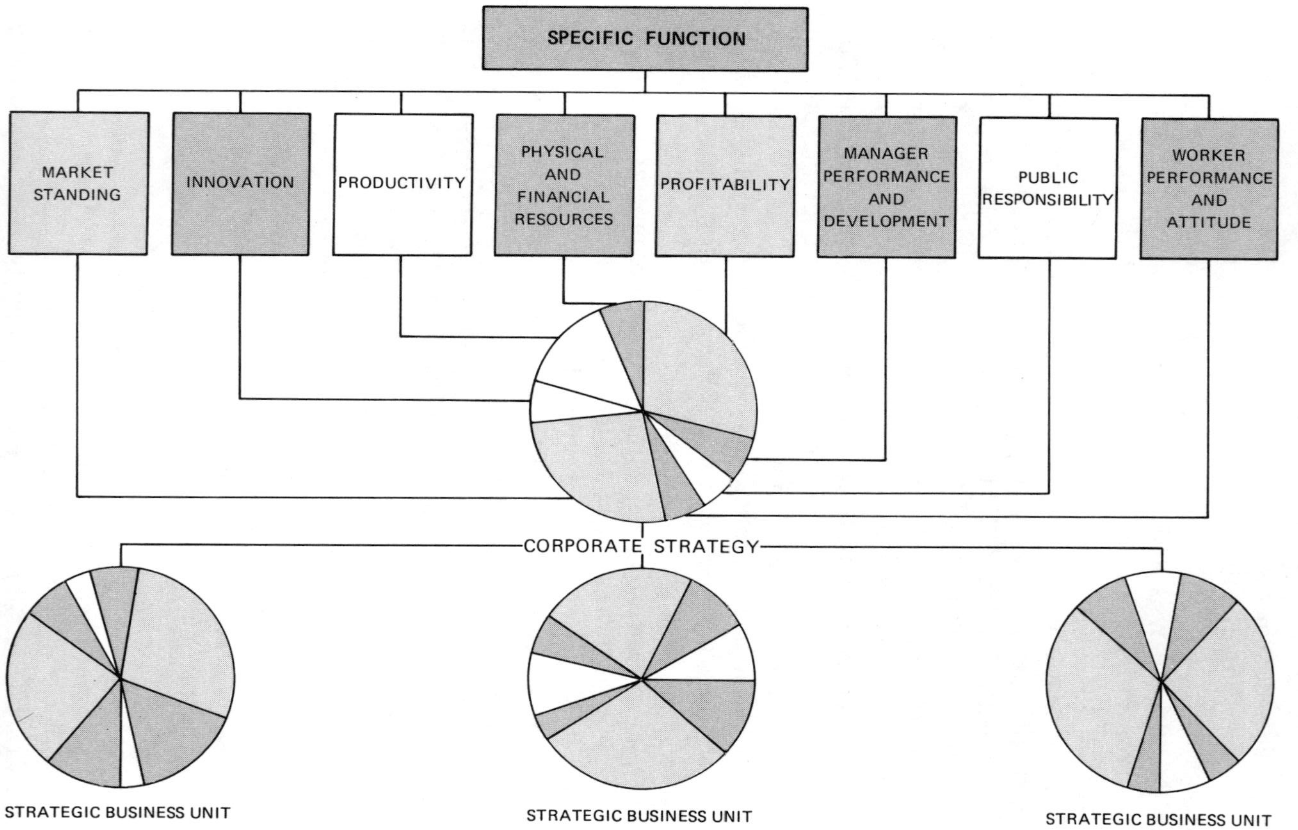

Exhibit 5-6 Corporate strategy as an evolution from the charter of objectives.

scribed in the charter of objectives, so does the balance of harmony flow into each business included in the corporate strategy.

THE STRATEGY CHRONICLE

The formulation of corporate strategy marks the completion of the chief executive officer's and his executive committee's initial role in the Strategy Management process. From here, the onus of responsibility is passed to middle management. Senior management will now settle into a passive role of supervising the efforts of middle management. As part of this transition of responsibility from senior to middle management, a formal communication or summary of the events to this point is required. The vehicle through which this knowledge is transferred is the strategy chronicle.

The strategy chronicle is used to bridge the communication gap between senior management and middle management. It is a documentation of senior management's activities and decisions pertaining to both the charter of objectives and corporate strategy formulation. The intention of the strategy chronicle is to clearly state the message which senior management wants to pass on to middle management while hopefully minimizing the possibility of misinterpretation.

Initially, the strategy chronicle is assembled in "draft format". This tentative presentation is used as an agenda or focal point of discussion for a "brainstorming" session involving senior and middle managers. This meeting will provide an opportunity for senior management to unveil their findings in an informal manner. Most importantly, this session gives middle management a chance to raise questions and express their feelings thereby providing a valuable source of input to these critical issues. Specifically, this "brainstorming" session is an occasion for senior management to test the integrity of their plans before they are firmly documented in an official strategy chronicle.

The "brainstorming" session should be expected to require a minimum of one day's attention and a maximum of two. It is normally a good idea to hold the meeting away from the organization's regular offices. This stresses the importance of the event and tends to minimize potential distractions. A meeting involving the middle and senior executive echelons of an organization is obviously a serious and expensive investment. Considering the importance of the situation, it is probably one of the best investments that an institution can make.

Promptly following the "brainstorming" session, the strategy chronicle should be put into a final format and published to all attendees of the meeting. The contents of the strategy chronicle would be as follows:

1. A full explanation of the charter of objectives of the organization.
2. An explanation of the current status of the organization's portfolio of businesses.
3. An explanation of the desired status of the organization's portfolio of businesses.
4. An explanation of the differences between the current and the desired status of the organization including a description of the intended strategic actions for each strategic business unit.
5. An explanation of how harmony among the eight categories of objectives is implanted into the strategic action plans of each respective strategic business unit.

By concernng itself with all of these five issues, the strategy chronicle becomes a comprehensive and articulate document summarizing senior management's aspirations for the institution. It is essential to establish this sound foundation as the primary sense of purpose and direction for the organization.

6

Strategic Business Unit Analysis

The organizational concept of a strategic business unit was presented in the previous chapter. It has been described as a discrete business in which an organization is or proposes to be involved. This definition retains its validity regardless of whether the strategic business unit occupies a formal position on the organization chart. The purpose of a strategic business unit is significantly different from that of corporate strategy formulation. Rather than focusing on the question of what business should be in the organization's stable, the strategic business unit is intimately concerned with how to best operate or compete within the specific business. Although this is a natural progression from corporate strategy, the issue of strategic business unit analysis is fundamentally unique. Coincidental with the graduation from the senior management to the middle management level, the strategic business unit analysis changes from a focus of "what" to a focus of "how". This alteration will be apparent in all components of the analysis.

In addition to changing the focus, the activities of the strategic business unit are also designed to bridge the communication and knowledge gap between senior and middle management. This is accomplished by incorporating a review of the corporate strategy pertaining to the strategic business unit within its own analysis. In effect, this is an expression of a second opinion about the direction of the strategic business unit. Combining this with its basic purpose, the mandate of the strategic business unit can be summarized as follows:

1. To confirm the validity of the corporate strategy formulated for the strategic business unit by ensuring that the industry attractiveness and competitive position have been accurately assessed and that the ensuing planned strategic action is appropriate and feasible.
2. To determine the optimum manner in which to conduct itself in support of this strategic action.

Strategic business unit analysis requires a thorough examination of all aspects of the business if these two objectives are to be met. This involves a significant amount of detail as compared to corporate strategy formulation. Most importantly, strategic business unit analysis demands a corresponding examination of the position of other organizations' businesses operating within the same industry. This external examination will permit the development of strategy only after full consideration of the complete operating environment has been achieved.

CONFIRMING INDUSTRY ATTRACTIVENESS

The strategic business unit's first task is to examine the attractiveness of the industry in which it participates. This is then followed by an assessment of the competitive position within it. This is a duplication of senior management's efforts but is nevertheless of significant value. The new mission will be approached from a fresh and unique point of view. It will also be a more comprehensive analysis performed by those executives intimately involved with the issues of concern.

Industry attractiveness is a relatively straight forward topic to evaluate at the strategic business unit level because only one industry is involved. However, this simplicity is somewhat negated by the fact that the issues of attractiveness are more numerous than those addressed when formulating corporate strategy. This expanded scope of analysis reflects the ability of strategic business unit managers to better understand and evaluate their businesses.

It is a reflection of their proximity to the situation.

The issues of industry attractiveness incorporated into the strategic business unit analysis should be consistent with those employed during corporate strategy formulation. The former are a natural outflow from the latter. As an example, industry profitability may be embellished into return on investment and cash generation issues at the strategic business unit level. Moreover, the relative importance of each of these issues should be similar to the pattern of importance utilized by senior management during the initial assessment of industry attractiveness. Significant discrepancies signal a disagreement between senior management and the strategic business unit personnel that require resolution before the analysis can proceed. A list of more detailed issues that a strategic business unit may want to consider in its examination of industry attractiveness is as follows:

Cash generation ability of industry.
Competition intensity of industry (absence of).
Currency rate fluctuation exposure (absence of).
Customer financial strength and reputation.
Domestic size of industry.
Energy consumption requirements (absence of).
Environmental protection requirements (absence of).
Growth rate of industry.
International size of industry.
Labour and material inflation potential (absence of).
Life cycle stage of industry.
Managerial talent availability.
Number of industry competitors (absence of).
Pricing flexibility of industry.
Public acceptability of industry.
Public appreciation of industry.
Return on investment potential.
Technology development rate.
Technology leverage potential.
Work force skill availability.

Every issue involved in the measurement of industry attractiveness deserves a great deal of attention. The strategic business unit should explain the results of its investigation pertaining to each of these issues in a written report, which serves as the formal confirmation of strategic position. An Industry Attractiveness Summary form similar to the one described in Exhibit 5-3 of the previous chapter can also be employed by the strategic business unit to present its findings. This helps to objectively express the conclusions of the assessment and makes them easily comparable with those of other strategic business units.

CONFIRMING COMPETITIVE POSITION

The assessment of competitive position is where the unique skills of the strategic business unit can be truly utilized. Because of their intimacy with the organization's operations, personnel of the strategic business unit have an exceptional ability to evaluate the competitive position of the business.

Although competitive position evaluation at the strategic business unit level is a confirmation of the work done during corporate strategy formulation, the scope of analysis is significantly different. The strategic business unit personnel examine their competitive position in a comprehensive and objective manner. The efforts are similar to the previous efforts of senior management, but the methods used to accomplish the assessment are radically modified.

Like industry attractiveness, the topics considered in the confirmation of competitive position are more numerous than those used in the initial formulation of corporate strategy. The precise criteria used reflect middle management's ability to work at a level requiring an increased attention to detail. The criteria for evaluating competitive position will be logical extensions of the issues addressed by senior management when formulating corporate strategy. Furthermore, the relative importance of each criterion will be strongly influenced by the pattern established by senior management. Some of the more detailed issues that a strategic business unit may want to consider in its examination and confirmation of competitive position are:

Capacity of physical resources.
Communication with and understanding of market.
Distribution outlet quantity.
Efficiency of operating equipment.
Geographical closeness to market.

Inventory reserve position.
Labour disruption potential (absence of).
Managerial orientation to risk and change.
Managerial understanding of industry.
Marketing effort effectiveness.
Market share.
Morale of work force.
Product/service average costs.
Raw material access and security.
Reliability of products/services.
Sales force size.
Skill level of work force.
Technology acceptance by work force.
Technology employment leadership.
Wage rate averages.

The strategic business unit should plan to expend much effort on its confirmation of competitive position. Each criterion of competitive strength warrants a thorough investigation if an accurate assessment is to result. A written report is used to formally document the efforts and findings of the strategic business unit as a conclusion to its evaluation. A Competitive Position Summary form similar in mechanics to the one described in Exhibit 5-4 of the previous chapter can also be prepared to help explain the results. This type of form expresses competitive position in numerical terms which facilitates a comparison among the various strategic business units of the organization.

CONFIRMING STRATEGIC POSITION

After the assessments of both industry attractiveness and competitive position have been completed, their proper presentation in the form of a business portfolio matrix is required. This is another concept that was first introduced during corporate strategy formulation. However, the business portfolio matrices used at the strategic business unit level are likely to be somewhat more elaborate and articulate.

To complement the illustration of the current strategic position, an historic, a projected and a desired business portfolio matrix should be constructed as well. The magnitude of this task is not simply restricted to the preparation of the appropriate diagrams. Each matrix represents a separate analysis effort by the strategic business unit. The matrix is used to summarize the results of these various investigations. Since only one industry is assessed by each strategic business unit, these four different matrices can be consolidated without causing confusion. Actually, consolidation produces a more meaningful picture of strategic position because the positions at various times can be related to one another. Exhibits 6-1 and 6-2 are examples of business portfolio matrices incorporating the historic, current, projected and desired points of view into one presentation. Exhibit 6-1 is a nine section matrix (3x3). Exhibit 6-2 is a fifteen section matrix[1] (5x3) using industry life cycle as one of its axes. Should either industry attractiveness or competitive position be clearly dominated by one factor, this factor could be represented by one of the axes. Exhibit 6-2 is one such case where the life cycle is the dominant factor in determining industry attractiveness.

APPRECIATING THE COMPETITION

The fundamental mandate of the strategic business unit has already been clearly described as one of determining how to best operate within the given industry. Confirming the accuracy of the organization's perception of its strategic position is only the first step towards achieving this goal. A more exhaustive effort of delving into the nature and status of competition will allow a strategic business unit to further progress towards the realization of its mandate.

A logical development in the exercise of discovering an optimum manner of behaviour is to extend the competitive position evaluation to the key competitors of the strategic business unit. The efforts that the strategic business unit expended while confirming its competitive position can be duplicated for each of the industry's prime participants. This results in a comparison between the strategic business unit's own competitive position and that of its industry foes. This comparison makes competitive position a relative issue not only to industry attract-

1 Hofer, Charles W. and Schendel, Dan, *Strategy Formulation: Analytical Concepts,* (St. Paul: West Publishing Company, 1978), page 34.

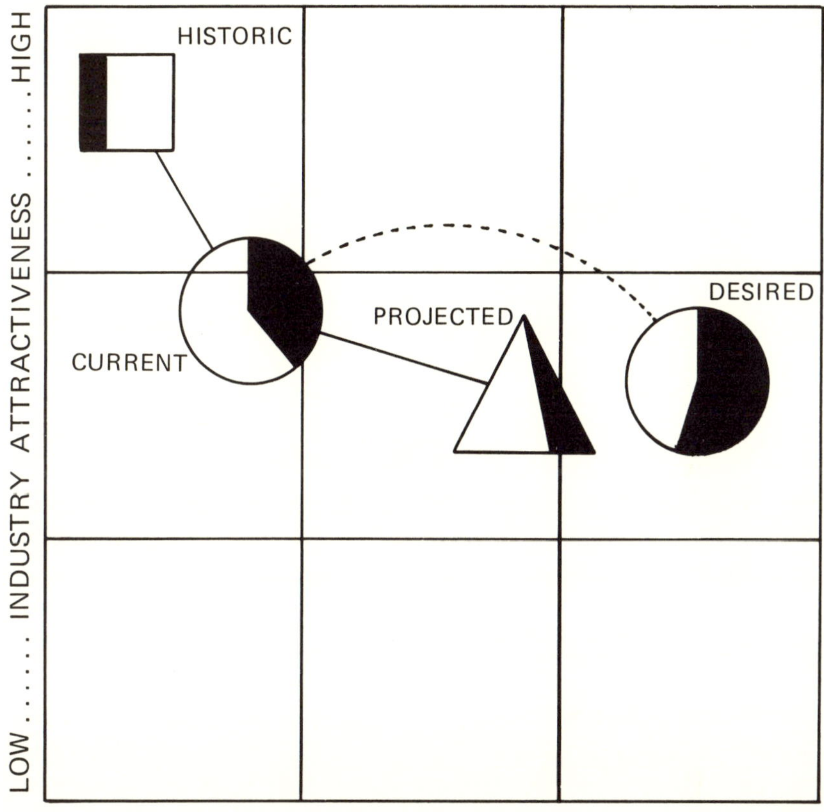

Exhibit 6-1 Example of a Business Portfolio Matrix using
traditional variables.

iveness but to neighboring organizations as well.

When an evaluation of competitive position has been repeated for each major industry participant, the findings need to
be presented in a format relevant to the strategic business unit.
A competitive position matrix can serve this purpose. The intention of the competitive position matrix is to visually illustrate the
characteristics of each industry participant's competitive stature
in one consolidated presentation. Exhibit 6-3 is an example of a
competitive position matrix where the two variable components
are overall competitive position and marketing capability. The

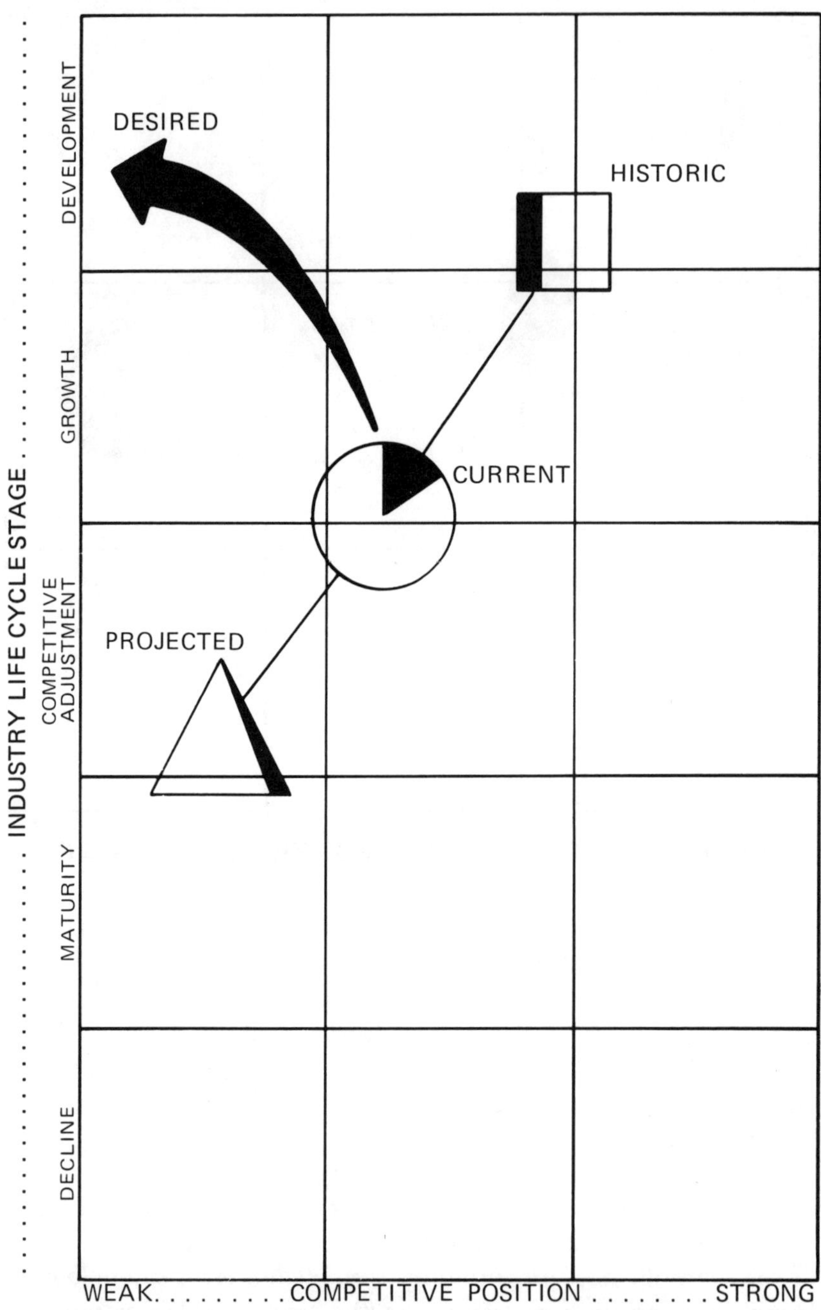

Exhibit 6-2 Example of a Business Portfolio Matrix using a dominant factor.

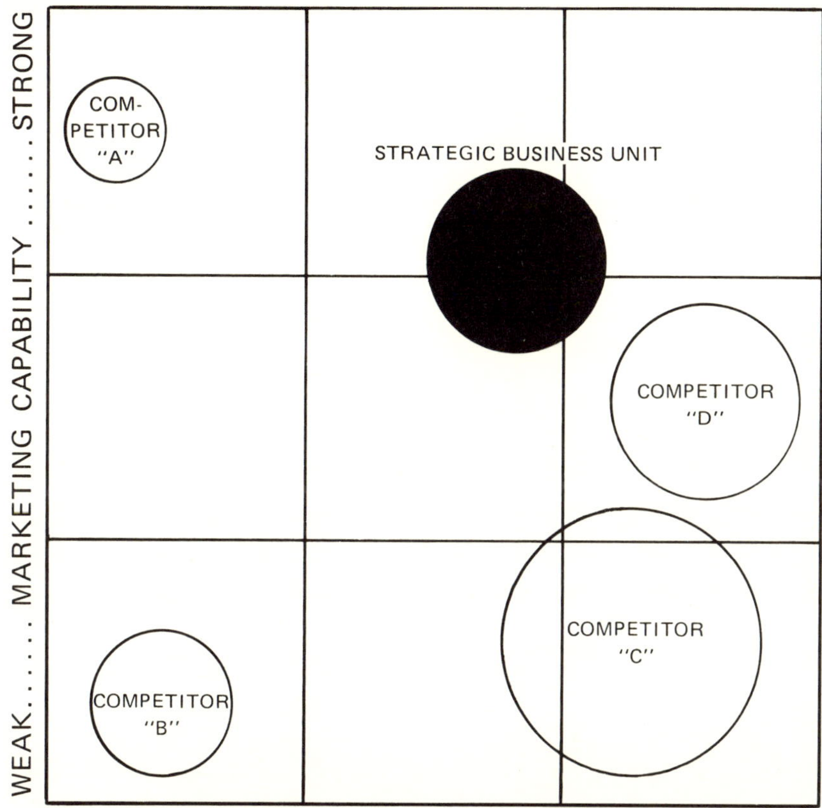

Exhibit 6-3 Example of a Competitive Position Matrix with one dominant factor.

circles contained within the matrix are proportional to the market share enjoyed by the respective organizations competing within the industry. The shaded circle represents the position of the strategic business unit performing the analysis. As the exhibit illustrates, the relative competitive strength of the individual players is easily appreciated.

Exhibit 6-3 uses marketing capability as a complementary matrix variable to overall competitive position. Any other issue which may dominate the assessment of competitive position can be substituted in its place. Furthermore, if two issues clearly

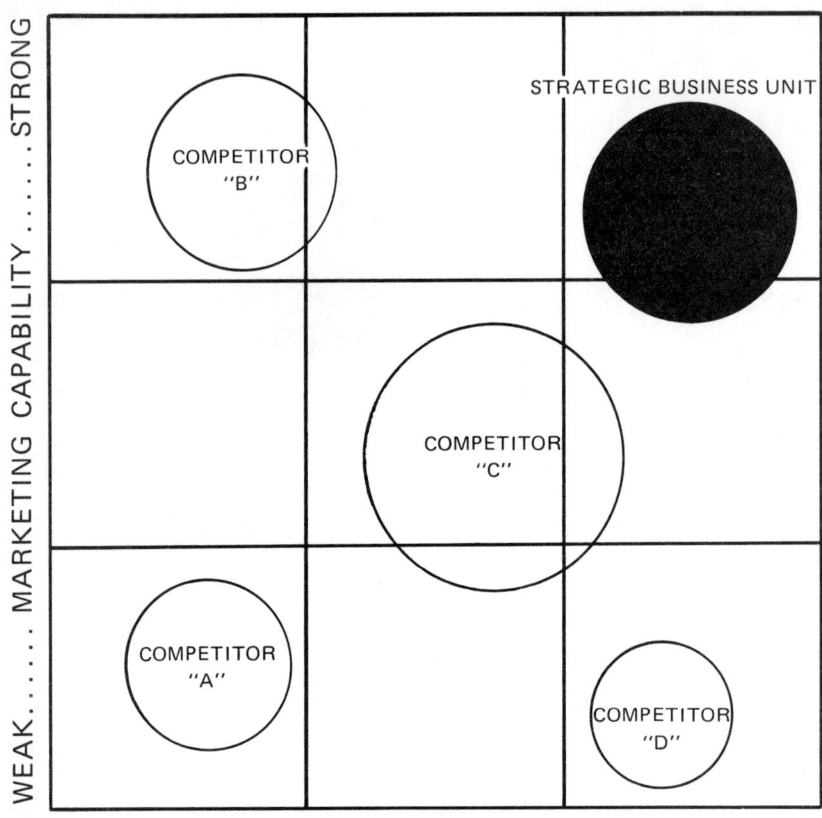

Exhibit 6-4 Example of a Competitive Position Matrix with two dominant factors.

dominate the consideration, they can be specially identified on each of the two individual axis of the matrix. Exhibit 6-4 is an example of such a situation where product or service quality and marketing capability have been judged as the two outstanding factors. The utilization of competitive position matrices in conjunction with business portfolio matrices provides an accurate description of the strategic business unit's sense of direction and relative strength. They are intended to create a solid foundation upon which the strategic business unit can begin to construct its plans for optimizing its competitive behaviour.

IDENTIFYING STRATEGIC OPPORTUNITIES

To this point in the chapter, we have directed our efforts towards confirming the accuracy of the strategic position described for each of the organization's major businesses during corporate strategy formulation. Attention will now be shifted to the efforts of the strategic business unit as it searches for the appropriate course of action which will allow it to progress from its current to its desired strategic position. Identification of major opportunities and impediments the business will encounter by taking this course of action is the fundamental task of the strategic business unit. This permits development of a strategy that both exploits the opportunities and minimizes the effects of the impediments while maximizing the contribution towards the objectives of the organization.

The objectives of the strategic business unit can be restated as follows:

1. The identification of those areas where the strategic business unit has unique advantages over others competing within the same industry. This is done for the purpose of possible exploitation.

2. The identification of those areas where others competing within the same industry have unique advantages over the strategic business unit. This is done for the purpose of possible protection.

When these objectives are achieved, a strategic business unit is in a position to understand what it possesses that competitors do not as well as what competitors possess that it does not. This knowledge is acquired through a series of profiles designed to determine the strengths and weaknesses of the business. A thorough understanding of what makes each industry participant unique is essential for any organization wishing to optimize its competitive position. These unique characteristics, expressed in terms of strategic opportunities and impediments, will strongly influence the type and substance of strategic action an organization will pursue.

FINANCIAL RESOURCE PROFILE

The most primitive form of resource which an organization possesses is its financial wealth. Financial resources are basic to all organizations and assume their value not from their intrinsic characteristics but from their ability to be readily converted into other forms of resources. Physical, human and organizational resources are all created using financial resources as the intermediary catalyst. For this reason, financial resources have an unusual importance and serve as a natural beginning place to examine the strategic business unit's and its competitor's unique dispositions.

The non-subjective nature of financial resources make them an easy subject to analyze. However, the difficulty of obtaining reliable information negates this advantage to a large degree. The examination of financial resources requires the construction of a profile concerning all major financial factors for both the strategic business unit in question and each of the primary competitors operating within the same industry. The purpose of this profile is to illustrate and compare the full spectrum of financial resource features possessed by the industry participants. This information will permit the strategic business unit to pursue its main objective of identifying the strengths and weaknesses of each industry member vis a vis the industry in total and the competition in particular.

One way to organize a financial resource profile is illustrated in Exhibit 6-5. This exhibit addresses a series of key financial issues that when considered individually and, most important, in total yield a thorough understanding of financial strength or weakness. This profile is constructed for the strategic business unit itself and as many major competitors as is appropriate. Each issue has an absolute answer which may be in the form of a ratio, a percentage or a dollar amount. Obviously, the information pertaining to competitors will in some cases be difficult to obtain. A variety of sources can be used to assemble this data. Less than perfect information about other organizations in the industry should be expected. A high degree of accuracy will suffice as a realistic goal. The absolute answers pertaining to each financial issue are ranked in their order of significance with the organiza-

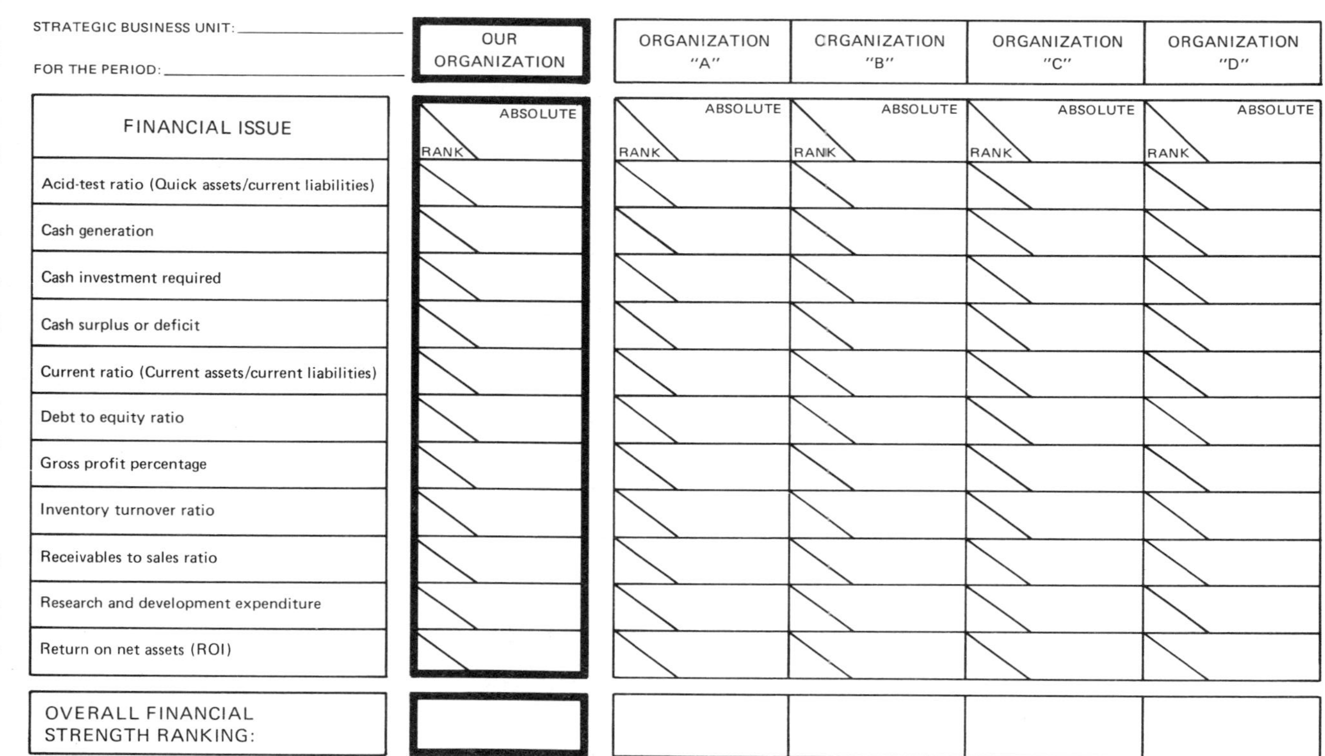

Exhibit 6-5 Example of a Financial Resource Profile form.

tion in the strongest position receiving the highest ranking. An overall financial strength ranking is used to summarize the relative position of each industry participant. This requires a somewhat subjective combination of all financial issues for each organization to arrive at this conclusion.

A series of financial resource profiles should be constructed by the strategic business unit. An historic, a current and a projected profile would be most appropriate. The current profile would correspond to the current year. An historic profile may cover the previous year or perhaps the previous three years, should this present a more meaningful analysis. Similarly, the projected financial resource profile would cover up to three or five years into the future and reflect the expected financial conditions, assuming no change in strategic action on the part of the industry participants. These profiles are intended to be constructed for the strategic business unit and the corresponding strategic business units of other organizations. However, a close examination of the financial issues contained in Exhibit 6-5 reveals that some issues, such as debt to equity ratio, will involve the total organization and not just the strategic business unit. When this broader scope is addressed, it is essential that the change in level for the financial issue be consistent for all competitors listed in the profile in order to protect the integrity of the analysis.

HUMAN RESOURCE PROFILE

Human resources, although not as quantitative as financial resources, are of extreme importance due to the high impact they can have upon the success of an institution. There is little doubt that some organizations possess a highly talented work force while others are saddled with a less than enthusiastic assembly of individuals. The difference between the two is difficult to measure in monetary terms. However, this presents little obstacle because the difference in value between the two is easily recognized.

The abilities of human resources will have a dramatic influence upon a strategic business unit's competitive position. Of greater importance, the competence of human resources will specifically dictate the range and magnitude of strategic action that an organization can realistically expect to achieve. These

circumstances highlight the importance of a thorough understanding of the human resources of each major participant in the
industry of which the strategic business unit is a part. It is only
with a clear and accurate perception of the human resource
strengths and weaknesses of itself and its competitors can a
strategic business unit arrive at proper decision for strategic
action.

A logical way to create an understanding of the strategic
business unit's human resources and those of its competitors is
to construct a human resource profile. Mechanically, this profile
is similar to a financial resource profile inasmuch as different areas
of concern are addressed for all major industry participants.
Exhibit 6-6 is an example of a Human Resource Profile Summary
form. This exhibit focuses on a series of human resource issues
designed to produce a comprehensive description of human
resource strength first for the strategic business unit and then
for each of its competitors. Because of the narrative nature of
these issues, there is insufficient space on the form to describe
their status. The form can act as a summary by referencing sections of a subsidiary report where a full discussion of the human
resource issue can be found. Most important, the form allows
us to appreciate the logistics behind the human resource profile
even if it is of only limited value in its summary/reference role.
The human resource status of each industry participant is ranked
in order of strength for each issue separately and then as an overall human resource summary. This overall summary of human
resource strength involves a subjective consolidation of all human
resource issues for each organization.

The human resource profile is intended to document the
status, nature, position or policy of a number of key issues having
a significant influence on the ability and willingness of a strategic
business unit's employees to act and to act properly. The issues
concern the strategic business unit as a whole and thus are qualita-
tive rather than functional in nature. Due to the importance of
human resources, an organization may wish to further explore its
strength and that of others in this area by segmenting human
resources into different functional categories. Exhibit 6-7 is an
example of a Human Resource Competence Profile Summary
form that can be used to assess strength within each functional

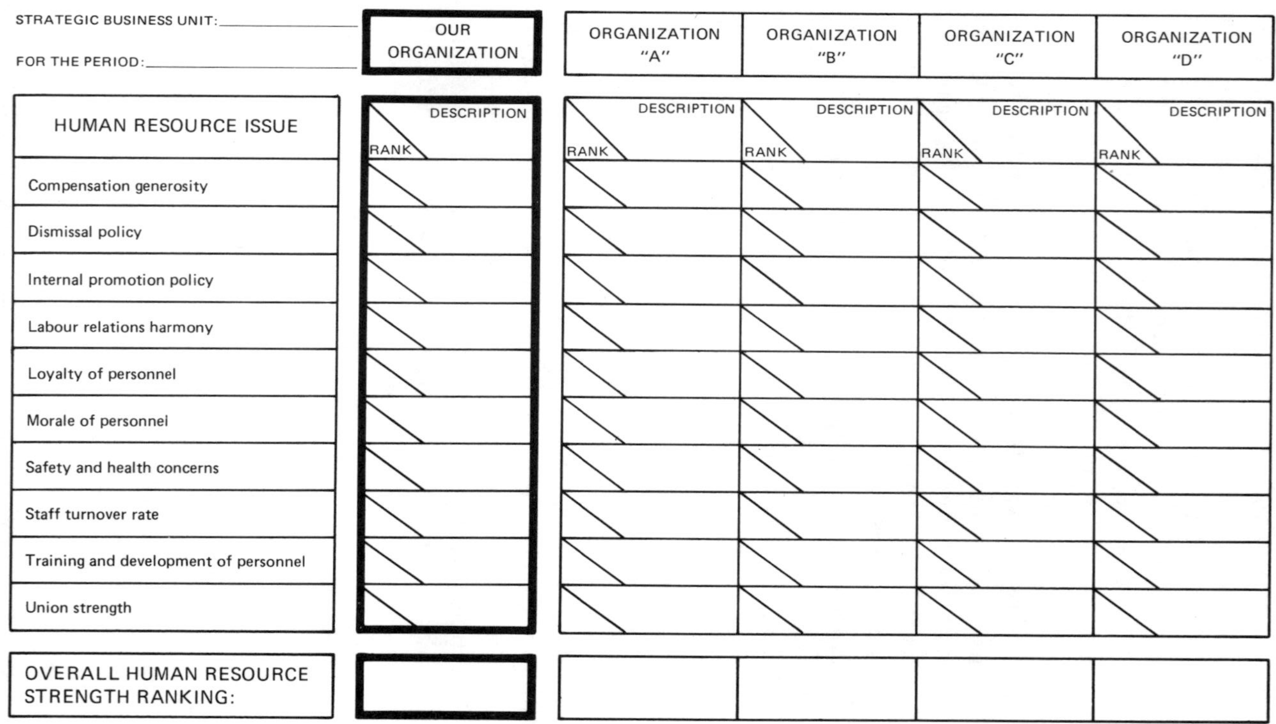

Exhibit 6-6 Example of a Human Resource Profile Summary form.

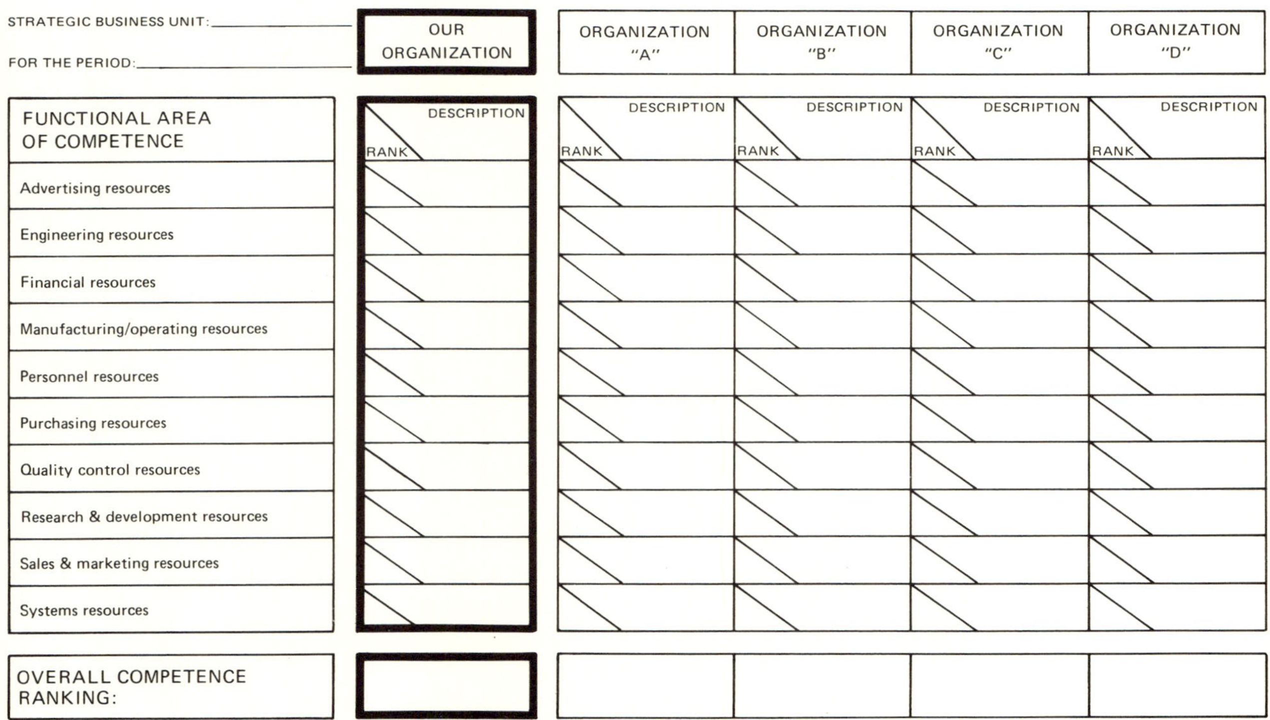

Exhibit 6-7 Example of a Human Resource Competence Profile Summary form.

category of the strategic business unit. This competence profile describes and ranks the competence of the strategic business unit and its competitors with respect to major operating disciplines. By doing so, a strategic business unit can more precisely identify its strengths and weaknesses and choose its subsequent strategic action from a position of greater knowledge. Once again, this form is referred to as a summary because space limitations do not permit a full discussion of the various areas of competence. References to a subsidiary report will be necessary to comprehensively present this human resource information.

When preparing the human resource profile and the human resource competence profile, special attention should be devoted to ensuring that the focus is on the strategic business unit and the corresponding strategic business units of other organizations. The strategic business unit is not being compared to the totality of other organizations participating in the industry — only their equivalent strategic business units. The possibility of making this inequitable comparison exists because some issues such as compensation generosity and union strength and some functional areas such as advertising and finance could have identical characteristics at both the strategic business unit and total organization levels. If there is a difference between the levels, it is imperative that the true position of the strategic business unit be the one included in the profiles.

As a final note concerning human resource profiles and competence profiles, the strategic business unit should construct its usual series of historic, current and projected analyses. This is a more complete examination which will add credibility to the identification of strengths and weaknesses associated with each individual industry participant.

PHYSICAL RESOURCE PROFILE

Physical resources refer to the fixed assets of the strategic business unit such as plants, equipment and buildings. They are a necessary ingredient in any organization's portfolio of resources — for without them an organization could not function. Physical resources are somewhat peculiar in comparison to the other forms of resources because their strength does not necessarily increase in direct proportion to quantity. If an organization — and a strategic business unit in particular — has an over abundance of physical resources, this is not likely to result in an advantage over its competitors. The carrying costs of such excess capacity may very well be a liability. At the other extreme of the spectrum where a strategic business unit is short on physical resources, a simple absence of competitive advantage no longer exists. Just the opposite, a strategic business unit with inadequate physical resources possesses a very serious weakness in comparison to other participants in the industry. Because of these circumstances, an analysis of physical resources is not likely to identify many strengths that a strategic business unit can exploit to improve its competitive position. However, such an analysis will reveal any weaknesses that the industry participants may have developed. Weaknesses in the area of physical resources can often be substantially exploited by other members of the industry to improve their competitive positions. The delay in employing physical resources permits this to occur.

A physical resource profile is prepared to examine the status of physical resources with the intention of discovering any surpluses or deficiencies. This profile initially examines the strategic business unit in question and then enlarges the analysis to include the industry's major participants. Exhibit 6-8 is an example of a Physical Resource Profile Summary form. This exhibit addresses a series of physical resource issues designed to produce an accurate picture of the strategic business unit's health in this area. The form is similar to the resource profiles described previously. There is inadequate space for a full narrative description of each physical resource issue of each industry participant. For this reason, the form is a summary and must be cross-referenced to a more detailed subsidiary report. The physical resource status of each industry participant is ranked in order of strength for each issue separately and then as an overall physical resource summary. The overall ranking requires a subjective summation of the different physical resource positions of the respective strategic business units.

While constructing the physical resource profile, it is important to remember that the focus is once again on strategic business units, not on complete organizations. The information document-

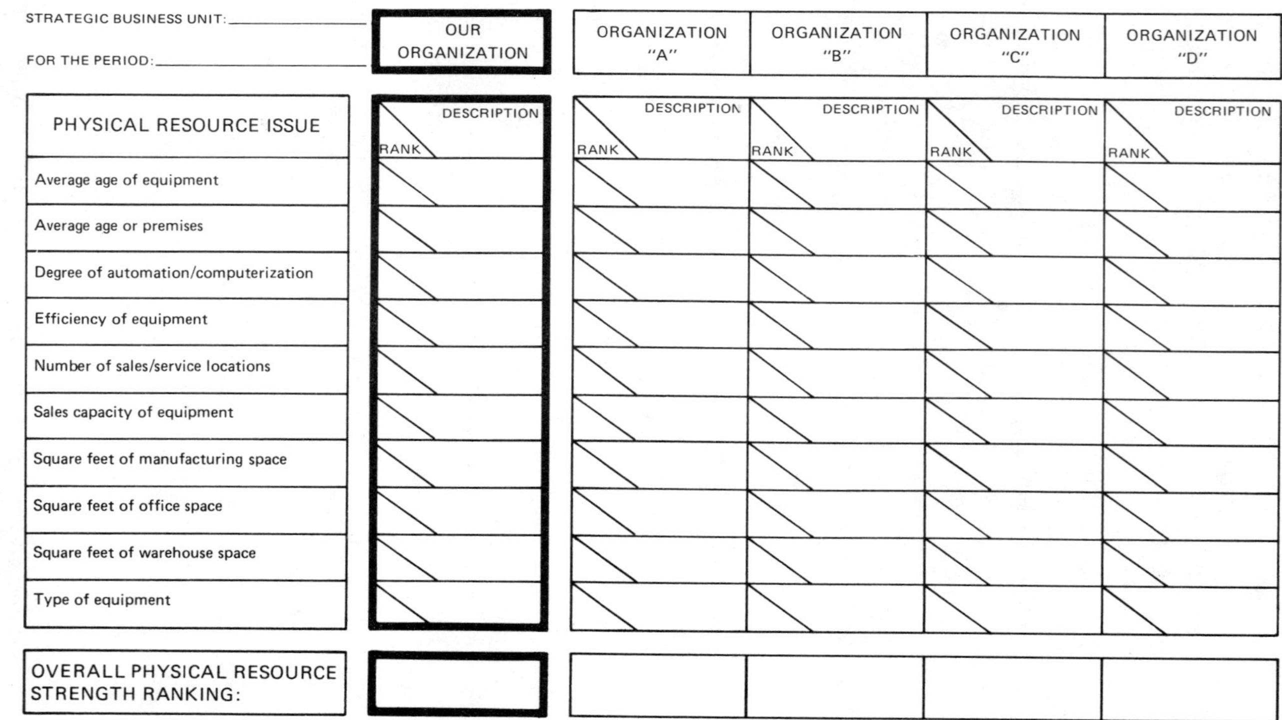

Exhibit 6-8 Example of a Physical Resource Profile Summary form.

ed for the competitors of the strategic business unit in question pertains to equivalent strategic business units rather than to the total organizations of which they are a part. This distinction is often difficult to make when examining physical resources because plant and equipment are not always clearly divided between the various strategic business units of an organization.

As with the preparation of other resource profiles, the physical resource profile should be triplicated to present an historic and projected point of view in addition to the current position. The historic and current physical resource profiles will form a basis for creating the projected analysis utilizing the assumption that no major shifts in strategic policy will be made by any of the industry participants. The current physical resource profile complemented by a projection will provide maximum ability for the strategic business unit to identify the strengths and weaknesses associated with each individual industry participant.

ORGANIZATIONAL RESOURCE PROFILE

Organizational resources refer to the systems, practices and procedures that a strategic business unit creates and maintains for itself. Unlike other forms of resources, organizational resources have intangible properties. They represent a sense of order that the human resources of the organization have developed. The purpose of organizational resources is to enhance the operating effectiveness of the organization and thereby better prepare it to realize its goals. Organizational resources are formal routines of management designed to optimize communication, direction and control. The value of organizational resources is difficult to document due to their intangible nature. What is the difference between a well run and poorly run organization? The answer to this question is the internal value of organizational resources. The external value of organizational resources can be measured by customer or public satsifaction with such procedures as billing, distribution and service. Together, the value of organizational resources can amount to a critical asset of an organization. For without strong organizational resources, an organization imposes restrictions on its ability to identify and execute appropriate courses of action.

The examination of organizational resources is best accomplished by preparing a profile for the strategic business unit and its relevant competitors. This profile will present a comprehensive illustration of the strengths and weaknesses of each industry participant for the various issues of organizational resources. Exhibit 6-9 is an example of an Organizational Resource Profile Summary form. This exhibit is a summary because the full scope of information cannot be accommodated on a single sheet of paper. The profile is concerned with the status of the key organizational resources within the various strategic business units. The strength of each industry participant is ranked for the respective organizational resource issues and is complemented by an overall ranking at the bottom of the form. When completed, the profile is intended to show the categorical and total organization resource strength of the key industry competitors in comparison with that of the strategic business unit in question.

As is customary when preparing resource profiles, the focus is specifically on the strategic business unit and presents historic, current and projected views of the situation. Many organizational resources will be shared across the full breadth of an institution. In these cases, the status of the organizational resource issue for the strategic business unit will correspond to that of the total organization. When performing a strategic business unit analysis, it is important to be alert to differences between the strategic business unit and the total organization because they are often sources of additional and significant strengths or weaknesses.

SEGMENTATION ANALYSIS

As part of its efforts to identify the opportunities and impediments which it faces, the strategic business unit has created a series of resource profiles. These profiles document the unique strengths and weaknesses of each industry participant pertaining to the four major resource categories of financial, human, physical and organizational. These resource categories are defined from an internal characteristic point of view. They represent different possessions of an organization. To complete the strategic business unit analysis, the opposite point of view needs to be considered as well. This is the external characteristic point of view for the given industry in which the strategic business unit operates.

THE ABC ORGANIZATION
ORGANIZATIONAL RESOURCE PROFILE SUMMARY

STRATEGIC BUSINESS UNIT: ____________

FOR THE PERIOD: ____________

ORGANIZATION RESOURCE ISSUE	OUR ORGANIZATION		ORGANIZATION "A"		ORGANIZATION "B"		ORGANIZATION "C"		ORGANIZATION "D"	
	RANK	DESCRIPTION	RANK	DESCRIPTION	RANK	DESCRIPTION	RANK	DESCRIPTION	RANK	DESCRIPTION
Ability to manage by objectives/results										
Clarity of organization structure										
Control ability/systems										
Inventory management ability/systems										
Management information systems										
Operating ability/systems										
Planning ability/systems										
Quality control ability/systems										
Research & development ability/direction										
Reward ability/systems										
OVERALL ORGANIZATIONAL RESOURCE RANKING:										

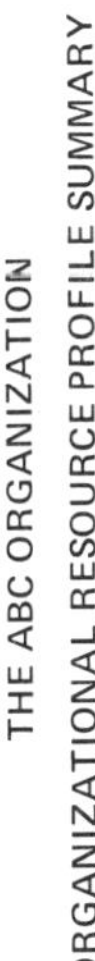

Exhibit 6-9 Example of an Organizational Resource Profile Summary form.

Externally, the industry or market can be segmented into a series of natural categories. A segment is any portion of an industry that is large enough to address in an economical fashion and which responds to a unique approach. Rather than defining strengths and weaknesses in terms of its own categories of resources, segmentation analysis requires strengths and weaknesses to be defined in terms of the industry traits. This double focus on strengths and weaknesses helps to ensure that no analytical omissions are made and that all possible opportunities to improve competitive position are uncovered.

Industry segmentation involves the selection of an appropriate level of detail. The number of choices facing a strategic business unit is infinite. For this reason, there is a very real danger that one can go overboard and simply segment industries as an academic exercise. When choosing the proper level of industry segmentation, it is important that the segments are of such a size that they are economically viable to serve in a differentiated manner. In addition, the industry should not be segmented beyond the point where strengths and weaknesses cannot be identified. Using these two criteria, a strategic business unit can decide upon the level of segmentation meaningful to the industry of which it is a part. To illustrate the nature of choices confronting a strategic business unit, an example of an industry segmentation exercise is presented in Exhibit 6-10. The exhibit shows how segmentation progresses from one level to another and leaves the impression that segmentation could be a never ending exercise. What the exhibit fails to show, however, is that the number of industry categories increases geometrically with the level of segmentation. This makes it more imperative that strategic business units be reasonable in the selection of their market segments for analysis.

When selecting industry segments, a strategic business unit should be constantly aware that entirely new segments may be developing. New industry segments often represent highly attractive opportunities for the strategic business unit. However, they are sometimes quite difficult to identify. A strategic business unit needs to be alert to any signs that new segments are forming. Market research is an excellent way in which to keep on top of these potential developments. Most new industry segments can be foreseen well in advance but the problem is in predicting "when".

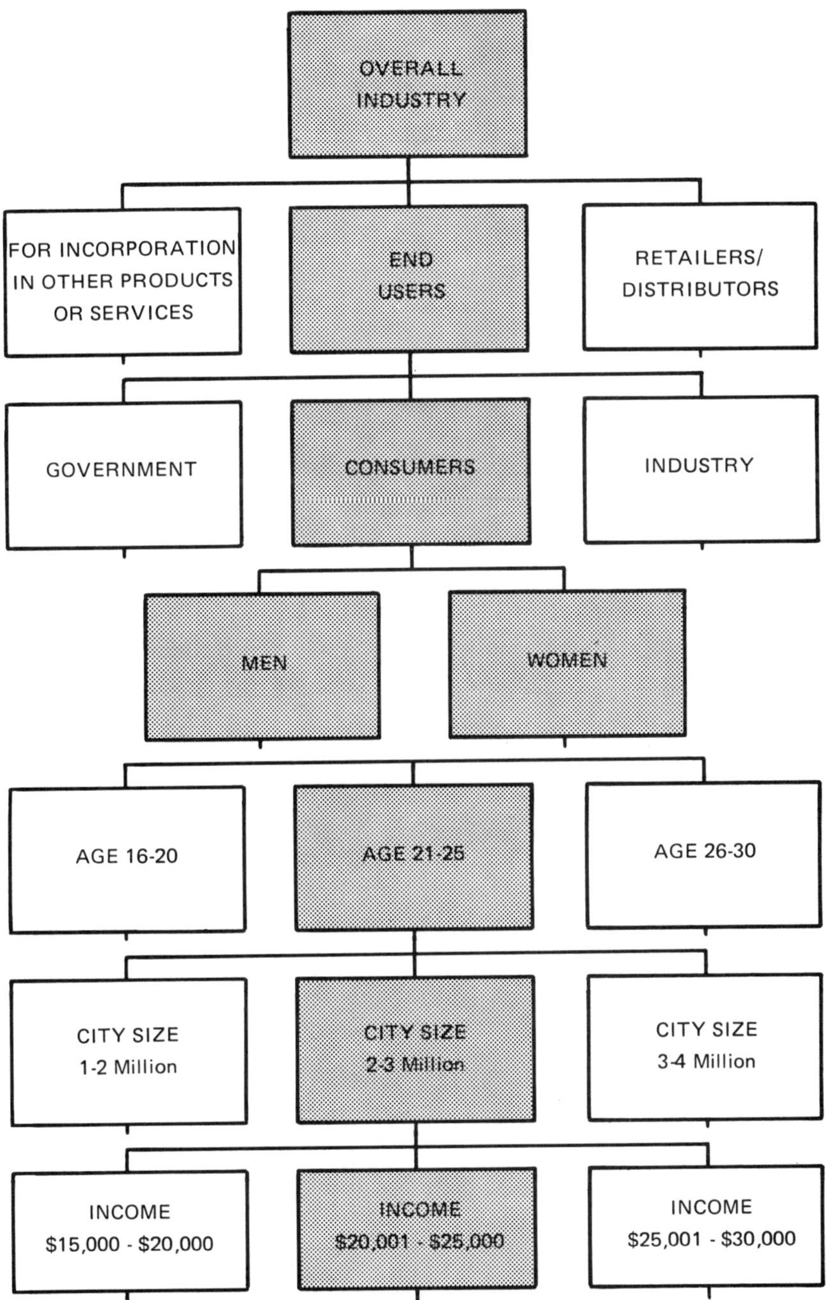

Exhibit 6-10 Example of an industry segmentation exercise.

Almost everyone will agree that someday every household will have its own personal computer or at least have access to one. However, the question is "when". It is important that strategic business units consider new market segments in their segmentation analysis simply because they present either an opportunity or impediment — the identification of which is the direct responsibility of the strategic business unit. New industry segments are high impact areas because they are certain to alter the competitive positions of industry participants.

Industry segmentation analysis is similar to the preparation of resource profiles inasmuch as the status of both the strategic business unit and each of its major competitors are considered. Exhibit 6-11 is an example of an Industry Segmentation Analysis form. The industry segments used in the example are very elementary in nature. Normally, a strategic business unit will use a more comprehensive list of industry segments in its analysis, both in terms of quantity and originality. However, the mechanics of the analysis can be sufficiently demonstrated using this example. The status of each industry segment includes a description of the **size** of the position (in dollar terms when possible) that the particular strategic business unit holds, the **share** of the segment to which this equates and the specific **growth rate** of that strategic business unit's share. In addition, the overall growth rate of the segment is entered on the form as well as the total size, share and growth rate for each industry member. Upon completion, the segmentation analysis will present a very explicit documentation of the strengths and weaknesses of each strategic business unit in relation to the logical sectors of the industry. For example, the segmentation analysis may indicate that females under the age of thirty represent a very high growth portion of the industry and that "Organization B" has almost complete share of this segment. If the physical resource profile indicates that "Organization B" is already operating at capacity, it may be a wise decision for "Our Organization" to focus attention on this market segment to meet the forthcoming demand and thereby improve competitive position.

Segmentation analysis will produce a wealth of information concerning an organization's own strategic business unit as well as those of competitors. Nevertheless, this information is acquired

THE ABC ORGANIZATION
INDUSTRY SEGMENTATION ANALYSIS

STRATEGIC BUSINESS UNIT: ______

FOR THE PERIOD: ______

INDUSTRY SEGMENT	SEGMENT GROWTH RATE	OUR ORGANIZATION			ORGANIZATION "A"			ORGANIZATION "B"			ORGANIZATION "C"			ORGANIZATION "D"		
		GROWTH RATE	SIZE	SHARE	GROWTH RATE	SIZE	SHARE	GROWTH RATE	SIZE	SHARE	GROWTH RATE	SIZE	SHARE	GROWTH RATE	SIZE	SHARE
Male population age 1-19																
Female population age 1-19																
Male population age 20-29																
Female population age 20-29																
Male population age 30-39																
Female population age 30-39																
Male population age 40-49																
Female population age 40-49																
Male population age 50 and over																
Female population age 50 and over																
TOTAL OF SEGMENTS:																

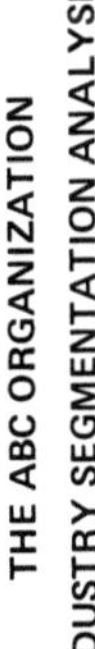

Exhibit 6-11 Example of an Industry Segmentation Analysis form.

as the result of much effort. The elementary example presented in Exhibit 6-11 contains 121 separate pieces of information and a further 55 calculations. Constructing a segmentation analysis is not a chore to be taken lightly.

As in the case of resource profiles, a series of segmentation analyses should be prepared. Due to the volatility of industry segments, changes in status can be expected to occur much more frequently than with resource profiles. The development of an historic, current and projected segmentation analysis will permit a strategic business unit to keep abreast of changes in all segments of the industry. Only timely and accurate information can be of value when assessing strengths and weaknesses in hope of improving competitive position.

THE SOURCES OF INFORMATION

A question which has been waiting in the wings since we focused on confirming industry attractiveness has now come to centre stage with the attention given to the creation of resource profiles and segmentation analyses. The question is: where do we get the information to include in the analyses? There is no simple answer and no magic formula that can solve this problem. A central registry where all the information is waiting to be had simply does not exist. The strategic business unit must use a variety of sources to provide it with the information that it needs. Some of the more useful sources are as follows:

1. Government information publications.
2. Corporate annual reports.
3. News releases.
4. Advertising material.
5. Sales force feedback.
6. Customer discussions.
7. Employees recruited from competitors.
8. Industry associations.
9. Direct contact with competitors.
10. Supplier discussions.

Of these sources, the most overlooked and sometimes the most valuable are the ones concerning the organization's own employees. It is surprising to see the wealth of information that already exists within an organization waiting to be mobilized. All that is needed is someone to recognize its value and to set about acquiring it.

For those organizations determined to receive optimum value from the information source of its employees, the establishment of a competitor information bureau could be a wise idea. A competitor information bureau brings formality to the function of collecting and digesting information from employees about the actions of competitors. The existence of such a bureau signifies that the organization is serious and highly regards the input of its employees. The competitor information bureau presents a high profile vehicle for employees to express themselves. It is a centralized collection and assimilation function for all competitor intelligence. The bureau should be staffed by a small number of people whose job is to encourage employee participation and then react to information upon presentation. This requires a close rapport with all levels of management so that the information can be passed along in a timely and effective manner. It also involves rewarding employees for their contribution. Rewards provide the reason why employees should take the time and make the effort to both collect the information and then deposit it with the competitor information bureau. The reward should have a dual focus. It should recognize the basic act of contribution and it should recognize the relative value of the information. As an example, an organization can award a prize or compensation for the three most valuable pieces of information contributed each month. Furthermore, each contribution (regardless of how insignificant) can entitle the employee to one chance for a prize or compensation decided by a drawing each month. These two forms of rewards encourage participation and produce valuable information. Such a system of rewards would ensure that all competitor information reaches the bureau and that an employee will not withhold such information, feeling it to be unimportant. This would permit more qualified personnel to judge the significance of the information.

Whether competitor information comes from a centralized bureau or any other source, it will not always be entirely complete and precisely up to date. It can never be perfect and should not be expected to be so. Strategic business unit personnel should strive for the best possible information to include in their deliberations. At the same time, they should realize that it is a matter of quality. Perfection is not required to make the proper strategic decisions. However, good quality information is fundamental. The ability of the strategic business unit to exploit its information sources will have an equally significant influence upon the success of its assessment and the analysis that is subsequently applied.

RATIONALIZING THE STRATEGIC BUSINESS UNIT ANALYSIS

At the outset of this chapter, the purpose of the strategic business unit analysis was described as an effort to determine the optimum manner of competition within the specified industry. The method of carrying out this mission was to construct an outline of the strengths and weaknesses of each of the industry's major participants. In the course of this action, four different resource profiles and a segmentation analysis were developed. Collectively, these exercises will generate an abundance of information. As a conclusion to the strategic business unit analysis, there is a need to sort out, interpret, explain and organize this information so that it can be applied in a meaningful way. This is a rationalization process.

The rationalization process begins with a review of all information assembled during the analysis. As part of the review, strategic business unit management will be searching for bits of information that have little or no contribution to potential strategic action. These bits of information will be a resource profile issue where none of the industry participants is in a clear position of advantage or disadvantage. For example, should the human resource profile indicate that all parties have an equal degree of labour relations harmony, this issue no longer represents a significant concern in the strategic business unit analysis. Issues with results of this nature should be weeded out of the analysis so that the amount of information is manageable and is confined exclusively to positions of strength or weakness. This is an act of management by exception.

Once the peripheral information has been extracted from the main body of the strategic business unit analysis, the final task is to arrange the remaining data into an intelligible format. This involves arranging the strength and weakness information into an order of importance. Importance is determined by ability to affect the competitive position of the strategic business unit. There are a number of different ways that a strategic business unit can go about arranging the analysis in this order of importance. One way is to review each piece of relevant data and then to classify it as high impact, medium impact or low impact. Following this initial sort, the final order of importance can be decided upon. Another way to arrange the analysis data is to assign a weight of importance to each separate item of either strength or weakness. A scale of from one to ten can be used as a basic sorting mechanism after which the final order of impact can be documented.

Arranging the strategic business unit analysis in order of its impact on competitive position is no easy chore. There are no forms or formulas that can be employed to calculate the proper answers. The number and quality of variables affecting the decision demand that a subjective response be developed. Only creative thinking and astute analysis can assist in this matter. matter.

The objective of the rationalization process is to arrive at a list of strengths and a list of weaknesses for the strategic business unit. These lists would contain a **description** of the strength or weakness instead of just a name. Both lists would be arranged in their order of importance as determined by impact on competitive position. As a result, the strategic business unit produces a documentation (in the form of a short story) of its unique characteristics expressed in competitive terminology. It now has an understanding of the industry in which it is operating, the position it holds within that industry and the opportunities and impediments both it and its competitors possess. From this position of knowledge, the strategic business unit is now prepared to decide upon its appropriate course of strategic action.

Exhibit 6-12 on the following page is a summary of the information components, the flow and the results of the strategic business unit analysis rationalization process. Although the middle circle of the exhibit is an over simplification of the management effort involved in the process, a sound appreciation of the mechanics can be derived from the illustration.

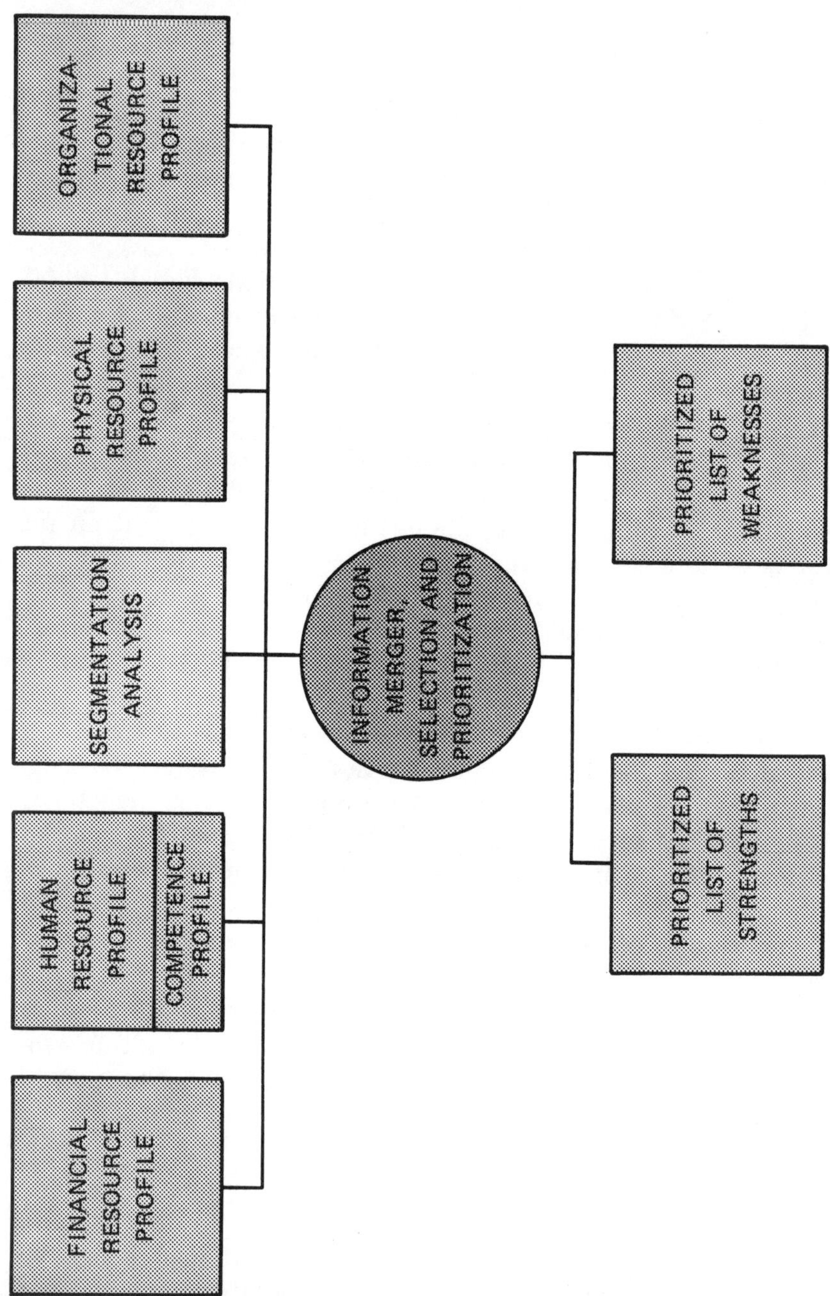

Exhibit 6-12 The strategic business unit analysis rationalization process.

7

Strategic Business Unit Recommendation

The previous chapter began with an explanation of the mandate of the strategic business unit. This was described as a mission to determine the optimum manner in which to compete within the particular industry. Inherently, this also involved a confirmation of the corporate strategy originally developed for the strategic business unit. The previous chapter also went to considerable lengths in its explanation of how various types of information are compiled with respect to the industry's major participants. The remaining task of the strategic business unit is to put this information to good use. This is largely a matter of exploitation whereby the strengths and weaknesses of the strategic business unit are utilized to both identify the appropriate course of strategic action as well as to formulate the individual components contained therein.

This chapter will focus on the different types of strategy recommendations that can result from the analysis efforts of the strategic business unit. As part of this focus, the purpose of the various strategy alternatives, the circumstances in which to best employ each and the presentation format of the recommendation will all be examined.

STRATEGY RECOMMENDATION FORMAT

In response to the information that a strategic business unit has assembled about itself and its competitors, there are four different types of strategic action which it may pursue. These four categories are as follows:

1. Build strategies.
2. Maintain strategies.
3. Harvest strategies.
4. Divestiture strategies.

There is a wide range of activity within each of these types of strategies that the strategic business unit can select as its means of operation. However, these are best seen as subsidiary components to the overall strategy recommendation. The selection of the appropriate strategy category is usually easy to make because it is largely determined by the current strategic position of industry attractiveness and competitive position. It is the question of how to carry out the strategy that will be extremely difficult to decide upon. In other words, the question of what to do is much easier answered than how to do it. The magnitude of benefit to be derived from addressing these two concerns will be directly related to the degree of difficulty experienced. Granted, Strategy Management will help an organization to alter its portfolio of strategic business units and the strategies which they are pursuing but the major improvement from the process will be a discovery of better ways in which to carry out their present competitive activities. This situation is less dramatic than making a series of key fundamental changes in an organization's makeup. Nevertheless, in no way should this detract from the significance of the result. With this in mind, the critical importance of the strategic business unit's description of how it proposes to carry out the selected category of strategic action can be fully appreciated.

The presentation of the strategy recommendation is intended to concurrently address both issues of what to do and how to do it. Based upon the analysis and interpretation of the data it has collected, the strategic business unit chooses its desired course of strategic action and then proceeds to describe the major processes to be utilized in its pursuit. These answers of "what" and "how" form the nucleus of the strategy recommendation presentation.

Peripheral information such as a description of strategic position, the reasoning supporting the strategic decision, performance targets and resource requirements are also necessary ingredients of the strategy recommendation.

Because of the small number and uniqueness of strategic business units within an organization, the recommendation would normally be prepared in an unstructured format. The topics to be addressed in the recommendation would be made clear and then the strategic business unit would proceed to construct its recommendation in a "free form" within these general constraints. The sequence and depth of discussion pertaining to each topic would be left to the discretion of the strategic business unit management. This flexibility can be used to best explain the strategy recommendation while at the same time considering the novelty of the strategic business unit's environment.

An organization may wish that its strategic business units use a more structured format when preparing their strategy recommendations. This would involve a **summary** of the strategy recommendation on a form specified by the organization. No form can adequately allow one, let alone all of the strategic business units, to present their strategy recommendations with the degree of comprehension suitable to the occasion. For this reason, any form used by a strategic business unit to document its strategy recommendation must be a summary.

Should an organization decide to adopt a structured summary, the form employed must be customized to best meet the needs and emphasis of the institution. When customizing the form, the variable components are the topics themselves and the space devoted to each. Different combinations of these variables will emphasize certain issues which the organization deems to be relevant. It is suggested that the form used to summarize the strategy recommendation be a single sheet of paper. A piece of paper eleven inches by seventeen inches folded in half yields four full pages of eight and one-half by eleven inches (standard page size) writing surfaces. Exhibit 7-1 is an example of such a four page Strategy Recommendation Summary form. The topics included in this exhibit are the ones which would normally be addressed by the strategy recommendation. Since every organization will customize the form in response to its own needs, this

**THE ABC ORGANIZATION
STRATEGY RECOMMENDATION SUMMARY**

STRATEGIC BUSINESS UNIT:. . . . . .DATE: . . . .

<table>
<tr><td>CURRENT STRATEGIC POSITION:</td><td>HISTORIC STRATEGIC POSITION</td></tr>
<tr><td>PROJECTED STRATEGIC POSITION:</td><td>DESIRED STRATEGIC POSITION:</td></tr>
<tr><td colspan="2">STRATEGIC ACTION RECOMMENDATION</td></tr>
<tr><td>DESCRIPTION:</td><td>QUALIFICATION AND TIMING:</td></tr>
</table>

Exhibit 7-1   Example of a Strategy Recommendation Summary
form (page 1 of 4).

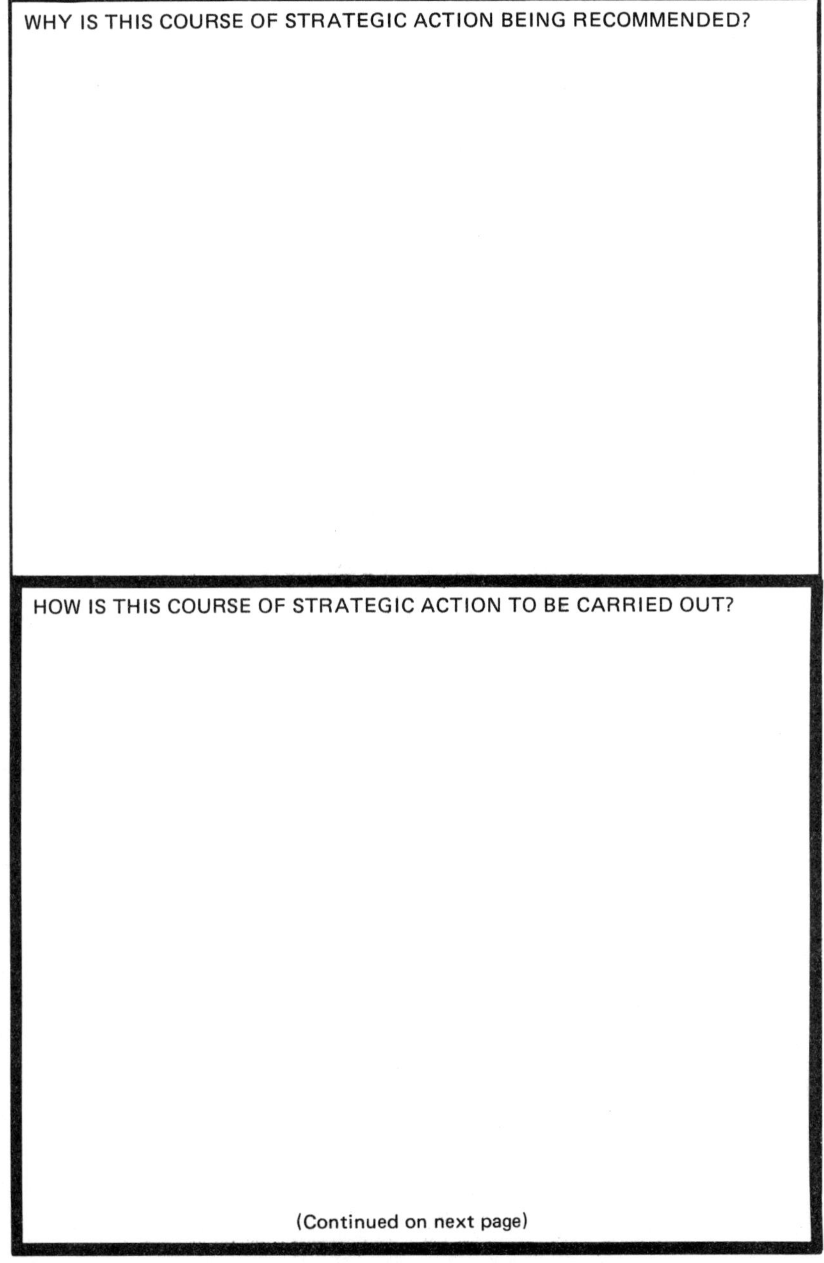

Exhibit 7-1 (Cont'd) Example of a Strategy Recommendation Summary form (page 2 of 4).

HOW IS THIS COURSE OF STRATEGIC ACTION TO BE CARRIED OUT?
(Continued)

STRATEGIC PERFORMANCE CHECKPOINTS:

ALTERNATIVE STRATEGIES CONSIDERED BUT REJECTED:

Exhibit 7-1 (Cont'd) Example of a Strategy Recommendation Summary form (page 3 of 4).

CORRECTIVE ACTION WARNING INDICATORS:

FINANCIAL RESOURCE REQUIREMENTS:

HUMAN RESOURCE REQUIREMENTS:

PHYSICAL RESOURCE REQUIREMENTS:

ORGANIZATIONAL RESOURCE REQUIREMENTS:

Exhibit 7-1 (Cont'd)   Example of a Strategy Recommendation Summary form (page 4 of 4).

example should not be viewed as a rigid demand for presenting the strategy recommendation.

As the exhibit illustrates, the strategy recommendation begins with a review of the strategic position enjoyed by the strategic business unit in question. A description of the industry attractiveness and the related competitive position from an historic, current, projected and desired point of view is fundamental to the recommendation. Particular emphasis should be devoted to illustrating the differences in competitive position for each of these points of view. Not only is this the issue which is more likely to see a substantial change, but it is the issue of prime importance for the strategic business unit. The strategic position is likely to include a description of the relationship with the key industry participants. Substantial changes instigated by competitors that have a direct effect upon competitive position are important issues to address if a thorough understanding of strategic position is to be attained. The precise time frames associated with each of the four strategic position points of view are essential pieces of information as well.

The difference between the current strategic position and the desired strategic position represents the intended course of strategic action. These intentions are formally documented under the topic of "strategic action recommendation." This section of the form is a central point of focus. It is here that the intentions of the strategic business unit are exposed. The strategic action recomendation is divided into two parts. One is a description of the recommendation where the strategic business unit would indicate that it intends to pursue a build, maintain, harvest or divestiture course of action. By itself, this description represents an open-ended type of objective and therefore is of only limited meaning. To make this description more expressive, the second part of the strategic action recommendation is concerned with a qualification of the strategic business unit's intentions and their linking to a specific time frame. This helps to express the recommended strategic action in terms of expected end results which not only clarifies the objectives of the strategic business unit but establishes a criteria against which the degree of their attainment can be subsequently evaluated.

Following the exposition of the recommended strategic

action, the exhibit focuses on a new topic entitled "why is this course of strategic action being recommended?" In this part of the form, the strategic business unit would illustrate the thought processes, rationalizations, assumptions and reasoning supporting its decision to recommend the course of action it has just revealed. This section of the form provides a check on the integrity and soundness of the decision making process applied to this recommendation. Most importantly, this section can be used to add strength and force to the message of the strategic action recommendation.

The most critical aspect of a strategic business unit's mandate is to develop a scheme or program for carrying out its recommended course of strategic action. The section of the form entitled "how is this course of strategic action to be carried out?" is where the strategic business unit unveils its scheme. At this time, the strategic business unit goes to great lengths to explain how it will exploit its knowledge of the strengths and weaknesses of each industry participant for the realization of its goals. The manner in which the strategic business unit plans to take advantage of the opportunities facing it is fully documented. Conversely, the manner in which the strategic business unit intends to cope with its impediments is also discussed. These documentations are what results from the exhaustive studies of the resource profiles and segmentation analysis illustrated in the previous chapter. Finally, this section of the form explains how the strategic business unit intends to address the eight categories of objectives (market standing, public responsibility, productivity, etc.) previously considered as part of the charter of objectives and corporate strategy formulation. Without question, this section is the heart of the strategy recommendation. Accordingly, it is awarded the most generous portion of the overall form.

The next topic of the strategy recommendation is "strategic performance checkpoints." This is an extension of a previous part of the form where the strategic action recommendation was quantified and related to a time frame. The purpose of strategic performance checkpoints is to establish a facility whereby the execution of the strategy can be effectively controlled. To do this, a series of strategic accomplishments and their expected time of realization are documented in this portion of the form. When the

Strategy Management process moves into its execution cycle, management will be able to evaluate the progress of each strategic business unit by a quick reference to the strategic performance checkpoints.

The description of how the strategic business unit proposes to pursue its recommendation as documented in that section of the form entitled "how is this course of strategic action to be carried out?" is supposed to be the optimum manner in which to do so. An optimum manner of performance is something that is direct, efficient and effective. It will exploit all of the strategic business unit's strengths and carefully guard against its weaknesses. To ensure that this course of action actually is best, the strategic business unit documents proof to this effect. The section of the form entitled "alternative strategies considered but rejected" is where the alternative strategies that were considered but dismissed as inferior to the current proposal are listed. This documentation produces evidence that a variety of strategies have been seriously considered and that the optimum one has been selected. This section also provides a source of valuable alternatives should conditions change in the future to warrant a refinement in strategy.

The primary thrust of the Strategy Management control effort is to assist strategic business units in attaining their objectives. However, another part of the control mandate is to determine when circumstances have changed to such a degree that the recommended course of strategic action is no longer appropriate. The "corrective action warning indicators" part of the strategy recommendation form is designed to produce this ability. In this section of the form, the strategic business unit would identify its control limits. Events within these limits would be viewed as consistent with the strategy recommendation. Events outside these control limits would indicate that the strategy recommendation now has to be reviewed in light of new events that have occurred. Here, the strategic business unit would list all of the possible events that could occur which would be in violation of the principles of the strategy recommendation. Should one or more of these events come to pass, it would act as a warning indicator that the strategic business unit did not count upon the occurence of the incident. Because it has come to be, an examination of the strategy recommendation is necessary. By identifying these issues in advance, an organization enhances its ability to react swiftly and confidently under the changing circumstances. It gives an organization flexibility and helps it to avoid a "management by crisis" method of behaviour.

The last part of the strategy recommendation form concerns the resource requirements necessary to enact the proposed strategy. These requirements pertain to financial resources, human resources, physical resources and organizational resources. Financial resources will be the key since it is in this area where constraints normally occur. An approximation of the financial investment and the degree to which this exceeds or falls short of the cash generating capacity of the strategic business unit needs to be documented. The magnitude of the other resource requirements and an explanation of whether this represents a surplus or deficiency in comparison to the current position completes the resource requirements section of the form. The intention is to identify the magnitude and incremental position of each resource category so that the required investment can be properly documented. A subsequent review of the strategy recommendation will ascertain whether these resources are available.

As a reminder, the strategy recommendation form acts as a **summary** for the strategic business unit's proposed course of action. It should be customized to reflect the needs of the particular organization and is suitable for any of the four categories of strategic action chosen.

BUILD STRATEGIES

For those strategic business units operating within an attractive industry and which are both dissatisfied with their current competitive position and possess an ability to improve it, a build strategy represents an attractive category of recommendation. The purpose of a build strategy is exactly as its name connotes. It is intended to significantly increase the market share of the industry held by the strategic business unit. This may mean building a strong competitor into a leader. More often, it means building a mediocre competitor into a strong industry participant.

A build strategy will require an additional – and usually

significant — investment of funds. It is important that these funds be put to good use. Simply spending money will not solve any problems. It is imperative that attractive opportunities exist and that when resources are applied to these opportunities, it will result in a better competitive position. As a complement to this philosophy of building upon one's strengths, a build strategy usually involves a fortification against weaknesses. The pursuit of a build strategy could include an investment to eliminate or reduce an existing weak point acting as a detriment to competitive position. Again, this is not a matter of simply spending money but of intelligently applying funds only after a good use has been discovered.

The strategic positions likely to be occupied by a strategic business unit recommending a build strategy are illustrated in Exhibit 7-2. The prime consideration for recommending this type of strategy is the involvement in an industry of relative attractiveness. Industries in a maturity or decline stage of their life cycle are not good candidates for build strategies. The next critical criterion for recommending this strategy is an awareness of how the unique opportunities and impediments facing both the strategic business unit and its competitors can be exploited and supported with investment to improve competitive position. For this reason, even strategic business units with weak competitive positions at the early stages of the industry life cycle are good candidates for build strategies.

Although the initial task of the strategic business unit is to decide which category of strategy recommendation is appropriate for its current strategic position and potential, most of the strategy recommendation contents will focus on the manner in which the strategy is intended to be executed. A build strategy is one of the most difficult types of recommendation to explain due to its aggressive nature. Targets and methods for attaining specific improvements all need to be fully exposed in the recommendation. It is the logic and soundness of the plans for achievement which will determine the quality of the strategy recommendation — not the name of the category which will eventually summarize the nature of the action.

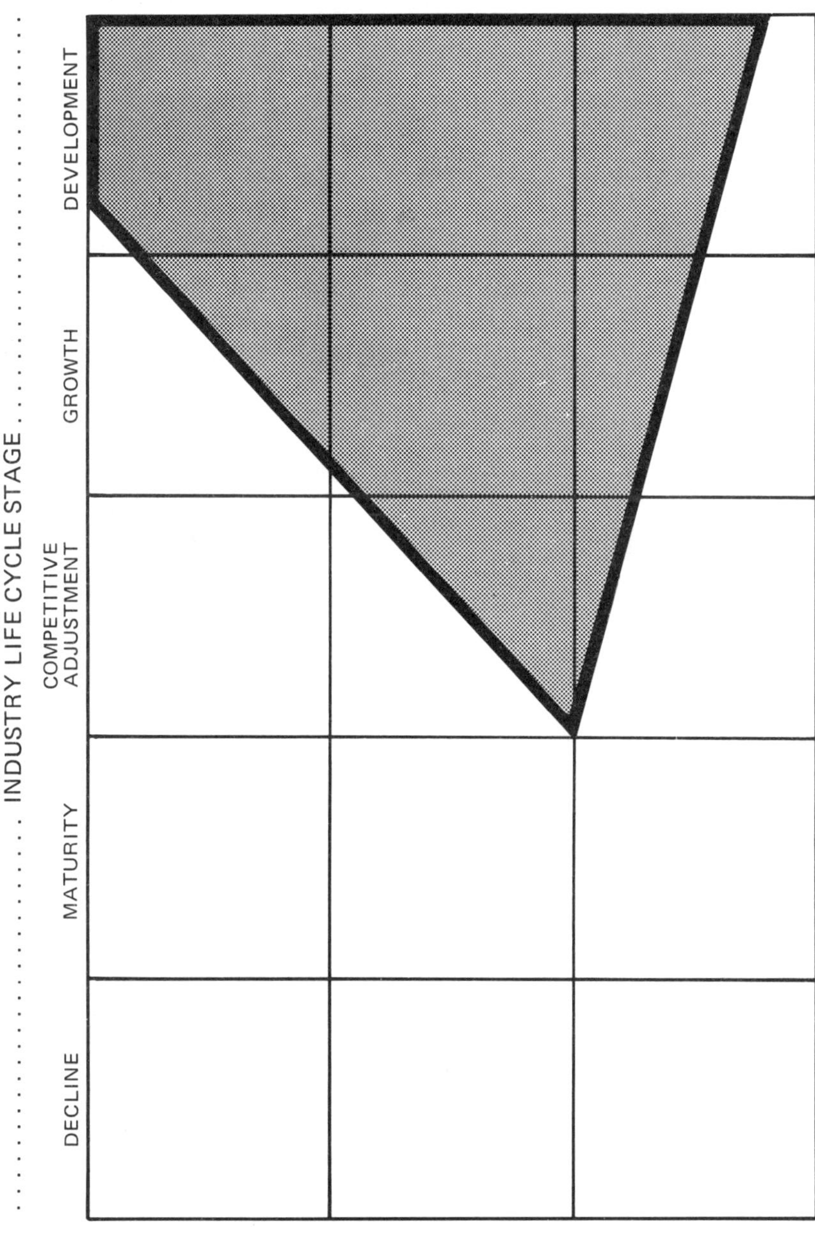

Exhibit 7-2 Positions in which a build strategy is likely to be employed.

MAINTAIN STRATEGIES

The purpose of a maintain strategy is to keep the competitive position now enjoyed by the strategic business unit intact while progressing through the normal stages of the industry life cycle. This type of strategy recommendation is particularly attractive to those strategic business units in relatively attractive industries holding a strong competitive position. Maintain strategies are used by those strategic business units which have little room to improve their competitive positions or by those strategic business units which believe the attractiveness of their industries no longer warrants the investment of a build strategy. Strategic business units in the latter situation would view the rewards of improved competitive position as not worth the efforts necessary to achieve them.

A maintain strategy is more frequently used in a growing market than in a maturing industry. Mature markets often see the employment of harvest or divestiture strategies. Should the industry in question be in the early stages of its life cycle, a maintain strategy is likely to entail a significant investment of additional resources. This investment is not required to improve competitive position but rather to hold the strategic business unit's own status within an expanding industry. Should the strategic business unit be in an industry which is in the later stages of its life cycle, resource investment can be expected to continue at the same level when pursuing a maintain strategy. An expanding industry will force the employment of a maintain strategy to assume many of the characteristics of a build strategy. Although additional funds will be required, they cannot be expended without careful consideration. Specific opportunities where the application of resources will result in meaningful benefits for the strategic business unit need to be identified. More importantly with maintain strategies, situations where resources can be used to deflate the impediments and bolster the weaknesses of the strategic business unit must be seen as prime targets for additional investment. The application of funds to exaggerate strengths and neutralize weaknesses is the only manner in which to carry out a maintain strategy within an expanding industry.

An illustration of the strategic positions where a maintain

strategy is likely to be an appropriate recommendation appears in Exhibit 7-3. The major prerequisite for recommending this type of strategy is a relatively strong competitive position on behalf of the strategic business unit. It does not make sense to recommend a maintain strategy for a weak competitive position. A weak position either has to be improved upon (a build strategy) or the strategic business unit should be withdrawn from the industry. For those industries well past their prime and in a definite state of decline, a maintain strategy is also not a wise recommendation. In cases such as this, the strategic business unit should be planning for its retirement from the industry in order to make the best of a deteriorating situation.

Like all other strategy recommendations, a simple selection of a maintain strategy is of little value by itself. To become meaningful, the strategy needs to be fashioned into specific execution procedures. The manner in which opportunities will be addressed and impediments will be immobilized are the principal concerns of the maintain strategy recommendation. The full strength of the strategy recommendation can only be appreciated when this exposition is made.

HARVEST STRATEGIES

The intent of a harvest strategy is to maximize the return on the strategic business unit's existing investment of resources. This is a very difficult strategy to recommend because it inherently represents the initial actions of the strategic business unit to leave the industry. Harvesting is a rational and preliminary effort to reduce investment in a strategic business unit with the expectation of rewards from prior investment and with the ultimate goal of withdrawal from the activity. In short, a harvest strategy involves recognition that the strategic business unit is now on a path which will end its participation in the industry and that while on the path the prime consideration is optimizing return on resources.

A harvest strategy requires a gradual withdrawal of resources from the strategic business unit. Gradually is the proper way to proceed because any abrupt action will act as an immediate signal to competitors and may very well frighten the clientele. These

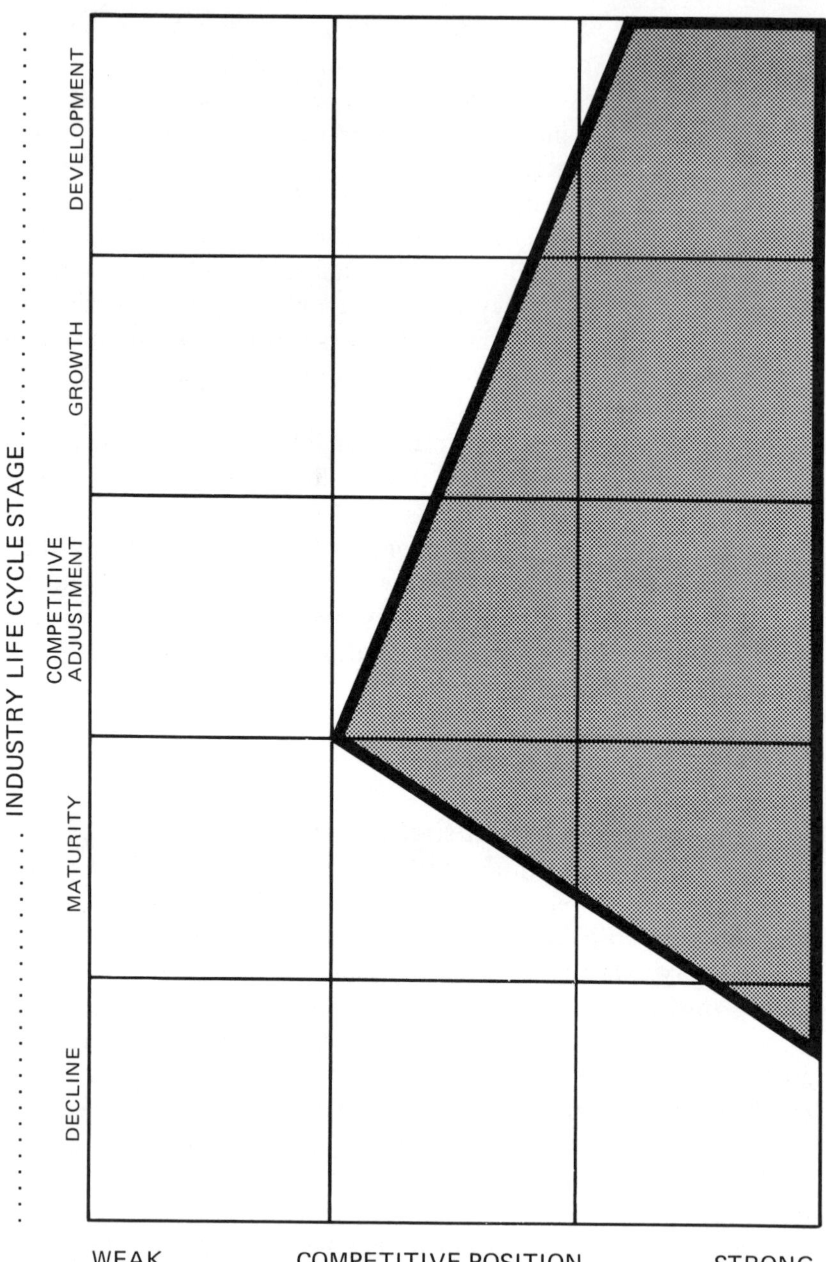

Exhibit 7-3 Positions in which a maintain strategy is likely to be employed.

two situations will certainly have an adverse effect on the strategic business unit's ability to maximize return on its existing operations. Harvesting is an attractive strategy recommendation for those strategic business units that have a weak competitive position and/or are functioning within an industry of low attractiveness. Low attractiveness is likely to be caused when the industry is in the final stage of its life cycle. Each or both of these strategic positions combined signal to the strategic business unit that the future is not very attractive. As a recourse, resource investments would be kept to a minimum and the strategic business unit would concentrate on making the best of what it has.

The reduction of the overall resource strength of a strategic business unit pursuing a harvest recommendation is not something that should be left to fate. A planned and orderly reduction of resources needs to be made. Otherwise, the most valuable and mobile resources, particularly human resources, could be the first ones to go. This may quickly cripple the total operation. Harvesting requires identification of those resources which will have the least effect on short-term benefits. Maintenance, research and development, advertising and training are good examples of activities that could be reduced or perhaps eliminated with only a minor impact on short-term results. A harvesting strategy should be formulated in such a manner that resources are withdrawn from the low impact functions before proceeding to areas of more serious consequences.

Exhibit 7-4 illustrates those strategic positions where a harvest strategy is most likely to be recommended. A weak competitive position or an unattractive industry are the key indications that a harvest strategy is needed. Although a combination of these circumstances can also necessitate a harvest strategy, a more prompt course of action in the form of a divestiture recommendation is normally more appropriate. The withdrawal of resources from strategic business units earmarked for harvesting can be expected to produce a positive and generous cash flow. As the name implies, harvesting is the day of reckoning for the strategic business unit when it begins to collect the rewards for all of its previous labours. The cash reaped from harvesting a strategic business unit can be immediately applied to nourish other strategic business units in the build or maintain time frames of their life

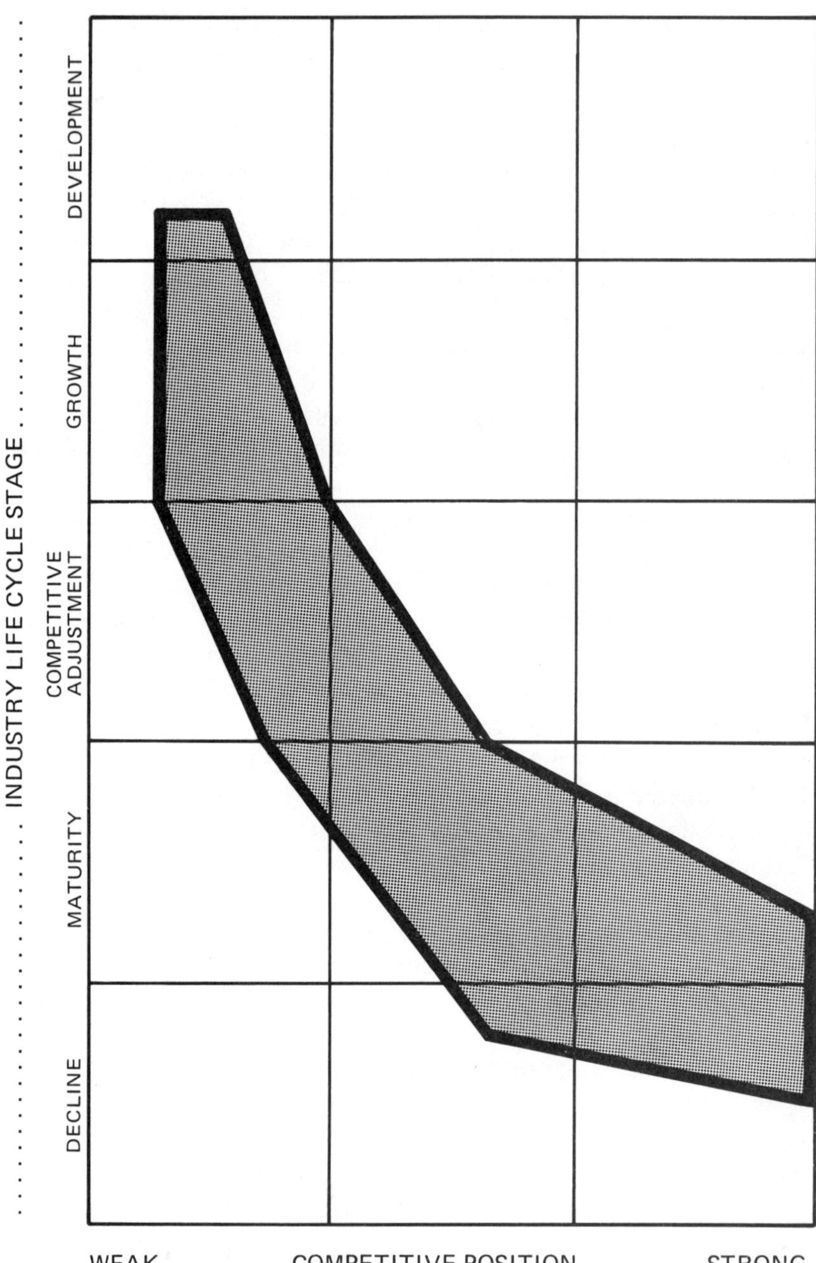

Exhibit 7-4 Positions in which a harvest strategy is likely to be employed.

cycle. This give and take relationship among strategic business units emphasizes the need for sound Strategy Management on behalf of all organizations.

DIVESTITURE STRATEGIES

The purpose of a divestiture strategy is to get out of an industry in an expedient fashion even if it means taking a loss. Divestiture strategies are recognitions that the strategic business unit is in a problem situation, probably losing money, and that prospects for a turnaround are bleak. There are two ways to proceed with a divestiture strategy. One is to liquidate the business. The other is to sell the business assuming that a buyer can be found. In either case, the least unprofitable or more positively, the most beneficial methods of realizing divestiture should be sought.

Divestiture strategies have the same ultimate goal of terminating participation in the industry as do harvest strategies. The difference is that divestiture is the final act of harvesting and is accomplished within a much shorter time interval. The criteria for recommending a divestiture strategy are basically the same as a harvesting strategy except the conditions are more serious. A very weak competitive position, an extremely unattractive industry or a combination of the two are prime ingredients for a divestiture strategy. Exhibit 7-5 illustrates these strategic positions where such action is appropriate. In comparison to the previous exhibit illustrating the positions related to harvesting strategies, Exhibit 7-5 reflects a more serious deterioration in strategic position towards the bottom left-hand quadrant of both weak competitive position and a completed life cycle. Divestiture strategies are designed to relieve an organization of problem strategic business units with no hope of recovery.

The choice when executing a divestiture strategy is between disposal and liquidation. This choice is not easy because both alternatives often appear to be equally unattractive. However, the choice has to be made as part of the strategy recommendation because both options cannot be pursued simultaneously. Should an organization be in the midst of negotiating a disposal for a strategic business unit, its efforts could be sabotaged when liquid-

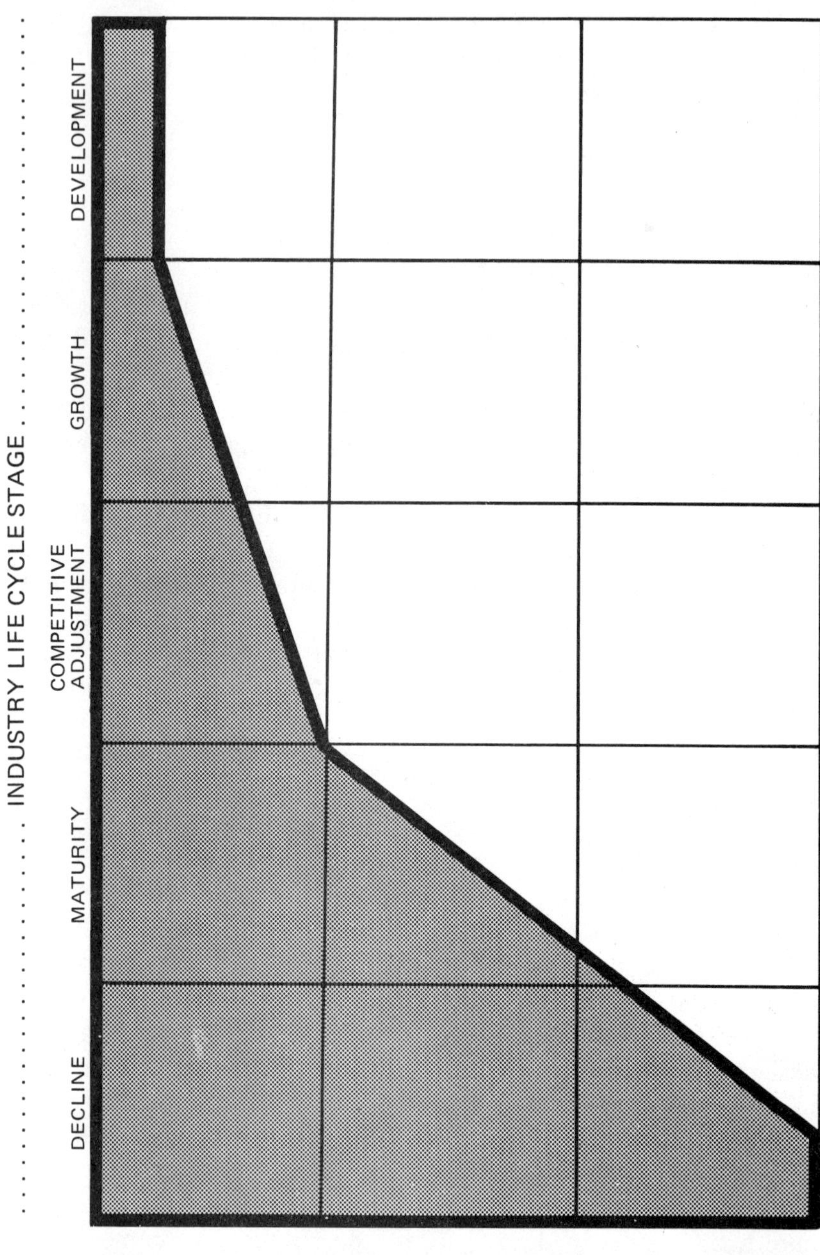

Exhibit 7-5 Positions in which a divestiture strategy is likely to be employed.

ating procedures are being taken at the same time. For a strategic business unit to be disposed of as a unified entity, and therefore realize optimum value, liquidation efforts to dismember it should be prevented. If liquidation is the desired course of action, the strategic business unit should plan for an orderly dismantling of resources. Constant attention should be given to the identification of resources which may be of benefit to other strategic business units of the organization in their expanding stages. It is more economical to transfer resources where possible than to reproduce them. The final decision between disposal and liquidation will be made on the basis of the short-term benefit that is obtainable from each. In either case, the strategy recommendation will contain explicit expositions of how the strategic business unit intends to bring its recommendations to fruition.

THE STRATEGY PRESENTATION

The final act of the strategic business unit is to formally present its strategy recommendation. We have just completed our review of the four main categories of strategy recommendation and the circumstances in which each is best employed. Prior to that, the strategy recommendation format giving particular attention to the Strategy Recommendation Summary form was reviewed. These are the main components of the strategic business unit's presentation. However, it is suggested that two subsidiary topics be incorporated into the presentation. One is a basic financial plan extending for a period of five years. The other is a comparison of the financial plan to the respective components of five year plans created in previous years.

A long-term financial plan is not an additional burden requiring development by the strategic business unit. It is simply a summary or reflection of the strategic plans that have just been prepared. A five year financial plan is a translation of the strategic intentions into the basic accounting classifications of a pro forma profit and loss statement for the strategic business unit. It is at this level of the organization and this stage of the Strategy Management process where sufficient information is available to permit a meaningful long-range financial plan to be assembled. Attempts to create a long-range plan at more detailed levels of the organization prove fruitless because the time frame is not in synchronization with the concerns of lower level managers. The five year financial plan not only displays the intended financial position of the strategic business unit but permits a total consolidation of the organization's financial future to be calculated and evaluated.

Comparing the five year plan to the ones created in previous years allows the strategic business unit to demonstrate the consistency or lack thereof in its planning efforts. An effective manner in which to build this comparison is through the use of a stair chart. Exhibit 7-6 is an illustration of how a stair chart can be used to compare the respective components of long-range financial plans. As the exhibit demonstrates, the first year of the long-range plan developed by the strategic business unit has four previous scenarios with which to compare itself. The pattern displayed by these views can bring either confidence or uncertainty to the ingredients of the newly created strategic plan. Regardless, a clearer perspective of the situation can certainly be realized

3 YEARS AGO	2 YEARS AGO	LAST YEAR	CURRENT YEAR	COMING YEAR	2 YEARS FROM NOW	3 YEARS FROM NOW	4 YEARS FROM NOW	5 YEARS FROM NOW
PLAN A YEAR 1	PLAN A YEAR 2	PLAN A YEAR 3	PLAN A YEAR 4	PLAN A YEAR 5				
	PLAN B YEAR 1	PLAN B YEAR 2	PLAN B YEAR 3	PLAN B YEAR 4	PLAN B YEAR 5			
		PLAN C YEAR 1	PLAN C YEAR 2	PLAN C YEAR 3	PLAN C YEAR 4	PLAN C YEAR 5		
			PLAN D YEAR 1	PLAN D YEAR 2	PLAN D YEAR 3	PLAN D YEAR 4	PLAN D YEAR 5	
				PLAN E YEAR 1	PLAN E YEAR 2	PLAN E YEAR 3	PLAN E YEAR 4	PLAN E YEAR 5

Exhibit 7-6 Example of the mechanics incorporated into a stair chart.

and followed up with appropriate action.

There is an important question still outstanding concerning the strategy presentation of the strategic business unit. Who receives the strategy recommendation and what do they do with it? The strategic business unit personnel present their recommendation to a strategy committee. This committee is made up of the top level executives of the organization and would most certainly include the chief executive officer. The strategy committee may very well be the existing executive committee of the organization. In some cases, other members of senior management may be invited to join the committee for the purpose of broadening the background of the committee as well as increasing its objectivity.

The strategy committee is the recipient of each recommendation prepared by the organization's strategic business units. A formal meeting between the strategy committee and the personnel of each strategic business unit is the vehicle for presentation. At this meeting, the strategic business unit reviews its analysis, explains its conclusions and unveils its recommendation. Prior to the meeting, each member of the strategy committee will have received a written text including any structured summary form of the strategic business unit's presentation to help it better prepare for the meeting. By asking questions and seeking backup data, the strategy committee first tests the integrity and accuracy of the strategic business unit's analysis. Once this base has been established and the precise strategic position of the strategic business unit has been confirmed, the logic behind the type of strategic action recommended is queried. The reasons why the strategic business unit personnel have concluded that their unique strengths and weaknesses are best exploited by following the recommended strategy are thoroughly investigated. The ramifications of pursuing any alternative types of strategy are also considered. Finally, a comprehensive examination of the strategic business unit's plan of how it will carry out its recommended course of action is made. Tests of logic, soundness and probability are made to assess the feasibility and quality of the plan. The strategy committee should bring intense scrutiny to this part of the presentation to ensure that the strategic business unit personnel unequivocally know what they are going to do. This is the final test and ultimate purpose of the strategic business unit's efforts.

By presenting its strategy recommendation in this manner, the strategic business unit is basically describing an investment opportunity (whether requiring cash or generating cash) to the strategy committee. It is an opportunity to sell itself and its operations to those persons who control the strategic resource allocation process of the organization.

STRATEGY RESOLUTIONS

Although the strategy recommendation presented by the strategic business unit can be loosely described as a sales effort, the strategy committee cannot accept the recommendation — at least not immediately. Before the strategy committee can either accept, reject or accept in a modified form, it must consider all of the recommendations presented by the other strategic business units of the organization. It's only after these considerations can the strategy committee create and review a confirmed version of the overall business portfolio for the enterprise. Most importantly, it is only at this time that the strategy committee gains a true perspective of the magnitude of resource requirements that the totality of the strategic business units is recommending. This may or may not be within the capabilities of the institution.

Chapter Five introduced the concept of business portfolio matrices to summarize the strategic positions of an organization's various businesses as represented by strategic business units. At that time, it was suggested that an ideal business portfolio matrix would have all of the organization's businesses clustered into that half of the matrix representing a strong competitive position. Furthermore a balance among the industry attractiveness of these business would exist. Exhibit 7-7 is an example of an ideal business portfolio matrix for an organization. The importance of having each strategic business unit's position in the right-hand side of the matrix is easy to understand. Of equal importance is the balance among the businesses on this side of the matrix. It is unlikely that an organization could meet the resource requirements of its strategic business units should they all be positioned in the top right-hand quadrant of the matrix. This is placing an over-emphasis on growth. Conversely, an organization with all of

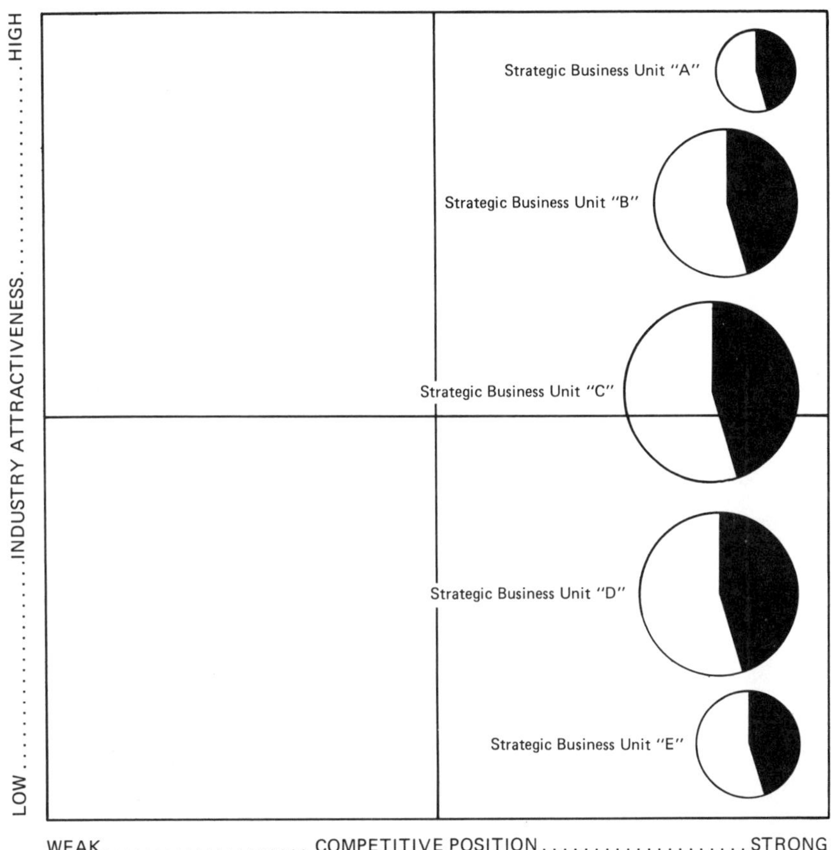

Exhibit 7-7 Example of an ideal Business Portfolio Matrix.

its strategic business units in the lower right-hand quadrant is quickly approaching extinction because it has no growing businesses to replace its maturing ones. Growth and mature businesses can expect to have a negative and positive cash flow respectively. For this reason alone, it is important that an organization plan its businesses so that the different cash flow situations can complement one another.

Exhibit 7-8 visually displays the behaviour of sales, profits and cash flow of a normal strategic business unit as it passes through the various stages of industry life cycle. Both profitability and cash flow can be expected to be in a negative position

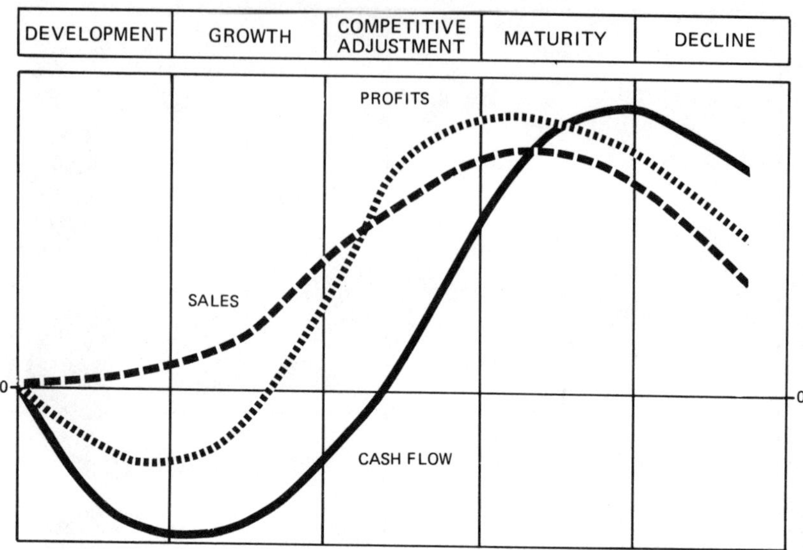

Exhibit 7-8 Example of change in sales, profit and cash flow characteristics by industry life cycle stage.

during the early life cycle stages. This is compensated in later stages when both of these topics become very positive. This display of the uneven timing of particularly cash flow emphasizes the need for an organization to intelligently manage its portfolio of businesses so that a complementary environment exists. It provides motivation for organizations to seek an ideal business portfolio matrix.

An extremely useful tool for organizations to use in the management of their business portfolios is presented in Exhibit 7-9. This is an example of a numerical business portfolio matrix describing the sales volume of the various strategic business units by categories of both industry life cycle and competitive position. Percentages are also calculated for each section of the matrix together with column totals for both axes. This type of matrix precisely describes the status of the overall organization by documenting its position in a numerical format. A year to year comparison of such matrices is particularly useful for illustrating an organization's progress towards an ideal business mix. This can be a valuable instrument for the strategy committee as it attempts to

. . . . COMPETITIVE POSITION . . . .

		VERY WEAK	WEAK	MODERATE	STRONG	VERY STRONG	TOTAL
INDUSTRY LIFE CYCLE STAGE	DEVELOPMENT	\$ – %	\$ – %	\$ – %	\$ – %	\$ – %	\$ – %
	GROWTH	\$ – %	\$ – %	\$ – %	\$ – %	\$ – %	\$ – %
	COMPETITIVE ADJUSTMENT	\$ – %	\$ – %	\$ – %	\$ – %	\$ – %	\$ – %
	MATURITY	\$ – %	\$ – %	\$ – %	\$ – %	\$ – %	\$ – %
	DECLINE	\$ – %	\$ – %	\$ – %	\$ – %	\$ – %	\$ – %
TOTAL		\$ – %	\$ – %	\$ – %	\$ – %	\$ – %	\$-100%

Exhibit 7-9   Example of a numerical Business Portfolio Matrix classifying sales volume by category of industry life cycle stage and competitive position.

comprehend the full breadth of the recommendations presented to it by the strategic business units.

In addition to simply balancing the cash flow of the organization, the strategy committee will be searching for synergy among the recommendations. How do the businesses and their planned strategic action complement one another? Are the recommendations fully consistent with the charter of objectives? These are examples of the questions that the strategy committee will ask itself. The acceptance of the strategic business unit recommendations will be dependent upon these factors as well as the organization's ability to provide the necessary resources — particularly financial.

After serious deliberation, the strategy committee will make and communicate its decisions regarding each strategic business unit recommendation. It is at this time that the strategic business units have their recommendations accepted either in whole or in part. It is also possible that a strategic business unit could be instructed to change the direction of its recommendation and to reconstruct a "how to" plan in support of these new goals. The end product of all these deliberations is an understanding of strategic objectives of each business within the organization.

When making these decisions, the strategy committee is likely to be creating an extension of the previously formulated corporate strategy. This involves a progression to the details of how the organization will perform within its prescribed businesses as opposed to a simple identification of the businesses and their direction. In certain cases, these decisions may represent an amendment to the corporate strategy based upon a more comprehensive spectrum of information. Regardless of whether the strategic resource allocation decisions are an extension of or amendment to the original corporate strategy formulation, an organization now has a consistent view of what it wants to do, how it intends to do it and the inherent logic behind its plans for all facets of its operations.

8

The Tactical Program —
Variable Components

The Strategy Management process to this point has worked itself down from the charter of objectives through corporate strategy to a position where planned strategic action has been mapped out at the strategic business unit level. These activities have intimately involved the senior management of the organization and in the latter stages, the middle management personnel of the strategic business units. However, the majority of persons in the organization have yet to come in contact with any of these ideas. The first line managers and all of their subordinates remain uneffected by these events. They have not enjoyed any benefits from the analysis and decisions undertaken by more senior management. All organizational activities, be they a change or a continuation, must be executed through the first line managers and their subordinates. It is imperative that these persons be brought into the mainstream of the organization's planning, execution and control activities.

The purpose of the tactical program in the Strategy Management process is to make this final step. The tactical program integrates lower level managers and subordinates initially into the planning process and subsequently into the execution and control aspects. The tactical program is intended to translate the strategic plans of the organization into a series of day to day action plans for each employee. The tactical program will identify each person's role within the total effort of realizing the organization's goals. It is the ultimate step of aligning the goals of the individual with those of the organization. For an organization to be co-ordinated and effective in realizing its goals, each employee must understand the role he or she is expected to play and what share this is of the total effort.

Although the tactical program will support the full scope of the organization's strategic plans, it will place special emphasis on short-term considerations. The time span of concern shortens at the lower levels of management. First line managers rarely live on more than a year to year basis. Because of this more immediate time focus, the tactical program will concentrate on the events planned to occur within the coming year. This focus coincides with that of what is traditionally called a budget. The tactical program has some radical differences from what is normally referred to as a budget and it is therefore somewhat inaccurate to label it as such. Nevertheless, the tactical program is broken out into variable components and discretionary components — much like a budget. This chapter will examine the variable components of the tactical program. The next chapter will examine the discretionary components.

COMMUNICATING THE STRATEGY

Progressing from the strategic business unit level to the first line of management may be done in one step or in progressive steps. The size of the organization and hence the number of management layers will have a lot to do with this. More importantly, however, is the position of the strategic business unit within the formal organizational framework. Should an organization already be arranged in a strategic business unit format as described in Exhibit 5-1 of Chapter Five, then a direct communication of strategy down to the first level of management is possible. Should the strategic business unit be an artificial organizational entity as described in Exhibit 5-2, then an indirect and more complex method of communicating the strategy must be employed. When the bridge between the strategic business unit and the first level of management involves one or more intermediate levels of authority, much caution needs to be taken so as not to distort the meaning of the strategy message as it is being communicated. Each level of management simply accepts the plans developed by the higher level of management, expands them into a finer level of detail with which it is accustomed to dealing and then re-communicates them to the next lower level of management. This process is progressively repeated and repeated until the first line manager and his or her subordinates know precisely what is expected of them.

The variable components of the tactical program are concerned with those issues closely related to the volume of business. From an accountant's point of view, these are revenue and direct costs. Of immediate interest in this chapter are those departments of the organization (sometimes called cost centres or responsibility centres) which deal with these two issues. Accordingly, the sales and manufacturing departments are the prime targets of the tactical program's variable components. The tactical program requires that the plans developed by the strategic business units be embellished and transferred to these organizational entities intimately involved with the variable issues.

THE REVENUE PROGRAM

The anticipated size of the industry and the market share which the strategic business unit intends to hold have both been detailed in the strategic business unit recommendation. By combining these two factors, the revenue goals of each strategic business unit and hence the total organization can be determined. It is these already developed factors that will provide both the guidance and the foundation for the variable components of the tactical program.

The first task when compiling the revenue portion of this tactical program is to allocate these total revenue goals into their various market segments. This revenue segmentation is done not only for the coming year but for the full scope of the strategy recommendation. The onus of preparing this part of the program rests with the first line manager responsible for generating the revenue. In most organizations, this is the manager of the sales department. Should the strategy recommendation call for the exploitation of certain market segments or the downgrading of others, the sales manager is expected to reflect these conditions in the creation of his revenue segmentation plan. In some cases, the sales manager may be fortunate enough to have this segmentation already made for his department. It is possible that the strategic business unit perceived it to be of such importance that it included a revenue segmentation plan in its recommendation. In this case, the sales manager can proceed directly to the next step of developing the revenue program.

After the revenue program has been divided into market segments, the next task is to extrapolate this information into individual products or services. While doing so, the integrity of the revenue segmentation is maintained so that the end result is a revenue program by product or service type within each market segment. Large organizations with an extremely high number of different products or services may be tempted to break out the revenue program by product or service **groups**. This is an acceptable practice, particularly for the later years of the revenue program. However, this should be seen only as a preliminary or intermediate stage. Eventually, specific product or service identification will be required to allow for the creation of a complementary operation or production plan. A simple matrix form can be used to document the relationship between market segments and individual products or services. Exhibit 8-1 is an example of such a form. There is nothing complicated about this form. It is designed to assist the sales department in the development of a revenue program which specifically supports and reflects the preceeding strategy recommendation.

As the next step in the preparation of the revenue program, the products or services associated with the various market segments are now further related to specific customers. The intention of this exercise is to establish clear objectives for the sales department by identifying precise combinations of customers and products or services. This final step is identical to the revenue budgeting procedures currently practiced by many institutions. However, the sense of direction flowing from the strategy recommendation through the revenue segmentation should make this exercise significantly more meaningful than traditional budgeting

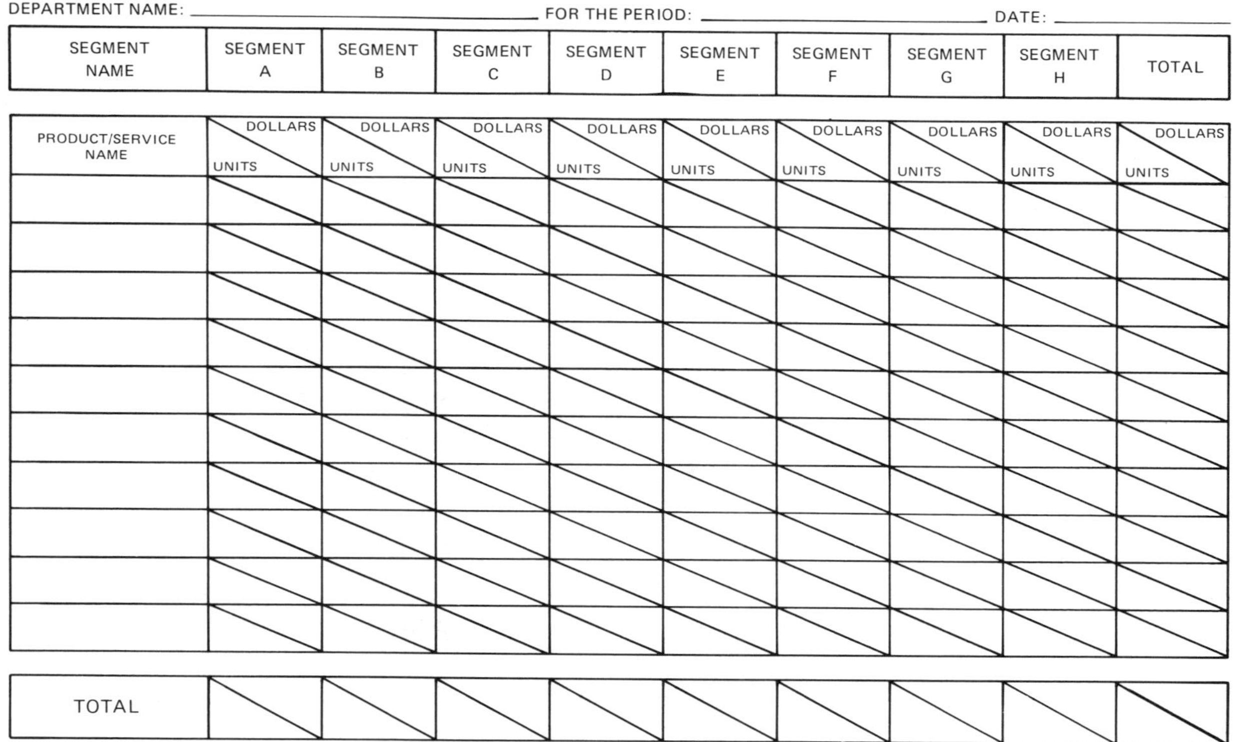

Exhibit 8-1 Example of a Revenue Program Segmentation form used to document the revenue program objectives by product/service types within market segment.

procedures. This final step often seems frustrating for sales personnel. From their point of view, it appears that they are being asked to precisely predict a series of events which the art of selling makes very difficult to do. Although this is the natural position to take, the focus should not be on prediction. The intention of the revenue program, and the budget portion of it in particular, is to establish targets and goals towards which the sales force can work. Predicting actual sales is something that borders on the impossible. Nevertheless, setting very specific performance objectives is the only way that the overall revenue program can be realized. This is one step (or customer) at a time.

Exhibit 8-2 is an example of a form that can be used to document the revenue objectives on a customer and product or service basis. As is the custom in many organizations today, this can be a computerized report forming the initial input to the budgeting process. Again when traditional procedures and facilities are used, it is important to be constantly aware of what makes the revenue portion of the tactical program unique — namely a complete subservience to a pre-established strategy. In some organizations, the revenue budget is "fudged" by breaking the desired level of revenue out over the established customer base. Financial allocations of this sort are not acceptable under the Strategy Management concept. The exercise is intended to be a sincere attempt to demonstrate the role of the sales department within the overall strategy of the organization. As well as adding and deleting from the present customer base, this will involve a change in status of many customers already doing business with the organization. These circumstances should be recognized and accordingly incorporated into the revenue program of performance objectives.

The ultimate goal of the revenue portion of the tactical program is to bridge the gap between the strategy recommendation and the action plans of the sales force. Inherently, this involves the creation of a revenue budget. In most organizations, a budget represents the short-term plans of the institution and as such is divided into monthly increments. Monthly increments allow for a timely review and control of actual events. As a final step in the preparation of the revenue program, the customer and product or service relationships previously documented are

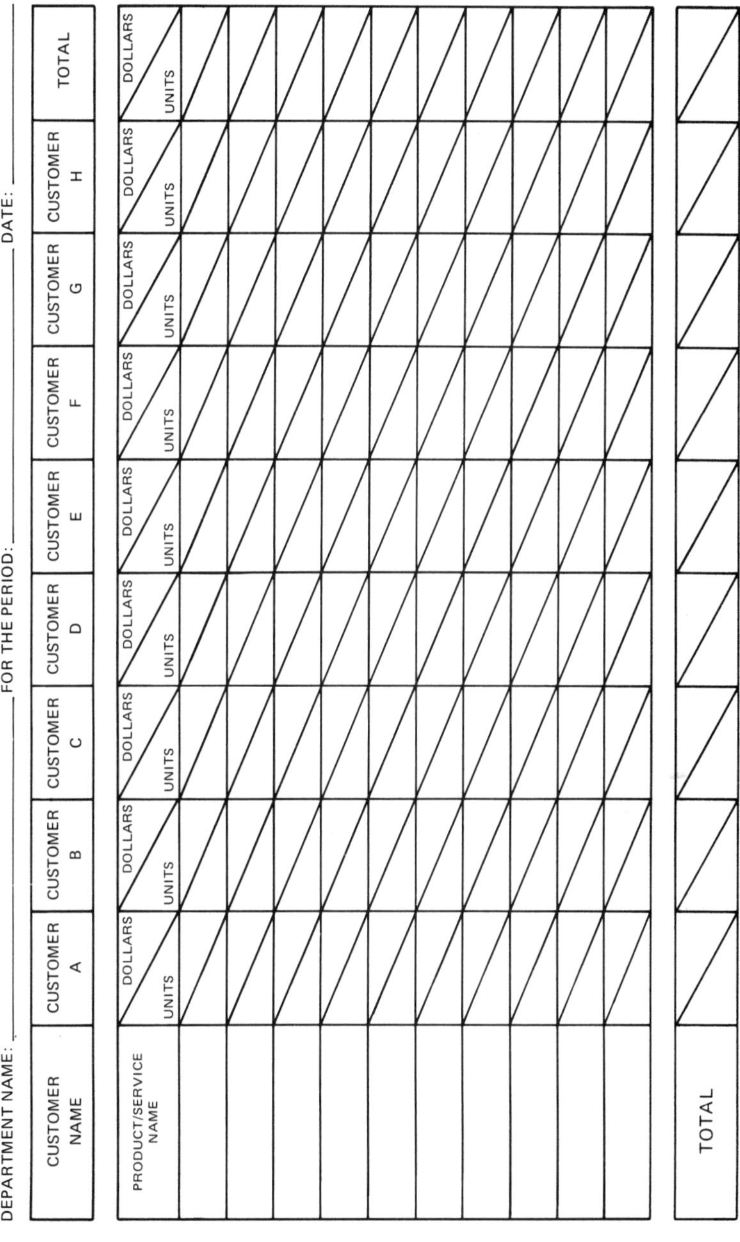

Exhibit 8-2 Example of a Revenue Budget form used to document the revenue program objectives by product/service types per customer.

linked to specific monthly intervals. Not only does this enhance the clarity of the performance objectives, but a foundation for the sales force to guide itself and prepare corrective action when needed becomes incorporated into the management process.

THE DIRECT COST PROGRAM

The remaining variable component of the tactical program is direct costs. By definition, direct costs are those which have a direct relationship to the volume of business being transacted. Direct costs are synonymous with variable costs. The words semi-fixed or semi-variable are sometimes used when describing costs. These cost categories will not be addressed either as part of the variable components or discretionary components of the tactical program because in reality they do not exist. Costs described in these terms have simply not been separated into their variable and discretionary elements. From an accountant's point of view, direct costs have two possible ingredients: direct labour and direct material. Preparing a plan for the utilization of these two ingredients is the specific purpose of the direct cost program.

The direct cost program is determined almost entirely by the revenue program. The latter flows into the former. When developing the revenue program, careful attention is given to identifying not only the various products or services included in the sales target but also the unit volumes of each. Exhibit 8-2 clearly indicates that both unit and dollar volumes must be associated with each product or service. The volume of products or services included in the revenue program equals the volume of products or services being produced and incurring direct costs in the manufacturing or operating departments of the organization. The only exception to this, assuming that the necessary physical resource capacity is in existence, is addition to or reduction of the current level of inventory. It is in this fashion that the revenue program and direct cost program of the overall tactical program complement one another.

Changes in inventory levels do not exist for service organizations since their production is sold immediately. However, in all manufacturing organizations, planned changes in inventory levels should be expected to change the production volume from that of the revenue program. How much of a change should be expected? That question can only be answered when the desired inventory level is compared to the current. Should a significant build-up or discharge of inventory be desirable, this would represent a notable change in resource requirements and should have been previously described in the strategic business unit recommendation. Insignificant changes in inventory levels would not form part of the strategy recommendation. Sales in conjunction with production personnel would assume the responsibility for determining these appropriate inventory levels. With this responsibility, they would specify any increases or decreases to the production plan in comparison to the revenue program. The key point to be made here is that in manufacturing organizations, the volume of products incurring direct costs will not be exactly equivalent to the volume of products in the sales program. After an intelligent determination of optimum inventory levels, the direct cost program will be modified for any surpluses or deficiencies with respect to the current inventory status.

Volume is only one-half of the direct cost equation. Anticipated unit costs make up the other part. Multiplying the expected operating volumes by the expected unit costs will produce a total dollar value for the direct cost program. Although this value will permit an organization to compute its gross profit, it does very little to assist the operating personnel with their chores. Rather than being an accounting instrument, the direct cost program needs to act as a vehicle through which operating personnel can receive direction and establish performance targets. Direct costs are constructed by calculating the labour and material ingredients of each component of activity comprising the complete unit of product or service. The construction of the direct cost program calls for a review of the steps involved in creating each different unit of output. Are all of the steps necessary? Are they in the optimum sequence? Can steps be combined to improve efficiency? These are examples of the types of questions operating personnel (probably with assistance from a cost accountant) will ask themselves as the initial task in developing the direct cost program. The intention of these questions is to ensure, through review, that the products or services are being produced with an optimum relationship between cost and quality.

After establishing the procedures to be followed in the production of each unit of product or service, projected costs are determined for each. In order to determine the direct labour component of each procedure, productivity rates and labour rates need to be established. Productivity refers not only to the time it takes to perform the activity but to the portion of the employee's paid time that will be available for actual work. Holidays, vacation, sickness and absenteeism are all factors that influence productivity. Labour rates refer to the remuneration, plus fringe benefits, that an employee receives per a given unit of time measure. The cost of material components for each procedure is usually very easy to identify. As part of the definition of how to produce the product or service, the input of various units of raw material is identified. These raw materials may range from mammoth hardware components in a manufacturing operation to postage and stationery in a service environment. Nevertheless, the individual costs of each can be isolated to determine the direct material cost of the various procedures. When the manner in which the product or service is to be constructed has been developed and costs have been determined for each procedural component, operating personnel will have an appreciation of the direct unit costs involved in their function. This is interesting information, but again provides little influence upon their performance.

To be meaningful, the direct cost program must tell operating personnel what to do and when to do it. When multiplying the production volumes derived from the revenue program by the components of the unit costs, these needs can be satisfied. The volumes for each production period can determine the type, quantity and cost of raw materials required as part of the direct cost program. Similarily, the type, quantity and cost of direct labour requirements can be ascertained. By performing these calculations, operating personnel can not only plan the input of resources into their departments but identify the manner in which they are to be employed. It is this knowledge which provides objectives and performance targets for operating personnel.

THE CONTRIBUTION TO DISCRETIONARY ACTIVITIES

The variable components of the tactical program are an

extension of the strategic business unit recommendation. Their value lies not in the form of a resulting financial budget but in the degree of coordination they bring to the organization. The variable components of the tactical program include discrete performance objectives for both sales and operating departments. Sales personnel gain a knowledge of what, where and when they need to sell in order to support their part of the approved strategy recommendation. Conversely, operating personnel become aware of what and when they must produce in terms of products and services to fulfill their mandate. It is this awareness of the expected performance objectives that is the fundamental purpose of the program. It creates an understanding of how sales and operating personnel are to work together in realizing the overall strategic goals.

The revenue program and the direct cost program both generate dollar values associated with their respective activities. By substracting the dollar value of the direct cost program from that of the revenue program, a residual amount of money to be applied to discretionary activities of the organization and/or profit can be identified. This calculation is an accounting activity. It is of extreme importance because the magnitude of this residue will have a profound influence on the nature and volume of discretionary activities in which the organization will subsequently engage.

Exhibit 8-3 on the following page is a summary of how the variable components of the tactical program are developed. It demonstrates how the three major results of performance objectives from the revenue program, performance objectives from the direct cost program and the amount of contribution to discretionary activities are determined.

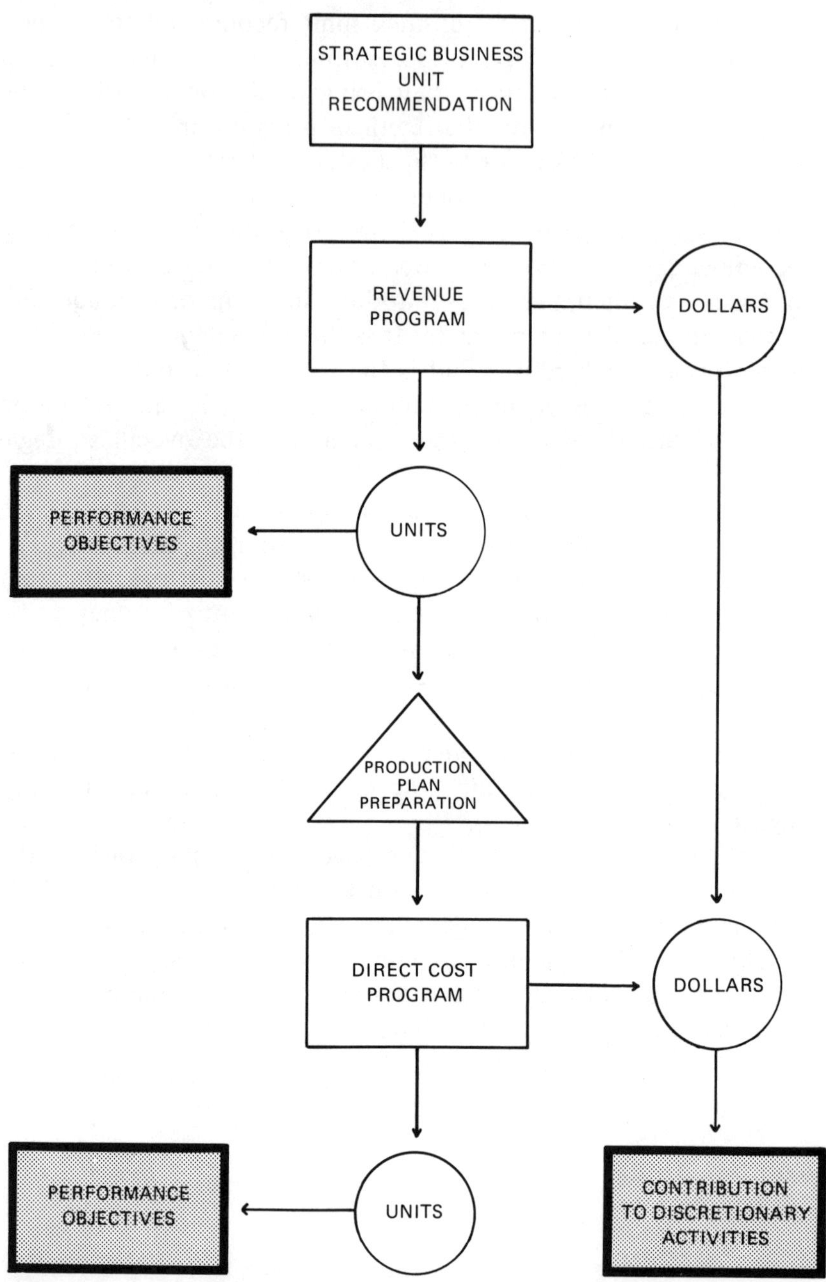

Exhibit 8-3 Developing the variable components of the tactical program.

9

The Tactical Program — Discretionary Components

The variable components of the tactical program focused on the revenue generating and production environments of the organization. Specifically, these were the sales departments and the operating departments. The discretionary components of the tactical program do not have such a limited scope. **Every department** in the organization has a role to play in this part of the tactical program. This role is intended to result in the expression of the planned strategic action in more detailed terms of understandable action plans for each employee.

The development of the discretionary components of the tactical program begins with an exercise of explaining the approved strategy recommendations of the organization to every department manager. As with the variable components, this is done in a progressive manner. The strategy is communicated to lower levels of the organization with each level expanding the message into the depth of detail commensurate with its operations. Should the strategic business units be a formal part of the organization's makeup, a direct communication of strategy can be made. Artificial strategic business units need an indirect and therefore more complex form of communication. Regardless, the objectives as outlined in the approved strategic business unit recommendations are passed down and down through the organization receiving further elaboration at each level.

An understanding of their contributions to the goals of the organization will eventually be developed by all departments. Many of these departments will not have direct operating responsibilities as do sales and production departments. Their role will be one of support or service to the main operating functions of the organization. Within this capacity, these departments will need to know the nature and particularly the volume of business that the operating departments will transact. This knowledge will permit the service departments to estimate the force of demands that will be placed upon them. As part of the exercise of progressively communicating and expanding the desired strategic action of the organization, information pertaining to key operating indicators should be filtered into the process as well. Not all support departments will require this operating information and those that do will likely need different types of data. It is important that this information be available and be included in the communication process so that various departments can make selections according to their unique needs. It is only with this complete spectrum of strategic goals and operating objectives can a department manager feel comfortable about what is expected of him.

The communication process which inaugurates the discretionary components of the tactical program is designed solely to inform each manager how he fits into the overall effort of the organization. This knowledge is critical from a coordination point of view. It also acts as a prelude or a foundation upon which each manager can determine the amount of resources required to execute his resulting action plans. Developing the discretionary components of the tactical program is a process whereby managers discover what it is they are required to do and how they will accomplish it. This involves the employment of resources. From a more global point of view, this part of the program can be described as a resource allocation exercise encompassing all non-operating activities — the discretionary activities of the organization. When put in this perspective, the importance of establishing clear and unequivocal performance objectives at the outset of the process is greatly magnified.

Simply providing this information to department managers is not good enough. The extreme importance of understanding these objectives means that managers must confirm that they possess an accurate perception of the issues at hand. This confirmation marks the initial active response by the first level managers in the Strategy Management process. It requires a formal documentation of their perceptions. This documentation should be in the form of two separate written statements:

1. A statement of mission, role or mandate.
2. A statement of action plans for the coming year.

The statement of mission, role or mandate is used to describe the manager's perception of the fundamental, long-term reason for being of his department. The statement of action plans for the coming year is used to describe when and what the department intends to do as support to the desired strategic action in the coming year. Upon preparation, both of these statements are reviewed by the next higher level of management. Further development of the tactical program is not permitted until concurrence on the validity of the accuracy of these statements is received.

CROSS IMPACT ANALYSIS

When each department manager has gained a clear understanding of what he must do, particularly in the coming year, it seems reasonable to expect that he is now in a position to prepare an explanation of how he proposes to do it and include the equivalent recommendation for funding. Traditionally, this is an exercise of budget preparation. Logical as it may seem, this is not the case. Before a manager can begin explaining his proposed operations and their related cost, an effort is required to sort out the interdependencies among the various departments of the organization. This exercise is called cross impact analysis.

A cross impact analysis is a preliminary task designed to help all managers identify the interdependencies among their departments. The exercise will determine and quantify in terms of timing, frequency and cost, each of the numerous internal support services in an organization. The omission of a cross impact analysis will seriously impair the coordination efforts of the organization.

Managers will forget to incorporate certain items in their plans and at other times include things which are not necessary. The result will be a sub-optimization pertaining to the efforts of the organization to execute its desired strategy.

The purpose of a cross impact analysis is to sort out and quantify who is doing what for whom within an organization in order to realize the planned strategy. This is accomplished by having each manager identify what services others will receive from him and what services others will supply to him in the coming year. A wealth of information is generated during this exercise. The most obvious benefit will be a discovery of any duplications in services. Similarly, redundant or unwanted activities can be highlighted and eliminated. The possibility of forgetting to build a needed service into the plan can be minimized. A cross impact analysis builds an awareness among managers of what they are doing, why they are doing it and the equivalent cost of their actions. As part of the process, managers are obliged to talk to one another and to exchange their ideas, problems and solutions. Opening up communication channels is a by-product of the cross impact analysis that is needed by all organizations.

As compared to the complexity of the interdependencies among departments in an organization, the procedures required to perform a cross impact analysis are deceptively simple. There are only three steps to performing a cross impact analysis. These steps are as follows:

1. A) Identify all departments that will receive services from your department in the coming year.
   B) Notify these departments of the services in terms of volume, timing, quality and estimated costs.
2. A) Identify all departments that will supply services to your department in the coming year.
   B) Notify these departments of the services in terms of volume, timing, quality and estimated costs.
3. A) Resolve the discrepancies between those whom your department has identified as receivers and those who have identified your department as a supplier.

The first step of the cross impact analysis requires each manager to identify the activities and services that other departments will receive from him in the coming year. These activities and services would be in response to the strategies of the organization. Once this identification has been completed, the specific departments receiving these actions would be determined. Reversal of these procedures can result in a less efficient approach to compiling a cross impact analysis.

The manager would contact each of the receiving departments and inform them of what activities and services they should expect to receive from him in the coming year. It is at this time that the manager would describe the volume, timing,quality and estimated cost of each service he expects the other department to receive.

The contact with the receiving department may be either formal or informal. In smaller organizations where communication often flows freely, an informal process may be sufficient. A telephone call or a short meeting may be all that is required. In larger organizations where communication requires much attention, a more formal process may be in order. A formal process involves the use of specially designed forms to make contact with the receivers. Exhibit 9-1 is an example of a Cross Impact Advice (To Receivers) form that can be used as the communication vehicle. One of these forms could be sent to each receiving department describing all of the activities or services involved.

The second step of the cross impact analysis requires each manager to identify the activities and services that other departments will supply to him in the coming year. These activities and services would also be in response to the strategies of the organization. Once this identification has been completed, the specific departments supplying these actions would be determined. Reversal of these procedures can result in a less efficient approach to compiling a cross impact analysis just as it would when identifying the receivers.

The manager would contact each of the supplying departments and inform them of what activities and services they should expect to supply to him in the coming year. At this time, the manager would describe the volume, timing, quality and estimated cost of each service he expects the other department to supply.

Similar to the process of identifying receivers, identifying suppliers may also be either formal or informal. A formal process

THE ABC ORGANIZATION
CROSS IMPACT ADVICE
(TO RECEIVERS)

TO: DEPARTMENT:

MANAGER:

ADDRESS:

FROM: DEPARTMENT:

MANAGER:

IN THE PREPARATION OF OUR TACTICAL PROGRAM, WE HAVE IDENTI-
FIED YOUR DEPARTMENT AS A RECEIVER OF OUR SERVICES IN THE
COMING YEAR. A BRIEF DESCRIPTION OF THE SERVICES WE INTEND
TO PROVIDE IS PRESENTED BELOW. PLEASE ADVISE IF THIS DATA IS
NOT CORRECT.

ESTIMATED
COST

Exhibit 9-1 Example of a Cross Impact Advice (To Receivers)
form.

could again use a special form to make the initial contact with the supplying department managers. This form would be mechanically identical to the one presented in Exhibit 9-1. The only difference would be the word "supplier" substituted for the word "receiver".

When performing a cross impact analysis, managers are often uncertain about the level of detail required. There is no absolutely right level of detail for a cross impact analysis. The main purpose of the exercise is to prevent items from being forgotten or "falling between the chairs." The likelihood of such an event occurring will determine the level of detail required. This involves discretionary judgement on behalf of the department manager.

Another problem that can be expected when performing a cross impact analysis is differences in terminology. A supplying department may use a different name from the one a receiving department uses for exactly the same service. Some minor translations can be expected to be made.

Department managers require a summary of the cross impact analysis which they have performed. One summary of the receivers and one summary of the suppliers is prepared. A simple matrix form listing the activities across the top axis and either the receivers or suppliers down the side axis can be used. The matrix would highlight each cross impact advice issued to either receivers or suppliers as the case may be. Exhibit 9-2 is an example of a Cross Impact Analysis form that could be used to summarize the receivers of a department's services. An identical form with the word "receivers" changed to "suppliers" could be used to summarize the suppliers of services to a department.

The third and last step of the cross impact analysis is to resolve discrepancies between those whom the department has identified as a receiver of services and those who have identified the department as a supplier of services. In step one, the manager has identified the receivers of his services. In step two, the manager has identified the suppliers of services to him. Therefore, for every service that a department manager identifies as being received from him in the coming year, the manager of the receiving department should be simultaneously identifying exactly the same service as being supplied to him in the coming year. Should any discrepancy exist, this is one of the items that would have "fallen between the chairs" in the tactical program.

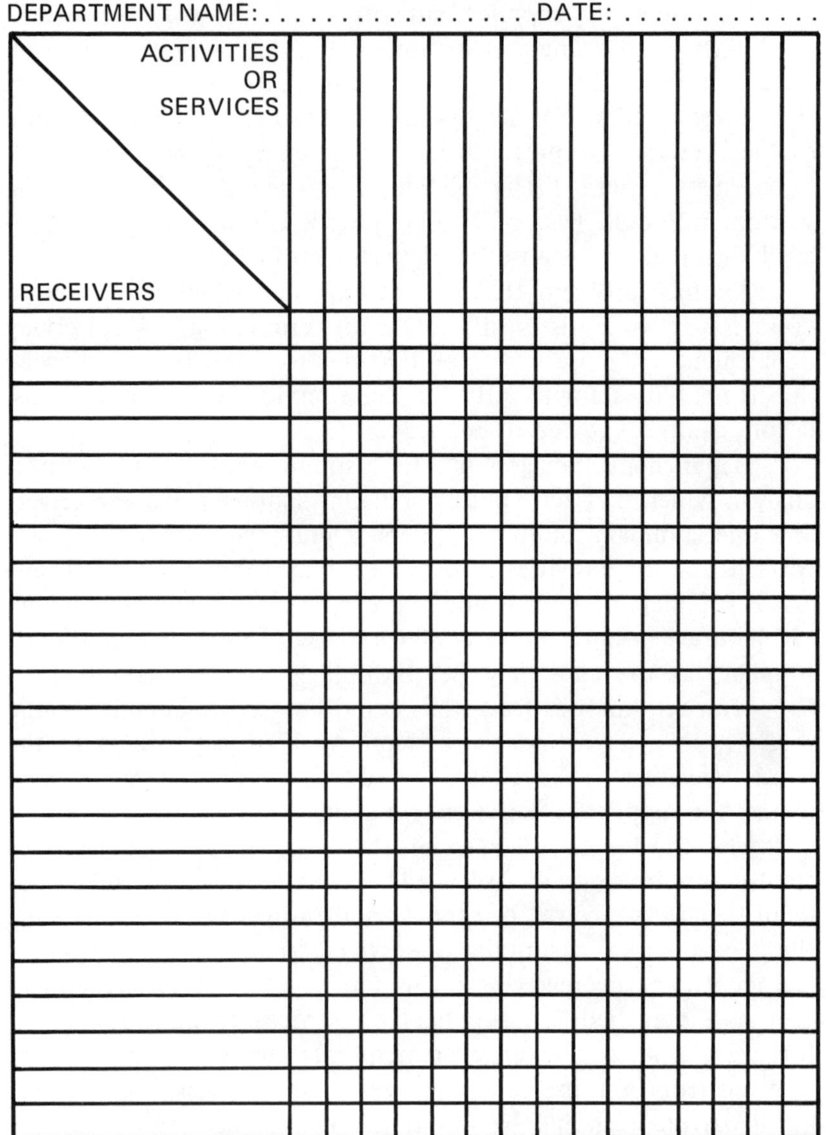

Exhibit 9-2 Example of a Cross Impact Analysis form (for receivers).

A significant amount of discussion among managers will be required to resolve these discrepancies. The costs and benefits of each interdependency can be expected to be fully examined. However, in the end, the cross impact analysis is a receiver driven exercise. It is the receiver that will have the ultimate authority to decide whether the service is to be included in the subsequent activity and funding recommendation to more senior management.

EXPENDITURE OPPORTUNITIES

Now that each manager has reached a stage in the tactical program where he knows what is expected of him as well as the the inherent interdependencies with other departments, he is in a position to describe **how** he proposes to do it together with the associated costs. This is the focal point of the tactical program's discretionary components. The manager accomplishes this task by constructing a recommendation consisting of a series of expenditure opportunities. The presentation of only one expenditure opportunity is not permitted. By definition, every department must prepare at least two expenditure opportunities, probably three, sometimes four, but never more than five. An expenditure opportunity is a small grouping of logically related activites upon which an absolute "go/no go" decision can be made. Aside from explaining the proposed operations of the department in digestible segments, the preparation of expenditure opportunities provides more senior management — through a selection process— with an ability to optimize the allocation of the organization's resources. A series of expenditure opportunities will provide a variety of alternatives to more senior management. They can intelligently increase or decrease the funding provided to any given department in order to maximize the contribution towards the objectives of the organization as described by the approved strategy recommendations. In addition, expenditure opportunities address the question of efficiency, which is always an important issue with discretionary or overhead activities.

The Expenditure Opportunity form serves as the communication vehicle between the department managers and senior management. Because of this role, the Expenditure Opportunity form must be designed with the utmost care and forethought. The form should reflect the needs of the organization and emphasize its aspirations while respecting the unique culture and habits of the institution.

Recognizing that a customized Expenditure Opportunity form is needed, there are nevertheless a series of issues which will be common to any design. To illustrate these basic topics, Exhibit 9-3 presents an example of a standard Expenditure Opportunity form. This example describes the basic ingredients of an expenditure opportunity by posing the following questions:

1. What is it that the manager is proposing to do?
2. How does he propose to do it?
3. What results or benefits can be expected from these actions?
4. Who will receive these benefits?
5. What will happen if it is not done?
6. What other ways of doing it have been considered but rejected in favour of this proposal?
7. What will happen if only a portion of the expenditure is provided?
8. How much will it cost?

The nature of these questions clearly illustrates that each expenditure opportunity is a comprehensive cost/benefit analysis. The intention of the discretionary components of the tactical program is to describe each proposed activity in a cost/benefit format so that its contribution to the organization's strategies can be assessed. The numerous peripheral issues surrounding the costs and benefits are intended to enhance understanding and therefore result in a more confident and accurate decision making process.

As Exhibit 9-3 illustrates, the first piece of information required is the expenditure opportunity name. The choice of name is left entirely to the discretion of the department manager. It should appropriately describe the activities and services contained in the expenditure opportunity. Above all, it should be unique and definitive to bring instant recognition to the expenditure opportunity. It may be easier to select an appropriate name after the balance of the expenditure opportunity has been prepared.

The section of the form entitled ". . . . of . . . . in depart-

BC ORGANIZATION

ITURE OPPORTUNITY

. . . . .DATE: . . . .

| TUNITY NAME | ____ OF ____
IN DEPARTMENT |

BENEFITS:

RECEIVERS:
1.
2.
3.
4.
5.
6.
7.
8.
9.
10.

CONSEQUENCES OF NOT APPROVING THE EXPENDITURE OPPORTUNITY:

ALTERNATIVES CONSIDERED BUT REJECTED:

Exhibit 9-3   Example of an Expenditure Opportunity form (front).

CONSEQUENCES OF APPROVING 1/3 OF EXPENDITURE OPPORTUNITY:

CONSEQUENCES OF APPROVING 2/3 OF EXPENDITURE OPPORTUNITY:

FISCAL 198X EXPENSE BREAKDOWN ($000)	1ST QTR.	2ND QTR.	3RD QTR.	4TH QTR.	198X BUDGET	198W BUDGET
STAFF						
SALARIES						
BENEFITS						
CONSULTANT FEES						
STATIONERY						
POSTAGE & PRINTING						
ADVERTISING						
TRAVEL						
ENTERTAINMENT						
COMMUNICATIONS						
ELECTRONIC DATA PROCESSING						
HEAT, LIGHT & POWER						
REPAIRS						
CLEANING & MAINTENANCE						
TAXES (OTHER THAN INCOME)						
BUILDING RENT						
DEPRECIATION						
EQUIPMENT EXPENSE UNDER $100						
MISCELLANEOUS						
TOTAL EXPENSES						

FISCAL 198X CAPITAL EXPENDITURE BREAKDOWN	1ST QTR.	2ND QTR.	3RD QTR.	4TH QTR.	198X BUDGET	198W BUDGET
FURNITURE						
OFFICE EQUIPMENT						
MACHINERY						
MISCELLANEOUS						
TOTAL CAPITAL EXPENDITURE						

Exhibit 9-3 (Cont'd) Example of an Expenditure Opportunity form (back).

ment" refers to the rank of importance that the manager assigns to the expenditure opportunity. He may indicate that it is 1 of 3 or 2 of 4, as the case may be, to identify the respective rank out of the total number of expenditure opportunities which he has prepared.

The statement of purpose acts as an introduction to the expenditure opportunity. It is in this section of the form that the manager exposes what it is that he proposes to do. This is a fundamental statement of intention.

The statement of program is a very significant portion of the expenditure opportunity. This section is used by the manager to reveal how he plans to accomplish that which he proposes. This is where the precise action plans of the department are documented.

The section of the form entitled "benefits" contains a description of the results that would be enjoyed by the organization should the expenditure opportunity be funded and executed. These benefits could be in the form of additional revenue, cost savings or non-monetary results. In all cases, benefits should be expressed in terms of **expected end results** that can later be measured. Furthermore, the benefits should always be expressed in a positive fashion rather than by listing all of the possibilities an organization would forfeit should it decide to fund only this particular expenditure opportunity. The purpose of this is two-fold. First, description of benefits will form half of the cost/benefit equation. Second, the benefits will act as performance measurements against which the manager can be subsequently evaluated. Within this context, the benefits section of the Expenditure Opportunity form establishes a basis from which to later exert control.

The receivers section of the expenditure opportunity form contains a list of those departments, if any, that would be recipients of the activities included in the statement of program. Should this expenditure opportunity not be affordable by the organization, the information contained in this section of the form will immediately signal what other departments are affected by such a decision.

The consequences of not approving the expenditure opportunity are used to alert senior management to the full ramifications of formulating a decision not to provide funding. Rather than repeating the benefits that could not be realized, the manager takes this opportunity to present a more global view of the impact upon the whole organization.

Each expenditure opportunity is expected to contain the best possible description of program or represent the optimum manner in which to realize the statement of purpose. The section of the form entitled "alternatives considered but rejected" is intended to address this issue. Here, each manager proves that his proposed statement of program is best by listing all of the alternatives that he has considered but rejected. This rigorous analysis introduces the concept of efficiency into the expenditure opportunity.

By examining the consequences of approving only 1/3 or 2/3 of the expenditure opportunity, additional alternatives are generated for senior management. More importantly, these sections of the form provide a deeper insight into the expenditure opportunity and act as a quality control check with respect to the ingredients.

The last section of the expenditure opportunity form is concerned with the resource requirements that the manager equates to his proposed activities. The requirements relate to staff, expenses and capital expenditures. There is a financial orientation because this information will eventually form the department's budget. This resource information is usually broken out by quarter with a comparison to last year should the expenditure opportunity have existed last year. The data is also segregated into as many line items as is feasible. The intention of this section of the form is to provide the other half of the cost/benefit equation as well as to provide managers with a framework in which to prepare their annual financial operating plan.

At the outset, it was mentioned that each manager will prepare a series of expenditure opportunities to explain how he proposes to accomplish his department objectives together with the related cost. The first one in the series is called the base expenditure opportunity. Subsequent ones are called incremental expenditure opportunities. Regardless of whether the expenditure opportunity is base or incremental, the form used and therefore the topics addressed will be identical for both. Incremental expenditure opportunities represent improvements in quality and/or frequency over the activities described in the base expenditure opportunity. By constructing the expenditure opportunity series in this fashion, an "either-and" question rather than an "either-or" question is presented. An incremental expenditure opportunity cannot be approved for funding before the base opportunity. This situation will be reflected in the rank of importance which the manager assigns to his expenditure opportunities.

The base expenditure opportunity has some unique characteristics — the understanding of which is vital to the success of an organization's tactical program. Some of the main characteristics are as follows:

1. The base expenditure opportunity will not likely be an attractive undertaking for the department manager by itself.

2. The base expenditure opportunity by itself will probably not permit the department manager to attain his objectives. (Incremental expenditure opportunities will be needed.)

3. The base expenditure opportunity must be conceivable and feasible and truly represent what would happen in the case of an emergency.

4. The base expenditure opportunity **must** be less than the current level of expenditure for the entire department (usually sixty to seventy percent.)

Of all these characteristics, the most emotional and therefore difficult to comprehend is that of limiting the size of the base expenditure opportunity to sixty or seventy percent of the department's current level of effort. This limitation is imperative if an organization wishes to create an ability to intelligently reallocate its resources in support of its targeted strategy. Without question, this is one of the major issues of the tactical program.

A manager would describe those activities and services of highest importance to the department in the base expenditure opportunity. This description would be in response to the question: What would be done if only sixty or seventy cents on the current dollar was available for spending? To managers, this is a distasteful question. It will involve a considerable amount of thought to arrive at a proper reply. The concept of limiting the size of the base expenditure opportunity to sixty or seventy cents on the current dollar emotionally agitates managers. They are reluctant to expose what they can do with less resources than they currently have for fear that someone may take them up on it. However, managers need to realize that these conditions are necessary to create the potential to optimize the allocation of the organization's resources.

The remainder of the department manager's series will consist of incremental expenditure opportunities. The exact number and the individual size of the incremental expenditure opportunities are left to the discretion of the manager. However, he must stay within the guideline limiting the total number of expenditure opportunities for any given department. He will build his incremental expenditure opportunities according to the natural analysis categories of his operations. When combined with the base expenditure opportunity, the incremental expenditure opportunities will represent sufficient resources to permit a manager to completely realize the objectives of his department.

Managers sometimes have difficulty understanding the incremental approach of these expenditure opportunities. The contents of the base expenditure opportunity, both in terms of cost and benefits, are not duplicated or included in the first incremental expenditure opportunity. It is a completely stand alone type of analysis. The same is true of further incremental expenditure opportunities. Only the additional activities with their related costs and benefits would be described in each. When approving expenditure opportunities later on in the process, it is not an "either - or" type of situation. It is a question of how many expenditure opportunities in total can be afforded by the organization.

THE RECOMMENDATION PACKAGE

When making his activity and funding recommendation, the department manager needs to present his documentation in an intelligible format. The forms which he has completed should be grouped and put in a sequence that will be meaningful to all interested parties, particularly senior management. This portfolio of documents can simply be called the department manager's recommendation package. This package includes every document that the manager intends to utilize in his explanation of how he proposes to accomplish his objectives as well as the related funding requirements. The portion of the tactical program's discretionary components addressed to this point will result in the following documents being included in the recommendation package:

1. Statement of Mission, Role or Mandate.
2. Statement of Action Plans For The Coming Year.
3. Cross Impact Analysis (For Receivers).
4. Cross Impact Analysis (For Suppliers).
5. Expenditure Opportunity Series (2 to 5 expenditure opportunities in the series).

The completion of the recommendation package requires the manager to prepare a small number of additional forms to more clearly establish the plans of the department and to arrange the resource requirements in a meaningful format. This process will result in the creation of the following documents:

1. Department Expenditure Summary.
2. Department Monthly Expenditure.
3. Organization Chart.
4. Job Descriptions.
5. Expenditure Opportunity Ranking.

The Department Expenditure Summary form and the Department Monthly Expenditure form are the final components of the financial operating plan. The department expenditure summary is nothing more than a consolidation of the resource requirements requested in each expenditure opportunity of the department's series. Exactly the same format used by the Expenditure Opportunity form is employed by the Department Expenditure Summary form. The Department Monthly Expenditure form is used for the final break-out of this information by month and by precise line item of expenditure. In effect, the department monthly expenditure is the financial operating budget of the department. The preparation of these two forms is largely a clerical effort. They are needed to create an ability to compare actual costs to the department plan as the coming year unfolds. Exhibits 9-4 and 9-5 are examples of these two respective forms.

A planned organization chart is an integral part of the tactical

THE ABC ORGANIZATION

DEPARTMENT EXPENDITURE SUMMARY

DEPARTMENT NAME: . . . . .DATE: . . . .

	1ST QTR.	2ND QTR.	3RD QTR.	4TH QTR.	198X BUDGET	198W BUDGET
	($000)	($000)	($000)	($000)	($000)	($000)
STAFF						
SALARIES						
BENEFITS						
CONSULTANT FEES						
STATIONERY						
POSTAGE & PRINTING						
ADVERTISING						
TRAVEL						
ENTERTAINMENT						
COMMUNICATIONS						
ELECTRONIC DATA PROCESSING						
HEAT, LIGHT & POWER						
REPAIRS						
CLEANING & MAINTENANCE						
TAXES (OTHER THAN INCOME)						
BUILDING RENT						
DEPRECIATION						
EQUIPMENT EXPENSE UNDER $100						
MISCELLANEOUS						
TOTAL EXPENSES						

	1ST QTR.	2ND QTR.	3RD QTR.	4TH QTR.	198X BUDGET	198W BUDGET
	($000)	($000)	($000)	($000)	($000)	($000)
FURNITURE						
OFFICE EQUIPMENT						
MACHINERY						
MISCELLANEOUS						
TOTAL CAPITAL EXPENDITURE						

Exhibit 9-4 Example of a Department Expenditure Summary form.

THE ABC ORGANIZATION

DEPARTMENT MONTHLY EXPENDITURE

DEPARTMENT NAME: ....DATE: ....

EXPENSE ELEMENTS	JAN. ($000)	FEB. ($000)	MAR. ($000)	APR. ($000)	MAY ($000)	JUNE ($000)	JULY ($000)	AUG. ($000)	SEPT. ($000)	OCT. ($000)	NOV. ($000)	DEC. ($000)	TOTAL 198X
STAFF													
SALARIES													
BENEFITS													
CONSULTANT FEES													
STATIONERY													
POSTAGE & PRINTING													
ADVERTISING													
TRAVEL													
ENTERTAINMENT													
COMMUNICATIONS													
ELECTRONIC DATA PROCESSING													
HEAT, LIGHT & POWER													
REPAIRS													
CLEANING & MAINTENANCE													
TAXES (OTHER THAN INCOME)													
BUILDING RENT													
DEPRECIATION													
EQUIPMENT EXPENSE UNDER $100													
MISCELLANEOUS													
TOTAL EXPENSES													

CAPITAL ELEMENTS	JAN. ($000)	FEB. ($000)	MAR. ($000)	APR. ($000)	MAY ($000)	JUNE ($000)	JULY ($000)	AUG. ($000)	SEPT. ($000)	OCT. ($000)	NOV. ($000)	DEC. ($000)	TOTAL 198X
FURNITURE													
OFFICE EQUIPMENT													
MACHINERY													
MISCELLANEOUS													
TOTAL CAPITAL EXPENDITURE													

Exhibit 9-5 Example of a Department Monthly Expenditure form.

program. It describes how the department's staff is expected to relate to one another. The staff requirements included in each expenditure opportunity are added up for the total department then displayed in an organization chart format. Job titles, employee names and lines of authority all form part of the planned organization chart. The intention of the organization chart is to encourage managers to consider their people management as well as their activity management responsibilities. It is constructed as of the end of the coming year with any additions above the present staff level being shown with dotted lines.

A department manager should also include planned job descriptions for each of his key employees in his recommendation package. These job descriptions will flow naturally from the organization chart of the department. They will force managers to tentatively allocate the activities and services contained in the expenditure opportunities to specific persons in the department. It translates the expenditure opportunities into action items for which persons can be held responsible. Planned job descriptions represent the final step in aligning the goals of the employee with those of the organization. It is the end of the communication cycle that emerged from the charter of objectives and now rests with performance targets for each individual. As a result of these job descriptions, employees should gain an appreciation of what is expected of them in the coming year and how this relates to the overall direction of the organization.

The last part of the recommendation package is an expenditure opportunity ranking. The expenditure opportunities represent the alternatives in the department manager's recommendation package. Each manager is required to go beyond this point and to arrange the expenditure opportunities in their order of priority. An Expenditure Opportunity Ranking form is used to document this information for each department. The ranking form would show the name of the expenditure opportunity together with its rank of importance. Summaries of the cost requirements for each expenditure opportunity would also be included on the form. Exhibit 9-6 is an example of an Expenditure Opportunity Ranking form incorporating these ingredients.

The department manager is assigned both the authority and the responsibility to rank the expenditure opportunities which

THE ABC ORGANIZATION
EXPENDITURE OPPORTUNITY RANKING

DEPARTMENT NAME: ....DATE: ....

R A N K	EXPENDITURE OPPORTUNITY NAME	198X			CUMULATIVE		
		STAFF DEC. 31	EXPENSE BUDGET ($000)	CAPITAL EXPEND. BUDGET ($000)	STAFF DEC. 31	EXPENSE BUDGET ($000)	CAPITAL EXPEND. BUDGET ($000)
	TOTAL DEPARTMENT:						

Exhibit 9-6 Example of an Expenditure Opportunity Ranking form.

he has prepared . The strategies of the organization expressed in action plans for the department will determine the importance of each. The department manager should experience little difficulty when ranking his own expenditure opportunities. The base opportunity would be considered the most important and would receive the number one ranking position. Incremental expenditure opportunities would be assigned progressively lower rankings. It is when the ranking process progresses beyond the boundaries of the department that difficulty begins to be encountered.

CONSOLIDATING EXPENDITURE OPPORTUNITY RANKINGS

The primary question to be answered by the department concerning the discretionary components of the tactical program is **how** it proposes to fulfill its role in attaining the desired strategy of the organization. The answer to this question will include a recommendation for resource employment. Because of this condition, the tactical program can also be viewed as a resource allocation process. To complete the tactical program, the remaining chore is to evaluate the expenditure opportunities prepared by the department managers. It is not likely that the organization will be able to afford all of the proposed expenditure opportunities. A process of identifying the high priority opportunities making the greatest contribution to the organization's strategy is needed. This selection process will ensure, regardless of the organization's level of affordability, that only the most beneficial activities available to the organization will be undertaken.

The process of identifying the organization's high priority expenditure opportunities involves a consolidation of the expenditure opportunity rankings already prepared at the departmental level. During this consolidation process, the expenditure opportunities are not summarized, combined or rewritten at any time. Neither are any expenditure opportunities approved for funding or discarded. The rankings prepared by each department are simply merged into a new and consolidated list of priorities. This merging effort is repeated and repeated at each higher level until a final consolidated list of expenditure opportunity rankings results for the total organization. Again, the major consideration during this consolidation process and hence the primary determinant of rank is contribution to the desired strategy of the organization.

The consolidation process is normally accomplished by holding a series of review meetings at each level of the organization. At the first level of consolidation, the attendees of the review meetings would be the department managers and their immediate superior. Each superior would chair the review meeting with his subordinates. At this time, the department managers would use their Expenditure Opportunity forms as an agenda to explain their proposed operations. After each manager has had a chance to present his expenditure opportunities and to respond to questions from his peers and superior, the meeting turns its attention to arranging the opportunities in order of priority. At this level of the organization, logical connections between the various expenditure opportunities can usually be established to determine the consolidated rank of priority. In any case, the superior is always present to settle those issues which may remain unresolved. An example of how this merger process at the first level of consolidation may result is presented in Exhibit 9-7. In this exhibit, a total of eleven expenditure opportunities from three different departments is consolidated into one ranking. It is important to note than no expenditure opportunities have been dropped or summarized. The existing departmental rankings are simply merged together.

This concept of merger through review meetings is duplicated at each higher level of the organization. A format of explaining the expenditure opportunities and then merging their rankings is retained. However, as the consolidation process gets higher and higher within the organization, clear cut answers will become more difficult to find and subjective decisions will be required. To help alleviate this situation, the review meetings may wish to employ some form of consensus determining mechanism. A voting procedure is often helpful in expediting the decision making process.

As the consolidation process progresses, higher levels of management in the organization can also be expected to look for shortcuts. It is logical for senior management to expend their energy on making ranking decisions that will truly count. For this reason, as the consolidation process moves to higher levels, man-

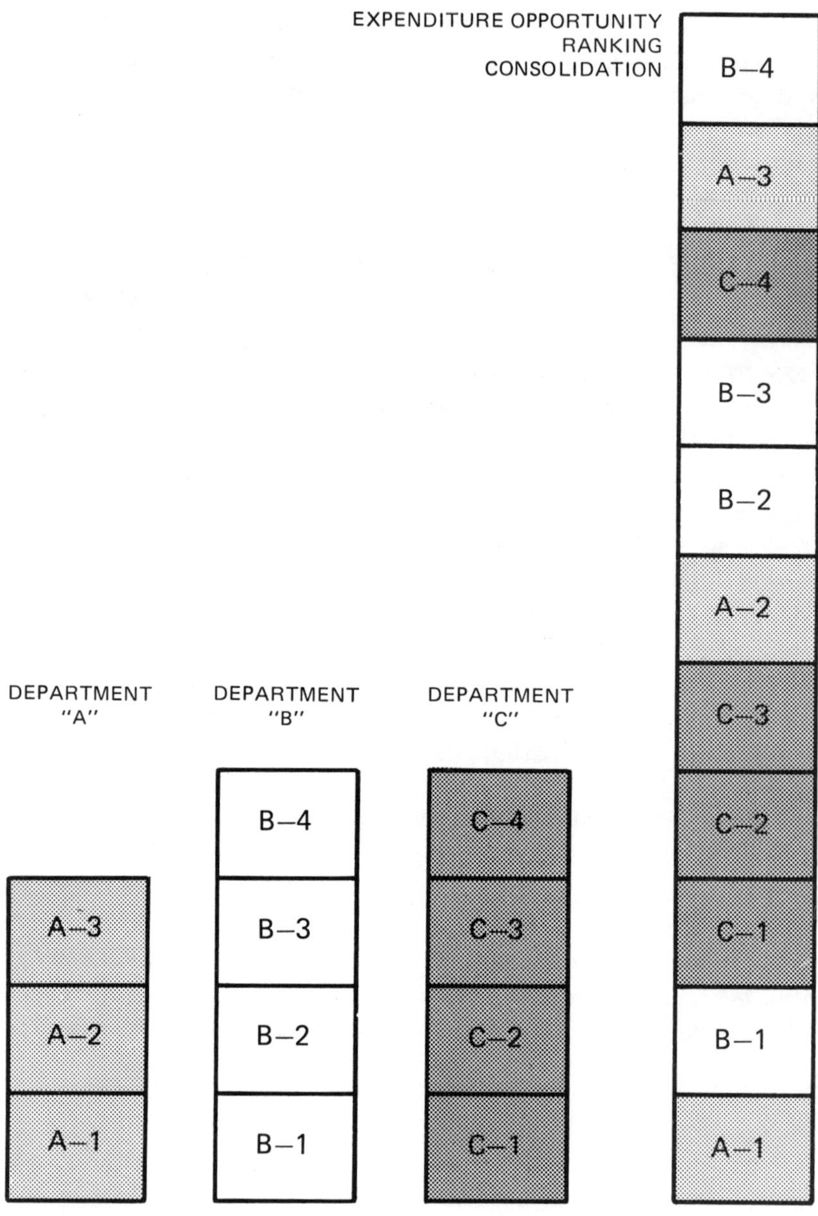

Exhibit 9-7 Example of a consolidation of expenditure opportunity rankings from three departments.

agement may want to restrict its focus by omitting consideration
of the highest priority expenditure opportunities. For example,
management may decide that the first thirty percent of expenditure opportunities is so important that its precise consolidation is not necessary. Time can be saved by arbitrarily putting
these expenditure opportunities into one block at the high priority end of the consolidated list. This practice of having senior
management concentrate its attention in those areas where efforts
will pay off is an intelligent way in which to accomplish the consolidation of expenditure opportunity rankings.

RESOURCE ALLOCATION

After the consolidation process has been completed and all
of the expenditure opportunities have been assembled into one
list according to importance, an organization is then in a position
to intelligently allocate its resources. The first question which
arises is how much funds are there to allocate in the first place.
The answer to this question is the expected revenue less direct
labour and material less any desired profit or loss. This equation
results in the amount of money that the organization can afford
to spend on discretionary activities.

The next step in the resource allocation process is to apply
the funds available to the deserving expenditure opportunities.
This is principally a clerical function. Beginning with the most
important expenditure opportunity, an organization would
accumulate the cost requirements by going down its list until a
point is reached where the costs of the next expenditure opportunity exceed the amount of funds available. This is the cutoff
point. All of the expenditure opportunities up to this point could
be afforded by the organization. As a result, they would be funded
and executed. Expenditure opportunities beyond this point have
been evaluated as not important enough to attract the limited
funds of the organization. Consequently, they would not be
approved or executed. Exhibit 9-8 is an example of how such a
cutoff point could be calculated for an organization. It emphasizes the simplicity of choosing which expenditure opportunities
an organization can afford to execute after they have been arranged in their order of importance.

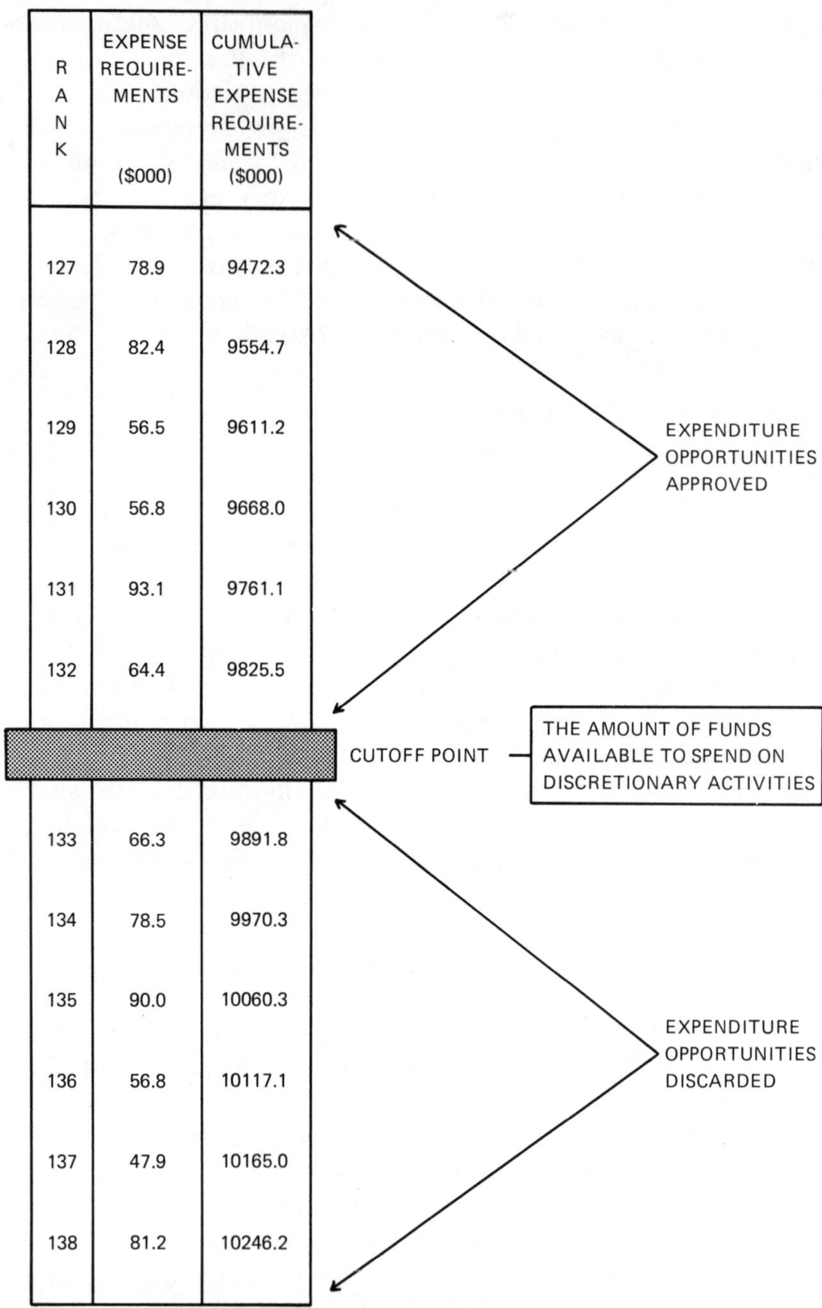

Exhibit 9-8   Example of a funding cutoff point calculation.

The expenditure opportunities unfortunate enough to fall into the range that could not be afforded are likely to come from a wide variety of departments. Regardless of their source, they represent the least important activities available for the organization to undertake. This resource allocation mechanism of the tactical program meticulously selects low priority activities to be deprived of funds. Inherently, this supplies resources to those activities which make the most generous contribution towards the desired strategy of the organization.

The results of the resource allocation decisions need to be communicated to department managers. Explaining the reasoning behind the decisions is also a courteous practice. Should a department manager discover that one or more of his expenditure opportunities has not been fortunate to attract funding, he will have to make modifications to his recommendation package. The cross impact analysis, organization chart, job descriptions and financial operating plan will all likely need adjustment. After these modifications have been made, the department manager then has an approved plan which will provide him with guidance for the coming year. This event marks the completion of the tactical program. The Strategy Management process is now prepared to move into the execution and control stage of its cycle.

10

Execution and Control

Over the years, various management techniques and processes have been hailed as the panacea to all that ails an organization. By adopting certain practices or systems, an organization sometimes believes that all of its problems will be solved. The truth of the matter is that no system or process, regardless of its credentials, can guarantee results. Strategy Management is no exception. Results can only be achieved through proper execution. Execution involves management action. There is no system or process than can force management to act against its will. To promise anything else is not realistic.

There is an old saying that you can bring a horse to water but you cannot make him drink it. This is a good analogy to the management situation. A horse can be prepared and instructed how to drink the water and even made aware of a reward that follows should he decide to execute the deed. Nevertheless, one cannot guarantee that the horse is going to drink the water. With managers, detailed planning, education and encouragement can be combined with a lively reward and punishment scheme to prompt execution. However, that spark which ignites execution comes from within and therefore managerial action is something that cannot be expected with absolute certainty.

Realizing these limitations, a good management process can

still have a positive influence upon the moment of execution. This is done by creating an environment which is conducive to execution. Such an environment will be free of any obstacles which might distract a manager from acting on his plans.

AN ACTION ENVIRONMENT

The execution environment includes the atmosphere both prior to and subsequent to the point of action. A sense that performance is encouraged permeates the execution environment. But this is not enough. The simple knowledge that one is expected to carry out his plans does not in itself make for an action environment. An organization has a fundamental need for an atmosphere that is free of distractions and confusion surrounding the point of execution. This state of affairs will permit the manager to concentrate exclusively on realizing his goals and minimize the amount of energy spent on subsidiary themes.

The time prior to the point of execution can generally be described as a planning stage. The removal of distractions and confusion in this stage calls for high quality plans. The Strategy Management process attempts to provide this by expressing in precise and unequivocal terms the detailed action plans of each manager. Moreover, it tries to relate these plans to the overall strategy and goals of the organization so that the manager can appreciate his role in the aggregate mission of the institution. By doing so, Strategy Management relieves much of the apprehension concerning what a manager is supposed to do. This frees him to focus his attention on the action of execution. Without this firm understanding and a sense of being comfortable with his action plans, a manager will naturally devote his energy towards "trying to understand the plans." These types of distractions are often used as explanations or excuses for failing to realize departmental goals. This failure is best described as a breakdown in execution.

The time subsequent to the point of execution can generally be described as a reward stage. The removal of distractions and confusion in this stage calls for both effective rewards and a complete understanding of them. A manager will not act, especially in the long-term, unless there is some personal benefit for him to do so. A good quality reward program realizes this fact and spares no effort in informing managers of the consequences of action or inaction with respect to their plans. Should the manager have doubts about the benefits or penalties confronting him, his energy will be misdirected towards alleviating this apprehension. Such a condition cannot help but detract from the probability of a proper execution. It is only by having clearly identified rewards combined with precise action plans can an environment be established in which a manager is free to devote his total energies towards a successful execution of his mandate.

MATCHING PEOPLE TO STRATEGY

Creating an atmosphere which encourages proper execution of plans and eliminates distractions immediately prior and subsequent to the point of execution has a significant influence upon managers. There are additional measures included in the Strategy Management process which will provide a further inducement to take charge. One of these is matching the proper people, particularly middle management, with the various approved strategies of the organization.

There is a radical difference between build and divestiture strategies. Although many organizations would like to think that their managers provide situational leadership, it is safe to assume that a manager with experience exclusively in build situations cannot execute a divestiture strategy as well as a manager who has had an extensive background in this area. It is simply a matter of bringing harmony between the nature of the person and the task he is about to carry out. Again, this will enhance the probability of achieving execution according to plan.

It is quite easy to assume that accountants are conservative by nature and make good candidates for harvest or divestiture strategies. Likewise, it is easy to assume that marketing people are go-getters and make good candidates for build strategies. These stereotypes are broad generalizations which cannot be used effectively. A person's nature is not determined by a profession. Each person is unique and should be treated as such. The personal and demonstrated skills of each manager need to be compared with the skill requirements of the respective strategy in order to determine if a suitable match exists. As a result, managers should be individually evaluated to determine their compatibility with the respective strategies.

Matching people with strategy is a goal that cannot always be realized. Because a wrong manager can be chosen or an appropriate manager may not be available, there is a possibility of a mismatch. To hedge against the consequences of such a situation, every key manager directly involved with the execution of the strategy should be thoroughly briefed about all of the peripheral reasoning and logic associated with the approval of the strategy recommendation. This will provide managers with a more global view of the desired strategy. This view is intended to weaken any natural resistance that the manager might have towards the desired strategy. Once again, this practice is designed to promote proper execution of the organization's plans.

EXPLOITING THE COLLECTIVE COMPETENCY

The final effort to create an action environment is not something that can be done at the time of execution. It is a policy or guideline that is used constantly throughout the Strategy Management process. This policy draws on the collective competency of subordinates.

A sizeable portion of managers believe that they know more than their subordinates. After all, isn't that the reason why **they** are the managers? It is this type of attitude which leads to decisions being made in isolation. In turn, this can also result in poor quality decisions. An individual manager may or may not be more knowledgeable than an individual subordinate. However, it is naive for a manager to believe that he knows more than all of his subordinates combined. Collectively, the knowledge possessed by subordinates is likely to greatly exceed that of an individual superior. Accepting this premise, it only makes sense to draw upon this competency at every available opportunity.

The Strategy Management process make extensive use of this principle. It is most evident during the tactical program preparation and the strategic business unit analysis. In both cases, the competence of subordinates is exploited to either confirm or amend the work done by the next higher level of management.

Drawing upon the collective competence of subordinates obviously forces responsibility and authority to lower levels of the organization. In essence, the role of the entrepreneur is shifted from senior management to strategic business unit personnel. Not only does this address a need for better planning; it fulfills the manager's need for more personal satisfaction. It also trains middle managers for the day when they become senior or chief executives. The greatest benefit from this practice is involvement. When managers become involved they assume ownership for their work. Ownership breeds motivation which is truly that inner spark which every manager needs to bridge that gap between planning and execution.

CONTROLLING COSTS AND RESULTS

Control is a tool that helps management to keep the activities of the organization on plan. It functions as a mechanism that warns management when activities are not being performed as they were intended. This warning mechanism is designed to trigger corrective action to get the organization back on course. It functions by closely comparing actual events to planned events. A good control facility will detect problems in their early stages when corrective action is still easily applied. A poor control system can only detect problems when they have become obvious and by that time usually difficult to correct.

The policing or detection aspects are only half of the purpose of control. A control system also acts as a form of "preventive medicine." By its very existence, a control facility will prevent a lot of problems from coming to fruition. The reason for this is human nature. When a manager knows that a control facility exists and that he will be regularly called upon to account for his actions, he is likely to take the necessary actions to see that actual results compare favourably to planned results. No manager wants to be seen as a fool or incompetent. When he is being monitored, there is an incentive to avoid being placed in this category. In this sense, a good control system has an intangible quality which will help minimize the number of problems that do come to the surface.

The most primitive and traditional manner in which to exert

control involves a departmental comparison of actual to planned costs on a monthly basis. There is nothing wrong with this type of procedure and accordingly it is incorporated into the Strategy Management process. However, it is by no means the only form of control that will be applied during the process. Monthly cost control is a small portion of the overall control scheme of Strategy Management.

The major thrust of the Strategy Management control facility is derived from two sources. One is the approved strategy recommendations of the organization's strategic business units. The other is the approved expenditure opportunities of the organization's departments. Costs and benefits are the key considerations included in the analyses and supporting forms used to address each of these issues. From **both the strategic and tactical** points of view, control is obtained by a **simultaneous focus on cost and benefit concerns.** This dual approach to long-term as well as short-term characteristics is the only way to achieve a truly comprehensive form of control. As an example, it is quite possible for a department to have actual costs closely in line with planned costs yet at the same time not be able to achieve its planned results. Conversely, it is quite possible for a department to have actual results closely in line with planned results and yet not be able to stay within its cost constraints. Individually, costs and benefits have a limited meaning. It is only when they are related to one another that they assume value. The control facility of Strategy Management recognizes this premise and uses such a dual approach in all of its control endeavours. It is important to note that this dual approach focuses on actual versus planned events rather than actual versus last year's events. Last year's events are not a reliable base from which to exert control. Consequently, they are not a prominent factor in this part of the Strategy Management process.

EXPENDITURE OPPORTUNITY PROGRESS REPORT

The Expenditure Opportunity form is the primary cost/ benefit document of the tactical program. It is the pinnacle of attention where the manager commits himself to attaining certain results and to employing certain resources. For this reason, the control process pertaining to the discretionary components of the tactical program will flow from these forms.

To complement the monthly departmental cost control efforts, managers should be asked to document their achievements with respect to each approved expenditure opportunity. Normally this is done on a quarterly basis. The form on which such a documentation could be made is an Expenditure Opportunity Progress Report. Exhibit 10-1 is an example of such a form.

The Expenditure Opportunity Progress Report is an elementary form of communication between the department manager and his superiors. It is a process of self-evaluation since it is initiated by the department manager himself. This lightens some of the burden on senior management because they only have to react to it rather than create or initiate it. The mechanics of the report are very simple. It begins with a re-statement of the planned costs and benefits. Next, the manager documents his actual costs and results. Finally, the manager describes any corrective action that he proposes should there be a discrepancy between actual and the plan.

The progress report prepared for each of the manager's approved expenditure opportunities provides an opportunity for a formal review. Formality is required to ensure that the proper attention will be paid to the report. An informal review process will very quickly retard to oblivion. Nevertheless, the report's formality does not mean that it is the only form of review or control exerted upon managers. A constant and informal dialogue between managers and their superiors culminating in the preparation of the Expenditure Opportunity Progress Report provides both a high quality and timely control process.

CONTROLLING VARIABLE COMPONENTS

In conjunction with the discretionary components, control needs to be extended to the variable components of the tactical program as well. Specifically, this refers to both the revenue program and direct cost program of the organization. This extension is consistent with the comprehensive philosophy of the Strategy Management control process. The logic is that if it was

THE ABC ORGANIZATION
EXPENDITURE OPPORTUNITY PROGRESS REPORT
FOR THE . . . . QUARTER

DEPARTMENT NAME: . . . . .DATE: . . . .

EXPENDITURE OPPORTUNITY NAME	_____ OF _____
	IN DEPARTMENT

BENEFITS:	STAFF LEVEL		
	ACTUAL	PLAN	VARIANCE
	EXPENSES INCURRED TO DATE		
	ACTUAL	PLAN	VARIANCE
	CAPITAL EXPENDITURES TO DATE		
	ACTUAL	PLAN	VARIANCE

PROGRESS ACCOMPLISHED TO DATE:

CORRECTIVE ACTION PLANNED:

Exhibit 10-1 Example of an Expenditure Opportunity Progress Report form.

included as part of the plan, then it must be important. If it is important, then it must be an issue for control.

The sales department will report on a quarterly basis the degree of success it is achieving with respect to costs and results. The vehicle for doing this is the Expenditure Opportunity Progress Report. In this report, the results discussed will almost completely concern the amount of revenue being generated. This focus of attention acts as a source of control on the revenue program. However, the strength of this control feature is not commensurate with the importance of the revenue program. Clearly, a more powerful monitoring process is needed.

To support the Expenditure Opportunity Progress Report in the revenue generating areas of the organization, an additional report comparing actual sales dollars and units to planned dollars and units needs to be instituted. This should be a monthly report with a quarterly summary. Attention to both dollars and units is necessary in order to address the question of average selling price or price per unit. Controlling unit prices is critical because of both the effect on contribution margin and the influence on dollar and unit volumes. The format of this Revenue Progress Report should be made to suit the needs of the particular organization. Normally a focus on sales of products or services within each market segment is what an organization will want. This monitors the revenue program at the stage of its development as described in Exhibit 8-1 of Chapter Eight. Comparing actual sales dollars and units to plan is nothing new for many organizations. Although it may appear to be somewhat mundane, it is nevertheless a critical component of the control process. It is the only way that an organization can ensure that its desired revenue levels and mix are being attained.

Control of the direct cost program can be a very elaborate exercise. Once again, the focus is not on controlling costs alone but on volume as well. The manner in which an organization controls its direct labour and direct material will be unique and will match its nature of operations. Although unique, an organization will monitor its operations by calculating a series of operating variations. These may be calculated daily, weekly or monthly as dictated by the relevant manufacturing or operating procedures. Operating variations normally include the following topics:

1. Material price variance.
2. Material usage variance.
3. Labour rate variance.
4. Labour efficiency variance.

Volume variances with respect to overhead application are also normal parts of the portfolio of operating variations. Yield variances can be extremely important factors for certain types of manufacturing corporations as well. Controlling direct costs through the calculation of operating variations is another long established practice in many organizations. The point to be made is that it has a natural role in the Strategy Management process.

STRATEGY PROGRESS REPORT

The final step in the Strategy Management control process focuses on the strategic business unit level and is concerned with the approved strategy recommendation. Of the many components of the approved strategy recommendation, two are of prime value for the purposes of control. One is the performance checkpoints. The other is the resource requirements. It is in these two areas that the strategic business unit personnel specifically commit themselves to achieving certain outputs and utilizing certain inputs. To help ensure that these two critical ingredients come to pass, control efforts will concentrate in these areas.

Control at the strategic business unit level is a perpetual process. As with other control efforts, its purpose is to prevent problems as well as to detect them. However, there is another important reason for control at the strategic business unit level. This is to constantly review the appropriateness from both an internal and an external point of view of the current strategy. Should issues or assumptions upon which the strategy is formulated prove to be defective, the strategy control process is intended to promptly identify the situation. This continuous assessment and search for improvement is a self-enhancing facility of the strategy control process. At this level of the monitoring process, improvements and reactions to change are more valuable to an organization than a policing effort. The nature of the strategic business unit makes this so.

Although the control process is a continual exercise, a degree of formality should be introduced. This should be in the form of a quarterly written report and review meeting. The review meeting would provide strategic business unit personnel with an opportunity to explain their progress and any proposed corrective action. The written report accompanying the meeting can serve as a documented summary or agenda. Formality is necessary to emphasize the importance of this portion of the control process.

An example of a Strategy Progress Report is presented in Exhibit 10-2. The report begins with a comparison between planned resource requirements and actual resource employments. This comparison is made for each of the four resource categories. Its purpose is to detect any discrepancies between the actual and planned levels of input. The report then goes on to document the performance checkpoints. This is a simple extraction from the equivalent section of the Strategy Recommendation Summary form. The next section of the form is used by the strategic business unit personnel to describe the progress accomplished to date. This is where the performance achievements are documented. This section of the form is followed by the strategy assumption discrepancies. It is here that strategic business unit personnel have an opportunity to identify any changes — both externally and internally — that may have occurred which affect the validity of the current strategy. This section is used to evaluate the appropriateness of the strategy by reviewing the integrity of the basis upon which it was formulated. There is a close relationship to the corrective action warning indicators section of the original Strategy Recommendation Summary form. Finally, the Strategy Progress Report deals with the issue of corrective action planned — if any. This section provides strategic business unit personnel with an opportunity to go beyond an assessment of actual versus the plan. They are asked to propose corrective measures which will restore an equilibrium between actual and planned events.

Working in concert, the monthly cost control efforts, the Expenditure Opportunity Progress Report, the revenue monitoring reports, the operating variations reports and the Strategy Progress Report provide a timely and comprehensive system of control. They are designed to fortify every major segment of the Strategy Management process and to provide direct input to the subsequent reward activities.

THE ABC ORGANIZATION

STRATEGY PROGRESS REPORT

FOR THE . . . . QUARTER

STRATEGIC BUSINESS UNIT: . . . . .DATE: . . . .

PLANNED RESOURCES	ACTUAL RESOURCES
FINANCIAL RESOURCES:	FINANCIAL RESOURCES:
HUMAN RESOURCES:	HUMAN RESOURCES:
PHYSICAL RESOURCES:	PHYSICAL RESOURCES:
ORGANIZATIONAL RESOURCES:	ORGANIZATIONAL RESOURCES:

PERFORMANCE CHECKPOINTS:

Exhibit 10-2   Example of a Strategy Progress Report form (front).

PROGRESS ACCOMPLISHED TO DATE:

STRATEGY ASSUMPTION DISCREPANCIES:

CORRECTIVE ACTION PLANNED:

Exhibit 10-2 (Cont'd) Example of a Strategy Progress Report form (back).

11

Reward and Compensation Issues

The last exercise in the Strategy Management cycle is dispensing rewards. It is the final link in the chain of events but should not be viewed as the least important. On the contrary, rewards are a very important part of the overall process. Without them, many of the other components will lose their vitality. Rewards provide the adrenalin that helps to energize every part of the system.

When examining the topic of execution, it was stated that the two requirements for proper action were precisely defined plans and unequivocal rewards. Rewards were understood to be both positive and negative. The importance of rewards as a component of the execution equation deserves reiteration at this time. For a manager to possess the desire and motivation both to construct his plans and then to carry them out, there needs to be a benefit or reward that will accrue to him upon doing so. Rewards are the fuel which makes managers act. Absence of rewards, both positive and negative, will stifle managers' incentive. Without rewards, an organization runs on the goodwill and pride of its employees. Such an environment attracts only a certain kind of individual and at best can provide short-term sustenance.

A creative and effective reward system is something very

frequently overlooked in today's organizations. This poses a severe problem because of the magnitude of the consequences it has throughout the entire institution. The plans and actions of many organizations are sabotaged because of the omission of an intelligent reward scheme. Without doubt, the Strategy Management process will be significantly impeded without a vibrant and comprehensive reward scheme as its final component.

TYPES OF REWARDS

Now that the importance of rewards has been established, it is an appropriate time to focus on the different types of rewards. People are paid for their work. Historically, money has been the medium of compensation. Other forms of remuneration have only come into widespread use within the last quarter century. More imaginative forms of rewards than money have been created to fit the personal situations of employees as well as to minimize the effect of government taxation. These two factors have resulted in an infinite variety of rewards ranging from free newspapers to use of company aircraft and with every possible combination in between. The intention is not to review any of the different types of rewards nor advocate one over the other. The intention is to simply draw attention to the vast array of possibilities and to make some collective observations.

The key concern with rewards is value. What is the value of a given reward to an employee? Is it the same value from the organization's point of view? Answers to these questions will provide significant insights to the issues of rewards and compensation. Many organizations believe that the value of the reward can be measured in one of two ways. The first is the complexity of calculating and delivering the reward. The more "kinky" that the reward is, the more is its value. Secondly, an organization may value a reward as the cost to itself. Both methods will almost certainly produce a different value from that which the employee will assign to the reward himself. The question then arises: which is the proper value? None of the three alternatives provides an absolutely accurate answer. However, the true value of the reward is likely to more closely reflect that assigned by the employee since only he can translate it into reality and become motivated by it.

To establish a logical valuation process, many behavioral scientists and compensation specialists rely on an understanding of personal need levels. To appreciate the employee's point of view, he is categorized into need levels ranging from survival to self-actualization. The form and value of rewards are determined by the need level which the employee currently possesses. Thus a person at a survival need level might be rewarded financially while a person at the self-actualization level might be rewarded with more personal autonomy. Any of these types of rewards may be appropriate considering the individual circumstances of the employee. However, there is a danger with an extreme focus on need levels and personality traits. Amid the confusion and arguments about what is the proper form of reward, it is easy to lose track of the prime motivator of people. This prime motivator is very basic and simple. It is called money. Fancy offices, long titles, public recognition and a pat on the back certainly mean something but none of them comes close to money. Money is a universal reward instrument which stands head and shoulders above its competitors. It is often poorly utilized as a reward mechanism by organizations perhaps because it seems so blunt and unsophisticated. Yet it is truly what a manager covets the most because it can be easily transformed into other tangible or intangible instruments for fulfilling his needs. Although it is important to recognize the portfolio of reward instruments that an organization can use and assess the value of each from the employee's point of view, any non-financial rewards should be viewed as peripheral. A cash bonus can be immediately translated into whatever the employee chooses to fulfill his needs and there is very little question of its relative value. A reward system needs to contain a variety of different reward instruments but money should always be its strongest influence.

THE PERFORMANCE EVALUATION

When dispensing rewards, the most critical question is how much does a particular manager deserve. Information to make this decision is collected through the control process. A manager is rewarded upon his performance and it is during the control portion of the Strategy Management cycle that performance is monitored and documented. On a regular basis, probably annually, the performance information concerning each manager is organized and reviewed for the purpose of assessing the magnitude of reward that the manager deserves. This process is formally and traditionally called the performance evaluation.

The performance evaluation is achieved with a review meeting between the manager and his superior. In some instances, a committee of superiors is used rather than one individual in the hope of arriving at a more objective evaluation. At this time, the manager and his superior reflect upon the events and performance of the just completed year. Most importantly, these accomplishments are compared to the original performance commitments prepared by the manager at the beginning of the fiscal cycle. This comparison will enable both parties to determine and agree upon the magnitude of any over-achievement or under-achievement with respect to the plan. The sources of input information to the performance evaluation can be quite numerous. In addition, the same sources will not be used for every manager. The level of authority (i.e. department versus strategic business unit) determines which sources of information are best employed. The sources of planned performance data and actual performance data considered during the evaluation are as follows:

1. Strategy recommendations (approved).
2. Expenditure opportunities (approved).
3. Planned job descriptions (approved).
4. Monthly cost/budget reports.
5. Expenditure opportunity progress reports.
6. Revenue progress reports (sales departments only).
7. Operating variation reports (production departments only).
8. Strategy progress reports.
9. Intangible (other) information.

The performance evaluation act itself needs to be fair and accurate which in turn means that it must be objective. The availability of these sources of input information combined with the formal requirement to utilize them allow for an honest and complete evaluation of performance. A strict comparison of actual achievements to planned commitments prevents emotion and subjectivity from clouding the picture. This enables the manager to be judged on his true merits. A structured performance evaluation based upon concrete terms of reference enhances the quality of the exercise by minimizing personal bias. The net result is a more reliable and meaningful assessment of the manager's behaviour.

The output from the performance evaluation will enable each manager to be classified into a special performance category. The extent of the favourable or unfavourable evaluation will identify which category is appropriate. Five or six performance categories are sufficient for classification purposes. A list of some possibilities is as follows:

1. Excellent (10%)
2. Superior competent (20%)
3. High competent (40%)
4. Competent (20%)
5. Unsatisfactory (10%)

The purpose of classifying a manager's performance in this manner is to allow for the calculation of the magnitude of reward to which he is entitled. The percentage associated with each category acts as a guideline for superiors conducting the performance evaluations. The percentage limits the portion of subordinates that can be classified into any single category. In effect, this forces a superior to rank the performances of his managers. Such a ranking instills a sense of competition among managers which once again promotes good behaviour. Without such guideline percentages for each category, the performance evaluation and reward process can become meaningless. As an example, if ninety percent of the evaluations were in the superior competent category, there would be no sense to the performance evaluation at all. No differentiated classes of behaviour that could be individually rewarded would be identified. For this reason, an organization is wise to establish a quota system for each performance category and insist that the guidelines be respected.

Different amounts of rewards need to be associated with each of the performance categories. The key in the reward scheme is to have the differences between categories large enough to provide an incentive for managers to progress from one to another. If all of the rewards are relatively the same, no motivation will be instilled. The rewards are likely to be comprised of both compensation and upward mobility or promotability. These two variables can be manipulated in such a way as to create ample incentive for managers.

An example of the performance evaluation and reward process is presented in Exhibit 11-1. This example illustrates the various sources of input coming into the performance evaluation and the resulting possible evaluation categories. The exhibit also suggests different levels of compensation for each category. Rewards of promotability, no promotability and possible termination are included in the exhibit as well. The whole process is designed to produce a fair and accurate performance evaluation supported with rewards commensurate with the manager's accomplishments.

DIRECT COMPENSATION

The idea of performance evaluation is not new to most organizations. However, the concept of assigning specific percentages to each evaluation category and then administering a notably different reward for each can be a radical change for many. The process seems logical and accurate and appears to generate sufficient incentive for managers to want to adjust their performance in order to get into the next higher classification. Nevertheless, there is a further action which organizations can take to reward their managers and executives. This is a more direct form of compensation where rewards are segmented according to the components of the strategy.

Direct compensation involves the selection of certain issues in either the approved strategy recommendations or the approved expenditure opportunities and rewarding managers for accomplishing those specific issues. For example, a strategic business unit manager pursuing a build strategy may receive rewards based upon sales volume or market share, whereas a strategic business unit manager pursuing a harvest strategy may receive rewards based upon cash flow or cost reduction. Using specific issues such as these increases the incentive for managers in those areas crucial to their job. Adding these procedures to the performance evaluation makes the whole reward and compensa-

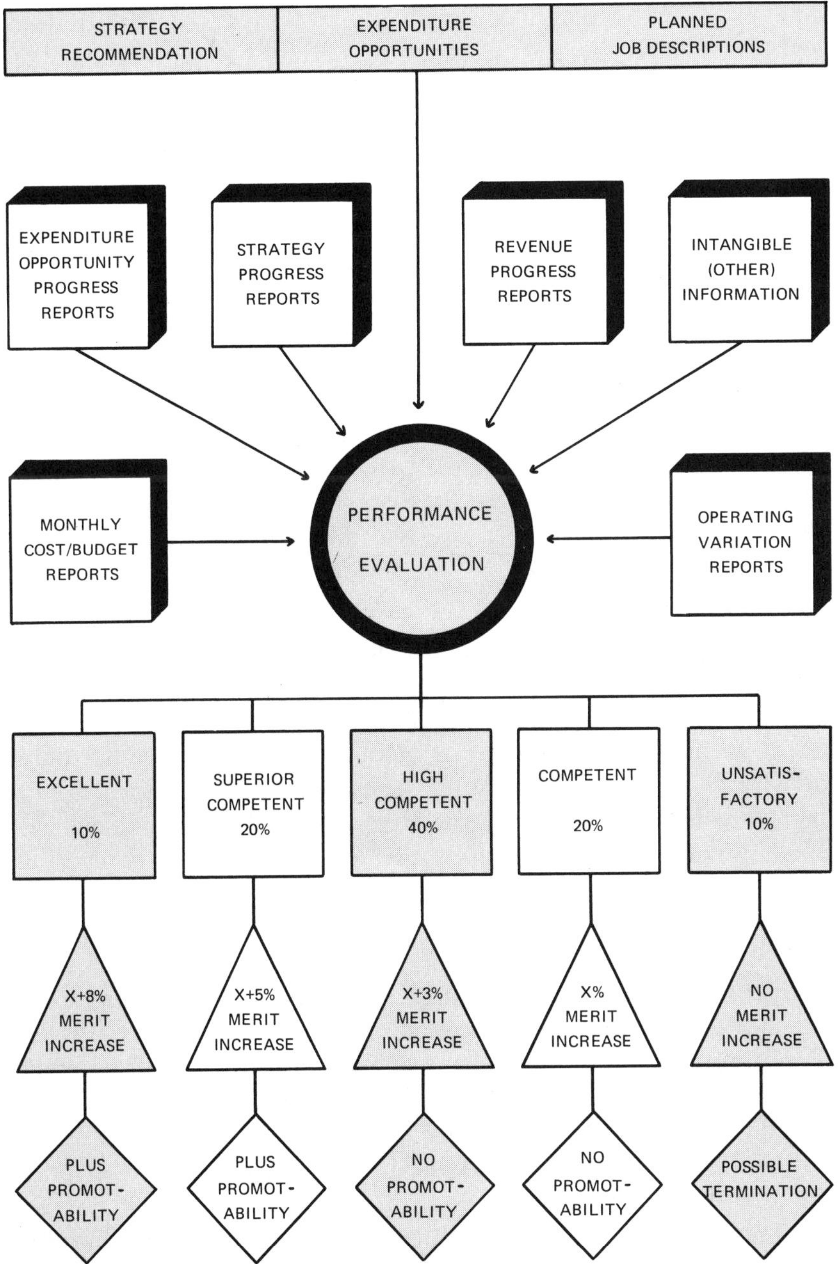

Exhibit 11-1 Example of a performance evaluation and reward scheme.

tion process just that more complex. However, the cost of this complexity may be a small price to pay for the motivation that can result.

Some organizations are currently following a practice of providing direct compensation, usually a bonus, to all managers who exceed a certain performance guideline such as a fifteen percent growth of return on net assets. This is an organizational wide target that does not recognize the unique circumstances or intentions of various strategic business units. For this reason, the application of such a policy can have an adverse effect on those organizations employing the concept of Strategy Management. Strategic business units with strategy recommendations of a maintain, harvest or divestiture nature may be enticed into abandoning their desired strategy in favour of such a universal target. Should this occur, the whole Strategy Management process would be undermined. This example serves to emphasize the importance of a well planned and thought-out reward system.

CUSTOMIZING THE COMPENSATION PACKAGE

Whether an organization uses a performance evaluation, a direct form of compensation or a combination of both, it would be wise to consider customizing the compensation package to suit the individual manager and the strategy which he is assigned to pursue. This statement suggests that certain forms of compensation are more effective and supportive of certain types of strategy. For example, providing a manager pursuing a harvest strategy with a wide assortment of perquisites is not an optimum form of compensation. When this manager is persistently cutting back expenditures all day and then steps into his chauffeur driven limousine to go home at night, a conflict of interest and possibly a mutiny is on his hands. On the other hand, a manager pursuing a build strategy is likely to find a lower salary and capital stock options to be a very comfortable form of compensation. It puts the accent on the future. Each of the four major types of strategy has unique characteristics which can be reflected in the composition of the reward and compensation package.

Exhibit 11-2 illustrates three different compensation packages each totalling $100,000. The $100,000 is chosen not so much

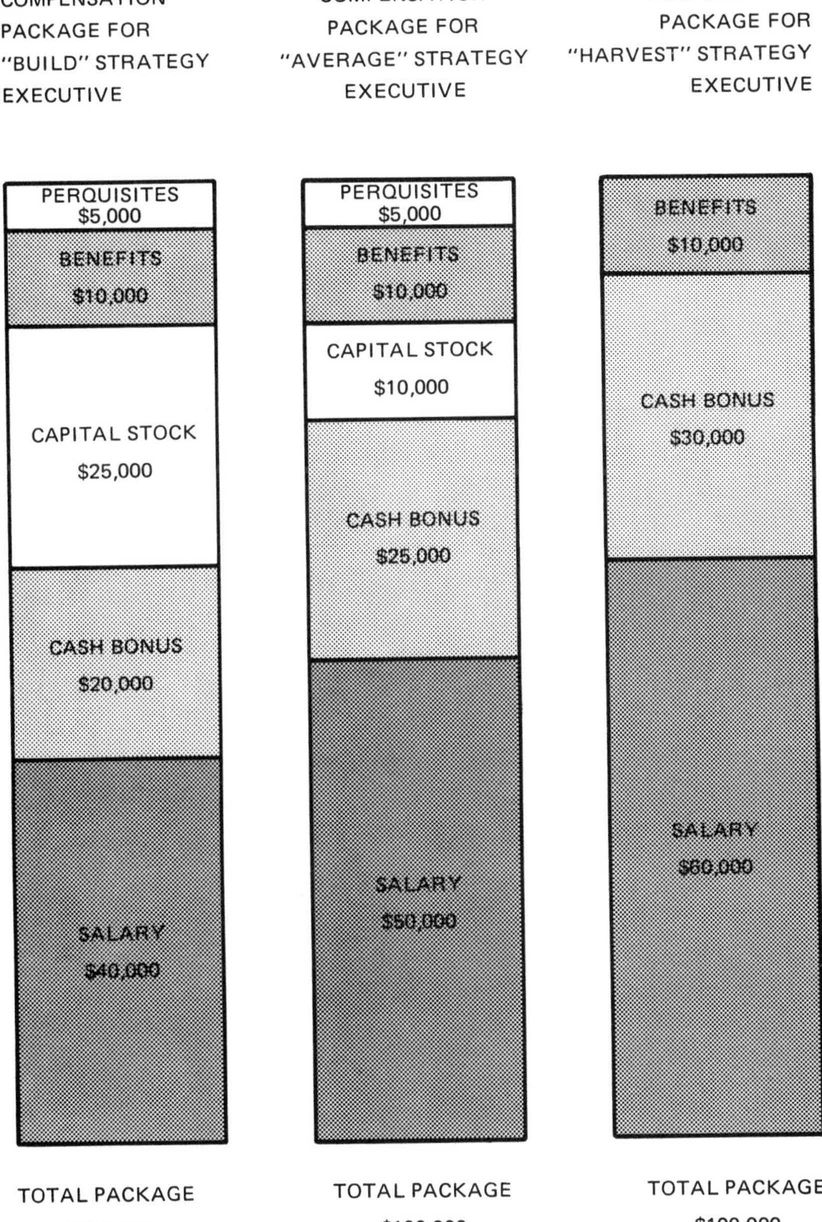

Exhibit 11-2 Example of customizing the compensation package to the approved strategy.

to reflect the appropriate reward levels of strategic business unit managers but to make the apportionments between the various divisions of the compensation package easy to identify. In the middle of the exhibit is an illustration of a compensation package for what might be described as an average strategic business unit executive. The illustrations on either side of this indicate how this average can be modified to suit the relevant strategy. The modifications stress longer-term considerations for the build strategy than they do for the harvest strategy.

In summary, the principles of the Strategy Management reward and compensation process are designed to make performance evaluation both legitimate and equitable. This is ensured by reliable input information concerning both actual and planned performance. The process also emphasizes the distribution of rewards based upon merit with enough of a difference between reward levels to promote better behavior from the managers. Finally, the process recognizes that different forms of rewards are suitable to different strategies and that an attempt should be made to match the two.

Rewards and compensation conclude the Strategy Management process. Since rewards and compensation are administered shortly after the end of the year, the new Strategy Management cycle will have already begun by this time. This overlap is a good example of how Strategy Management can naturally be a fundamental and perpetual undercurrent of the entire management environment.

12

The Implementation Plan

The critical point of the Strategy Management implementation process is securing senior management support for the concept. Senior management includes the executive committee of the organization and in particular its chief executive officer. Before any action can be taken, these persons must understand the idea of Strategy Management, be willing to assume their respective roles and allocate resources in sufficient quantity and quality to realize both a proper implementation and operation. Without this commitment, the process cannot proceed.

Obtaining senior management concurrence is likely to be a major task for many organizations. First of all, it requires an opportunity to present the concept to these executives for consideration. Secondly, it requires an effective presentation. When senior management are exposed to the idea of Strategy Management, their overriding question will be: why should we change our present ways? To find the answer to this question, senior management will attempt to appreciate the cost/benefit characteristics of the process. Based upon the attractiveness of this equation, a decision to accept or reject can be formulated.

The manner in which to construct a cost/benefit understanding of Strategy Management is to fully explain the principles that the process entails. Senior management needs to know how and why it works. When they realize the logic and natural behaviour upon which it is based, senior management can then become comfortable with the process. This in turn will reduce any natural resistance to change and permit a sound evaluation of the concept to be made.

The costs associated with Strategy Management have already been presented in the third chapter. They were classified into three separate categories of time costs, paper costs and management costs. Management costs refer to the discipline and effort required to face and make the hard decisions brought to the forefront during the process. To help counter these costs are the cost savings that can be enjoyed through the integration and streamlining of many existing management techniques. This entire consideration of costs needs to be adequately presented to senior management if they are to properly comprehend the true effort required to implement and operate a Strategy Management program.

The benefits associated with Strategy Management were also presented in the third chapter. This presentation consisted of numerous topics — both tangible and intangible. When presenting the concept to senior management, it is best to illustrate the full spectrum of these available benefits. Such an illustration will demonstrate the complete scope and flexibility of the concept and show how Strategy Management can be a long-term asset to the organization as it progresses through different stages of development and need. Special emphasis should be given to those benefits that are perceived to have the most current significance to the organization. An immediate problem can be used as the catalyst to convince senior management of the merits of a Strategy Management program. It is not by coincidence that most organizations take action only when they find themselves boxed in. This form of motivation should be well understood because it can be positively exploited when trying to enlist the support of senior management.

The most positive form of senior management commitment will belong to those organizations whose chief executive officer already believes in the concept or who actually introduces the idea himself. This is the most sincere form of involvement due to its top down nature. The chief executive officer assumes ownership of the process and takes the necessary steps to ensure a successful implementation. However, not all organizations are fortunate enough to find themselves in such circumstances. They are in a position where the interest of the chief executive officer needs to be cultivated and nurtured to finally gain acceptance for the idea.

Should senior management and the chief executive officer be unwilling to break the institutional inertia and make the change to Strategy Management, where does that leave an organization? In cases like this, the persons advocating the use of the concept within the organization can still derive some positive results from the venture. These results are referred to as incremental victories. Managers at different levels of the organization can experiment with certain facets or modules of the overall Strategy Management process by employing various components within their own sphere of authority and control. This, in effect, is a scaled down version of the concept but at least it will result in some positive action. Should the experiment prove beneficial and other parts of the organization decide to follow suit, senior management may then want to re-examine its overall position towards the Strategy Management concept.

The possibility of such a turn in events using incremental victories should act as a source of motivation for all managers. Those components of Strategy Management which are within the manager's realm of authority can serve as the initial steps towards a more inclusive change in organizational behaviour. Taking one small step at a time is more desirable than failing at an attempt to make a single giant leap forward.

IMPLEMENTATION VARIATIONS

Once an organization has decided to proceed with a Strategy Management program, it is faced with a series of questions. When should the implementation be made? How should the implementation be organized? What will the implementation involve? The question of when will be answered after the organization has determined how quickly it can assemble the required resources and how quickly it wants to begin enjoying the benefits. The question of organization is the main topic of the remainder of this chapter. Before we get to this question, let us address the issue of what the implementation involves.

Because Strategy Management is an integrated approach to planning, execution and control, it represents an extensive undertaking. It is precisely this degree of integration which lends value to the process. Nevertheless, some organizations will look at the full scope of the program and be overwhelmed by the size of the implementation task before them. It is in circumstances like this that the question of what the implementation involves becomes relevant. An organization may wish to phase the Strategy Management concept into its operations over a period of time — perhaps over two or three years. This breaks the implementation and operation tasks into "chewable chunks" so that the organization can manage the change and properly digest the new ideas. Should this approach be desired a decision is required with respect to what facets of the concept are to be employed and in what sequence are they to be introduced.

Although this book presents the concept of Strategy Management in a sequence that corresponds to its natural flow, it is not absolutely essential that the implementation follow this exact pattern. To maximize the benefit from the process, particularly when only limited implementation resources are available, an organization may choose to first implement those components with the highest impact upon performance. For example, an organization with an adequate long-range planning function and a weak budgeting function may decide to implement the tactical program before any other components of the Strategy Management process. Similarly, an organization with a strong budgeting function may decide to implement the pre-tactical program components or the control and rewards components before anything else. The factor which will help to make these decisions is the magnitude of benefit each option can provide to the short-term performance of the organization. These considerations are unique to each organization and are valid reasons for altering the implementation sequence of the overall Strategy Management program.

In later sections of this chapter, the sequence of implementation will be of more immediate importance. At those times, we will refer to the utopian implementation plan of beginning with the charter of objectives and ending with a reward scheme. However, it is important to keep in mind that organizations do have flexibility and can vary the implementation process to best suit the needs of the real world in which they operate.

FORMING THE IMPLEMENTATION TEAM

When senior management commitment has been secured for the Strategy Management program, the initial task is to create a project team to carry out the implementation mandate. This team would be responsible to both plan and execute the actions required to set the process in motion. The project implementation team is an extension of senior management and reports accordingly. The selection of the team members is a critical activity of the implementation process. Much authority and responsibility will be entrusted to these persons, thereby emphasizing the need for their careful selection. Each team member will possess a combination of technical and personal skills. From a technical point of view, it is difficult to find an expert in the field of Strategy Management. The concept is very encompassing and incorporates many different disciplines. If any technical background can be stated as a preference, those people of a general management upbringing possessing a wide variety of talents are normally the best candidates for the implementation team. People who are conversant (not expert) in a number of areas such as management by objectives, financial planning and performance appraisal bring a diverse background to the project team and are most likely to appreciate the integrated approach of the concept. The project team should also be formed with a consideration for balance among the dominant talents of the members. An implementation team does not want to become overloaded with a certain type of proficiency that could result in an over emphasis directed towards a certain Strategy Management component.

The personal or people skills of potential members take precedence over all others when making the team selection. The primary function of the project implementation team is to effectively spread knowledge throughout the organization. With this in mind, two key qualities that every team member should possess are:

1. Good interpersonal communication skills.

2. Enthusiasm concerning Strategy Management.

The degree of enthusiasm that a potential team member displays towards Strategy Management can be a good indicator of how he would perform on the job. Part of his job will be to instill a sense of enthusiasm into those managers participating in the program. This only becomes possible when the team member possesses a true sense of spirit himself. This quality will act as a strong indication of the candidate's suitability for the coming implementation task.

THE PROJECT LEADER

The Strategy Management implementation team needs a leader. An executive conversant in the area of planning and budgeting would be a prime candidate for this. Should an organization be large enough to employ a vice-president of planning, he would be a likely choice. Sometimes the controller or the vice-president of administration would be the logical selection. Nevertheless, a person who would likely be available to guide the Strategy Management process in the second year of operation as well would be an attractive possibility. This will provide continuity and protect the investment which the organization is making in its Strategy Management program.

The project leader will be responsible for coordinating and guiding the efforts of all the team members. He will also be the person directly accountable to senior management for the success of the project. He will normally be called upon to periodically report his progress to senior management and to alert them to any problems requiring their assistance. The project leader should possess an abundance of interpersonal and technical skills. He should be a well respected individual in the organization. Other team members should be proud to be associated with him. He needs to present an image of confidence, patience and determination. Based upon these characteristics, it is easy to see that the project leader needs to be an unusual person. Only this type of person can be entrusted with the responsibilities associated with a Strategy Management program implementation.

For some implementations, an organization may choose to engage the services of an external management consultant. The management consultant would probably assume the role of co-leader of the project. He would offer guidance but would usually be free of the routine administrative chores associated with a project. There are two main reasons why an organization would decide to secure the services of a consultant:

1. A consultant specializing in Strategy Management should possess a fair amount of knowledge about the subject. Rather than delaying the realization of the benefits from a Strategy Management program by researching and building its own expertise, an organization may choose to import the talent and to proceed without further procrastination.
2. The consultant should have developed enough experience with Strategy Management to allow him to predict where problems are likely to develop and which areas need careful attention. An organization may choose to minimize the risk involved with implementing the process by relying on the guidance of a consultant.

The management consultant should be selected with as much care as the project leader. Each will occupy a high profile position. The competence of the consultant or consultants should be thoroughly investigated. The ability of any junior members of the consulting firm to be assigned to the project should be examined. If these persons do not specialize in Strategy Management implementations, they can only be of little value to the organization. References should be checked and past work should be reviewed. The reputation of the consulting firm can be a good measure of competence providing that it was built in the area of Strategy Management.

PROJECT ADMINISTRATION

After the project implementation team has been selected, a program to upgrade their knowledge of Strategy Management should be promptly enacted. This program would usually involve the presentation of a mini-seminar. The members of the team would be assembled for a day-long education session concerning both the operation and implementation of Strategy Management. This mini-seminar would be conducted by the project leader or the management consultant should one have been engaged. The presentation will give the team members their own opportunity to discuss and question each facet of the process. This will prepare them to assume their guidance role when the strategic business unit and department managers become involved in the process.

As part of the administrative chores of the project team, two different logs or diaries should be established. These logs would be used to record key information about both the Strategy Management implementation and first year of operation. One log is called a trouble log. The other is a time log. The trouble log is used to record all of the problems encountered during the process. Members of the implementation team as well as the strategic business unit and department managers are invited to contribute to this log. The mechanics and purpose of maintaining the trouble log are discussed in greater depth in the last chapter of this book.

The time log is used to record the effort expended on the project by the implementation team members. The purpose of this log is twofold. It provides information that can be presented to senior management when reporting the progress of the implementation effort by the project leader. It also allows the organization to accurately calculate its actual investment in the Strategy Management program. This is a sound practice for any major project undertaking.

Another fundamental task for the project team is to identify the strategic business units and departments that will be participating in the program. The identification of strategic business units has already been examined in Chapter Five. In that chapter, both artificial strategic business units and strategic business units that conform to the formal organization chart were reviewed. The identification of the departments which will be participating in the program can also be made from the organization chart. The optimum size department for the purposes of the tactical program should be limited to about fifteen persons. Departments with a significantly larger staff may be treated as exceptions and be divided into two or more parts for the Strategy Management program. However, production line departments incurring direct labour and material need not be so restricted. Relative similarity in department size is only meaningful in regard to the discretionary components of the tactical program. The purpose of identifying the strategic business units and departments is to determine which managers will be participating in the Strategy Management process as well as to gain an understanding of the respective areas of the organization they will be representing.

Once the participants have been identified, it is appropriate to contact them formally through the use of an introduction letter. The introduction letter would come from the leader of the organization and would formally inaugurate the Strategy Management program. The letter would declare the organization's intentions to adopt the concept and explain to the managers what benefits are expected from doing so. The letter should also identify some of the positive reasons why managers should be anxious to participate and warmly encourage them to lend their support. In closing, the introduction letter should invite each manager to attend a training seminar on the subject of Strategy Management. At this time, the person who will be conducting the seminar — namely the project leader — should be identified along with the remainder of the project implementation team. The exact date and location of the seminar should be made clear so that managers can plan well in advance to devote an entire day to the event.

The final administrative task of the project team is to assign counsellors to the respective managers participating in the program. Each strategic business unit and department manager should have one member of the implementation team assigned specifically to him as a counsellor. This person will be the manager's personal instructor. All questions and problems would be directed initially to this counsellor for resolution. This arrangement will allow managers to receive special attention during the process. It also defines the scope of responsibility for the individual project team member. These counsellor assignments need to be made in a logical fashion. Each team member should be assigned responsibility for those areas of the organization with which he is most familiar and competent. As an example, if one member of the project team is a sales manager, it would be logical for him to be the counsellor for the entire sales division and perhaps a related area such as advertising or marketing. This will aid the team member in establishing a rapport with the managers and promoting his acceptance. A better communication flow is likely to exist between persons of mutual interests and understanding.

THE OPERATING MANUAL

Fundamental to any important and large scale management process is the support of an operating manual. The preparation of a Strategy Management operating manual will represent a very major endeavour by the project implementation team. It is a critical document from the point of view of all concerned. The effort required to prepare the operating manual can be divided almost evenly between writing the instructions and constructing the examples. The team members assigned to the preparation of the manual can divide their responsibilities and time accordingly.

The examples used in the operating manual should be as close to real life as possible with input being collected from the appropriate strategic business unit and department managers. Ample time should be allowed for typing (or typesetting), proof reading, correcting and printing. These are menial chores but at the same time are quite energy consuming. The preparation of the operating manual will almost certainly form the critical time path for the implementation team. Tight control will be necessary if this part of the project is to be completed on schedule. A full explanation of the purpose and contents of the Strategy Management operating manual is presented in the next chapter.

THE TRAINING SEMINAR

The date of the first training seminar for strategic business unit and department managers would act as the deadline for completing all previous implementation activities. From this point forward, the implementation team will concentrate exclusively on serving the needs of participating managers. The managers' education process will be the sole centre of attention.

The training seminar is the main event in the entire implementation process. The program's success is likely to be directly influenced by the impact of the training seminar. Since it is the managers' first legitimate exposure to Strategy Management, it will have a permanent influence on the program. An effective training seminar will pay dividends many times over. A poor seminar can do irreparable damage. All precautions should be taken to ensure that the training seminar is a complete success.

The training seminar should consist of three main parts. The first would be an introduction to the process stating the history, definition, costs and benefits of Strategy Management. The middle section would be a detailed explanation of the procedures involved. The last section would be a discussion of the implementation plan including the schedule of events for the program.

The detailed procedures section would represent about seventy percent of the seminar content. It would be revealed in the same sequence as that followed by the Strategy Management cycle. Each component of this section should be thoroughly examined in an informal manner with questions being encouraged. A workshop session would follow each component to provide managers with practice opportunity. The workshops are a dry run of the Strategy Management exercise. They are designed to assist the managers' learning process by presenting a chance to make mistakes prior to the commencement of the official program. These practice sessions will be the most valuable portions of the seminar-workshop. Hence, they will be the main thrust of the managers' entire education process. The components of the detailed procedures section of the seminar that should be complemented by workshop exercises are:

1. Documenting the charter of objectives.
2. Formulating corporate strategy.
3. Strategic business unit analysis.
4. Preparing the tactical program.

During these workshop exercises, the counsellors of the project implementation team would guide their respective managers in the preparation of their work. The documentation produced by the managers in their workshops should be retained. By saving this material, it can be used as a starting point for managers when the time comes to begin the Strategy Management program in earnest.

Serious attention should be directed towards the forthcoming implementation schedule of events. Managers need to be made aware of the exact dates on which they will be required to submit each completed form as well as the date on which the overall process should be concluded. Managers should realize that their work will be inspected for quality at regular intervals after each key event has been reached. The importance of adhering to the schedule of events should be firmly impressed upon all managers.

As a follow-up to the seminar, the counsellors would visit the strategic business unit and department managers within the next few days. The operating manuals can be delivered at this time. The team members should solicit feedback with respect to the training seminar and attempt to clarify any outstanding items of concern. After these visits, meetings with the managers will be informal on an "as needed" basis.

IMPLEMENTATION CHECKPOINTS

With the training of strategic business unit and department managers completed, the Strategy Management program is ready to move into the operation stage. The schedule of events presented at the training seminar and included in the operating manual will act as the guiding force at this time. The project implementation team will be looking for both quality in the managers' work and strict adherence to the schedule.

The operation stage of the program should be taken one step at a time. Upon completion of each step, the work of the respective strategic business unit or department manager should be inspected for quality. Due to the building block approach of Strategy Management, it is important that the initial activities in the process be done correctly. Otherwise, the errors will be perpetuated and magnified throughout the remainder of the program. The project implementation team cannot afford to wait until the completion of the tactical program to inspect the work of the managers. By that time it is much too late. The process is so far advanced that not enough time is left for managers to retrench and rectify the situation.

The more checkpoints that an organization builds into its implementation schedule, the more control it will have over the process. Accordingly, it is suggested that checkpoints be placed after every major component of the Strategy Management program. To be more specific, checkpoints should appear after each of the following steps:

1. Documentation of the charter of objectives.
2. Formulation of corporate strategy.

3. Strategic business unit analysis.
4. Strategic business unit recommendation.
5. Preparation of the variable components of the tactical program.
6. Preparation of the discretionary components of the tactical program:
   A. Confirmation of action plans for the coming year.
   B. Cross impact analysis.
   C. Expenditure opportunity preparation.

The quality checking needs to be done quickly to allow managers to proceed to the next step without delay. Good performance should be recognized and commended. Managers should be told when they have done a good job and others should be made aware of these achievements. Poor quality work should also be identified. The manager should be made aware of any problems so that he can correct them and improve himself. He should know that mediocre work is not acceptable. If a quality problem arises that is beyond the ability of the project team to correct, there should be no hesitation in calling upon senior management for assistance. Such a call for assistance should not be construed as a sign of weakness on the part of the project team. A wise project leader will use all the tools available to him when the situation is appropriate.

Exhibit 12-1 on the following two pages is a sample schedule of events for a Strategy Management program. The timing of the events would likely suit a medium size institution. The proper time allocations will vary somewhat from organization to organization due to the unique competencies and needs involved.

On the next three pages are Exhibits 12-2 and 12-3. These are examples of bar charts describing the implementation schedule (again for a medium size institution). The first exhibit includes the preparations made by the project implementation team while the second exhibit focuses on the operation stage of the program.

THE ABC ORGANIZATION
STRATEGY MANAGEMENT PROGRAM
SCHEDULE OF EVENTS

		COMPLETION DATE
1.	Document charter of objectives for organization.	01–03–8W
2.	Assess industry attractiveness of current and proposed strategic business units.	15–03–8W
3.	Assess competitive position of current and proposed strategic business units.	31–03–8W
4.	Present business portfolio matrices associated with corporate strategy.	15–04–8W
5.	Draft strategy chronicle.	25–04–8W
6.	Hold "brainstorming" session among senior and strategic business unit managers.	30–04–8W
7.	Finalize and publish strategy chronicle.	05–05–8W
8.	Confirm strategic position at strategic business unit level.	15–05–8W
9.	Construct financial resource profiles.	31–05–8W
10.	Construct human resource profiles.	15–06–8W
11.	Construct physical resource profiles.	30–06–8W
12.	Construct organizational resource profiles.	15–07–8W
13.	Perform segmentation analysis.	31–07–8W
14.	Rationalize the strategic business unit analysis.	05–08–8W
15.	Prepare strategic business unit recommendation.	15–08–8W

Exhibit 12-1 Sample schedule of events for a medium size organization.

16. Present strategic business unit recommendation to strategy committee.   25–08–8W

17. Approve portfolio of strategic business unit recommendations.   31–08–8W

18. Communicate desired strategic action down to department level.   10–09–8W

19. Prepare revenue program.   30–09–8W

20. Prepare direct cost program.   30–09–8W

21. Document departmental statement of mission, role or mandate.   05–10–8W

22. Document departmental statement of action plans for coming year.   10–10–8W

23. Perform cross impact analysis.   20–10–8W

24. Resolve discrepancies between interdependent departments.   31–10–8W

25. Prepare expenditure opportunity series.   15–11–8W

26. Extrapolate financial operating plan.   18–11–8W

27. Prepare departmental organization chart.   20–11–8W

28. Provide job descriptions for key employees.   27–11–8W

29. Assemble recommendation package.   30–11–8W

30. Consolidate expenditure opportunity rankings.   15–12–8W

31. Allocate resources to high priority expenditure opportunities.   31–12–8W

32. Prepare expenditure opportunity progress reports.   –8X

33. Prepare strategy progress reports.   –8X

34. Conduct performance evaluations.   31–01–8Y

35. Dispense appropriate rewards.   15–02–8Y

Exhibit 12-1 (Cont'd) Sample schedule of events for a medium size organization.

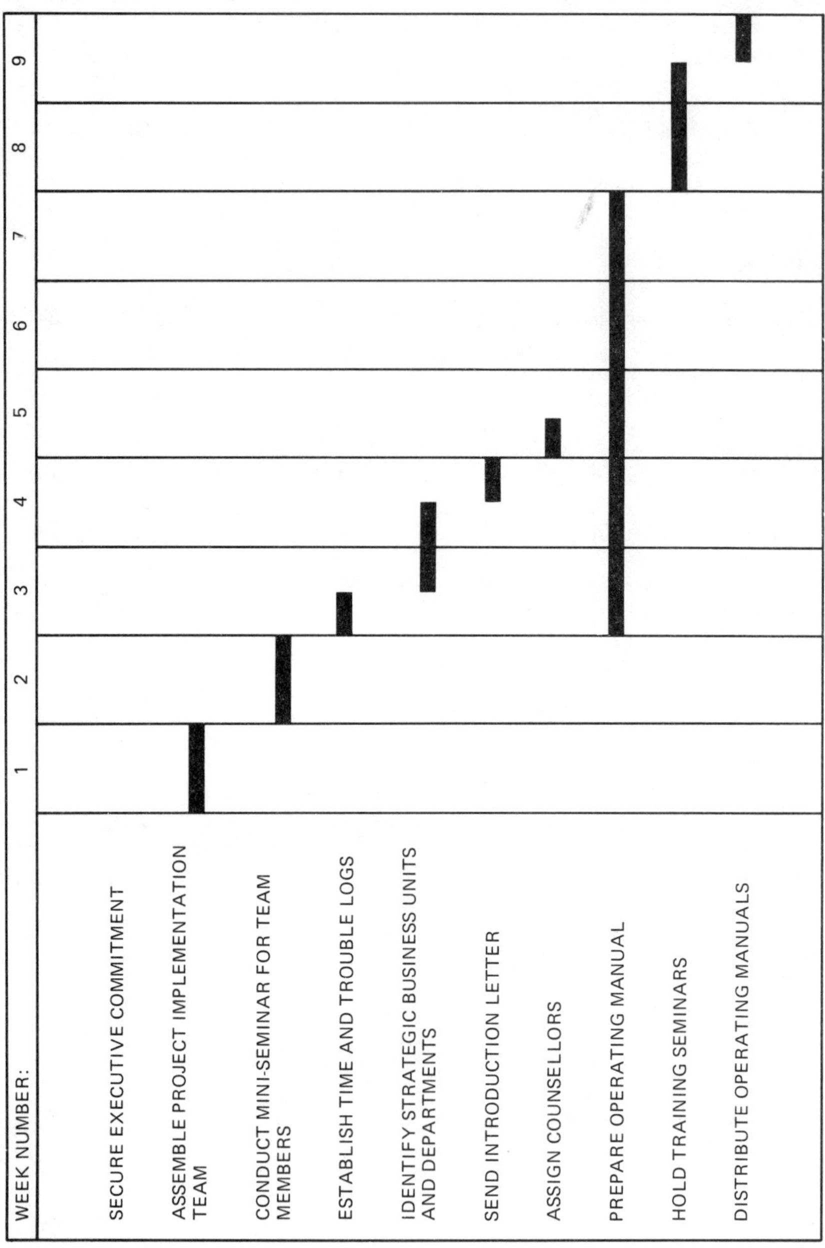

Exhibit 12-2 Example of a bar chart plan to implement Strategy Management concerning the efforts of the project implementation team.

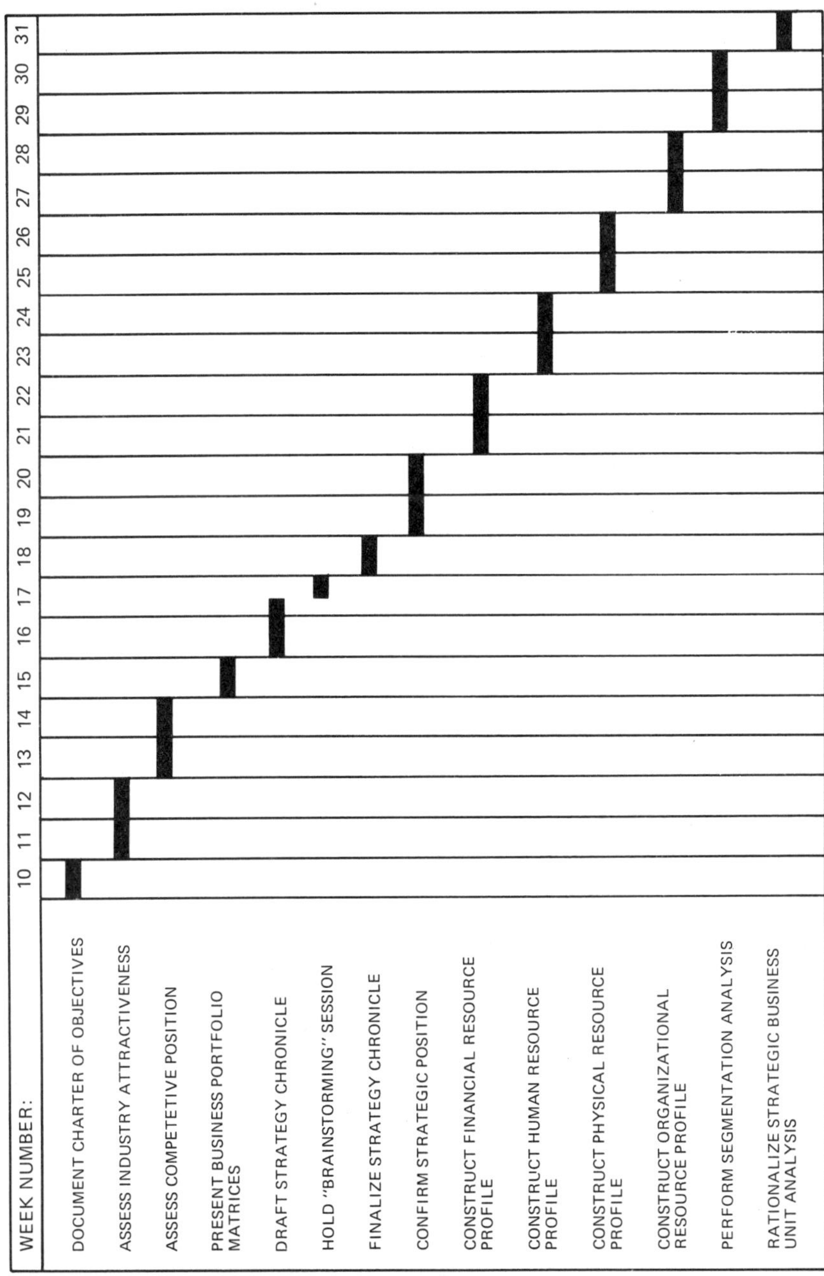

Exhibit 12-3 Example of a bar chart plan to implement Strategy Management concerning the first cycle of execution.

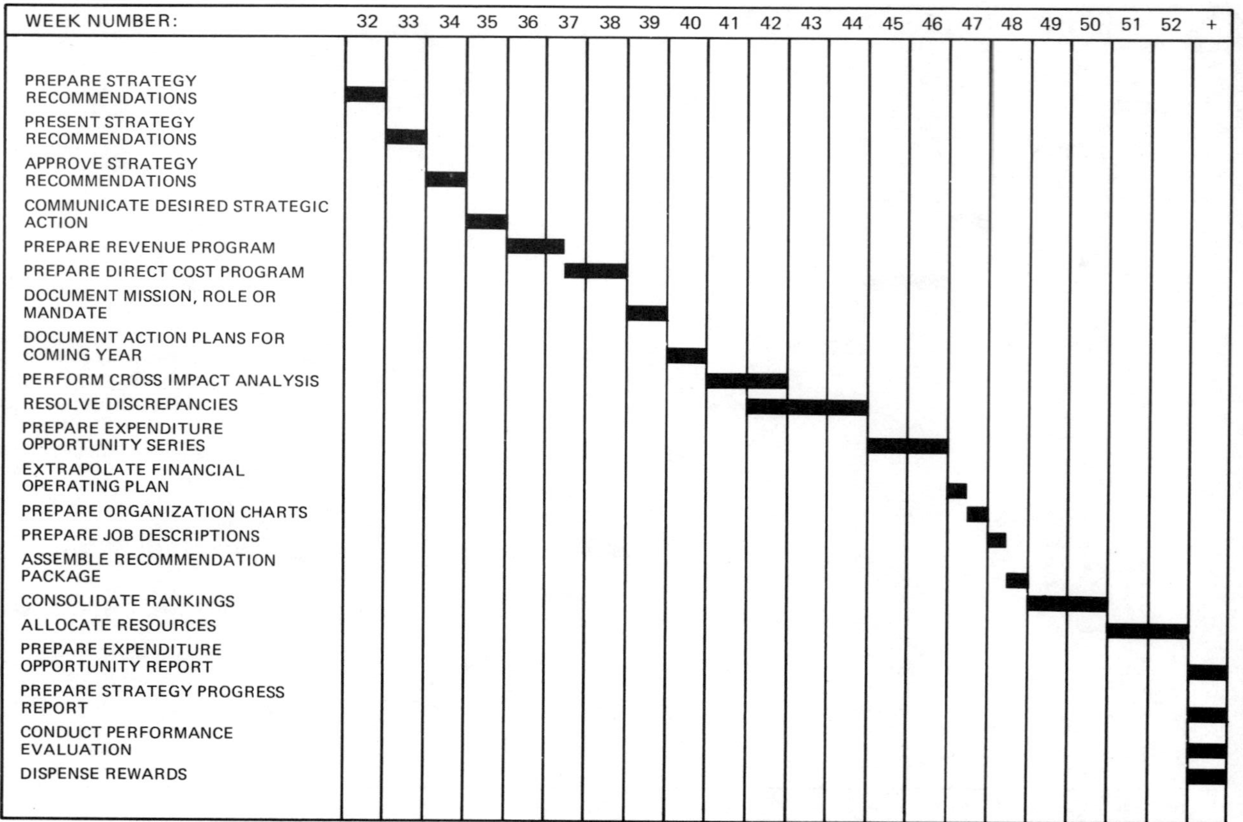

Exhibit 12-3 (Cont'd)   Example of a bar chart plan to implement Strategy Management concerning the first cycle of execution.

13

The Operating Manual

Every Strategy Management program should be supported by an operating manual. Aside from bringing a degree of formality to the process, the operating manual has two main purposes. The first purpose is to act as a sales document. As stated in the previous chapter, the operating manual can be used as a vehicle to communicate the detailed procedures of Strategy Management throughout the organization. The contents of the manual will provide all concerned with a good understanding of the mechanics involved. Most importantly, the operating manual would be used to sell the idea of the tactical program to the department managers. The manual can form the backbone of their education process. It would explain how the process works, why certain events are planned, what they will have to contribute, what happens to their documentation and what the overall process will do for them. This information is vital to relieve the apprehension most department managers will have about Strategy Management.

The second purpose of the operating manual is to act as a reference document. While the Strategy Management process is unfolding, strategic business unit and department managers will need some kind of document to which they can refer. The manual will show them how to prepare certain forms, when the completion deadlines are and other such administrative information. A central source of such information in the form of a Strategy Management operating manual is most convenient and effective.

These two purposes of the operating manual are quite compatible. Both can be achieved by addressing the same issues. Only the tone of the manual needs to be adjusted to accommodate both points of view.

The tone of the operating manual will be as important as the actual contents themselves. How the concept is explained will produce different responses from the audience. The manual should never be authoritarian. This will only build resistance. It should be informative and helpful. Its purpose is to explain the concept of Strategy Management and not to act as a book of rules or laws. The operating manual should be written with the recognition that the majority of its audience will be department managers, followed by strategic business unit managers. It should anticipate their problem areas and be particularly clear on these points. The operating manual is not intended to be a list of restrictions placed upon managers. It is there to aid them in understanding and executing the concept.

Since the primary audience of the operating manual is the department managers, it should be written in layman's language with a minimum of technical terminology. Abbreviations and special jargon should be avoided. A simple presentation of the information is all that is required. A basic style will be much appreciated by the managers and will allow them to concentrate on the facts without being encumbered by peripheral considerations.

THE LAYOUT OF THE OPERATING MANUAL

The physical layout of the operating manual deserves a good deal of attention. Of critical importance is the size of the manual. It should be strictly limited so that a manager can be reasonably expected to take time to read it. An average size manual with spaciously laid out type and illustrations would be one hundred pages in length. This is a concise document that at the same time will provide ample opportunity to get the message across. The operating manual is normally placed in a three ring binder custom made for the organization. It would identify the organization's name as well as the fact that it is the Strategy Management operating manual. In conjunction with this binder, the contents would normally be typeset to give it a professional appearance. This makes for an impressive product and indicates to all managers that it is a serious venture. Many people may argue that this is a needless waste of money. They feel uncomfortable going to such lengths for internal programs of the organization. However, such an approach has proven results. Selling the concept of Strategy Management to the different level managers of the organization is no different than selling products and services to the public. Disorganized advertising and instructional material will not be taken seriously and will result in poor acceptance of the product. There is too much at stake with a Strategy Management program to risk poor acceptance due to a frugal implementation approach.

As a final note on the appearance of the operating manual, an organization may wish to use a special colour coding for certain sections. This colour coding could help to emphasize the level of management responsibility for different parts of the Strategy Management process. Three special colour codes could be used in the following areas:

1. A. Charter of objectives.
   B. Corporate strategy formulation.
2. A. Strategic business unit analysis.
   B. Strategic business unit recommendation.
3. A. Tactical program – variable components.
   B. Tactical program – discretionary components.

The levels of responsibility designated by these components are senior management, strategic business unit management and department management respectively. The purpose of this colour coding is simply to make the operating manual more "digestible" from the individual manager's point of view.

THE INTRODUCTION

The operating manual should begin by explaining the organization's objectives in using a Strategy Management program. This will tell all concerned why a change in operations is being made and what the organization intends to accomplish by doing so. Managers should be made aware of why an improvement is desirable and how Strategy Management can help. This will allow all managers to better appreciate why the concept deserves their attention. This information will act as the introduction of the operating manual.

The contents of this first section of the manual should summarize the various benefits and results which the organization hopes to achieve as a consequence of the Strategy Management program. A complete list of potential benefits has already been presented in the third chapter of this book. This introduction section of the operating manual should highlight those benefits of particular concern to the organization. The intention is to provide a rationale for the program and therefore make it more acceptable to all managers.

To lend further weight to the operating manual's introduction, it's also a good idea to include a copy of the introduction letter from the leader of the organization. This is the letter that initiated the program and was distributed to all managers participating in the process. The introduction letter can be used to effectively fortify the message of the introduction section by giving it increased credibility. The inclusion of the introduction letter demonstrates the unequivocal support of the chief executive officer and connotes an expectation that all other managers are to follow suit.

THE PROGRAM OVERVIEW

The second section of the operating manual would normally contain an overview of the Strategy Management process. This would be a high level summary of the concept providing managers with an appreciation of how the process works before they examine each component in detail. It should give managers a good understanding of how the different components of a Strategy Management program relate to one another. This will permit managers to comprehend the size and nature of the task before them.

The overview section of the operating manual would briefly explain the function of the charter of objectives. It would illustrate how corporate strategy flows from the charter and results in the identification of the businesses in which the organization ought to be involved. The overview section should then describe how the strategic business unit analysis, culminating in a concrete recommendation, responds to the corporate strategy by determining how to best operate within these businesses. An important point for the overview to address is the bridge between the tactical program and the strategy recommendation. The manner in which the revenue program and direct cost program are influenced by the desired strategic action needs explanation. The discretionary components of the tactical program deserve extra special attention. The cross impact analysis will be of interest to managers as will the preparation of an expenditure opportunity series. Managers should be made aware that the expenditure opportunities are ranked in their order of importance and that the highest priority expenditure opportunities are the ones that will attract funding. The manner in which control is exerted upon the various components should also be discussed. Finally, the comprehensiveness of the reward scheme should be illustrated. This will provide an exposure to the complete Strategy Management process.

The responsibilities of different individuals in the process and the schedule of events are an important part of the overview section of the operating manual. The outline of the different responsibilities will demonstrate the degree of involvement expected from the various levels of management. It will show how they are expected to relate to one another as the process progresses. The schedule of events will play a very key role throughout the program. Managers will constantly refer to it as the cycle unfolds. A note emphasizing the importance of strictly adhering to the schedule should always be included.

OPERATING PROCEDURES

The next part of the Strategy Management operating manual explains the detailed operating procedures and is accordingly the heart of the manual. Following the logical flow of the process, the operating manual describes how to perform each exercise and how to complete each form. Most importantly, the reasons for each component are explained. Due to the importance and extent of these operating procedures, a separate section or chapter of the manual should be created for each of the Strategy Management components. This will allow the material to be absorbed and referenced in a meaningful manner. This part of the operating manual will likely be organized into the following sections:

1. Charter of objectives.
2. Corporate strategy formulation.
3. Strategic business unit analysis.
4. Strategic business unit recommendation.
5. Tactical program — variable components.
6. Tactical program — discretionary components.
7. Control.
8. Rewards and compensation.

The names of these sections correspond almost exactly to those of the middle chapters of this book. It is the logical sequence in which to present the Strategy Management idea.

Each of these sections of the operating manual should begin with detailed instructions of how to perform the task at hand. An explanation of how the task fits into the overall flow of the process should also be made. When it is necessary to prepare forms, completed examples must be presented as well. The completed examples will provide managers with a picture of how the final product should look. These examples will be a critical learning vehicle within the operating manual.

The examples should be as true to life as possible. Consistency among the examples is also important. It is best to use one strategic business unit and one department as examples for the various completed forms. Consistency is necessary to indicate how each part of the Strategy Management process relates to the other. It is fundamental to demonstrate the information flow in this manner. The inclusion of blank forms in the operating manual is also a good idea. Managers find it handy to make photocopies from these blanks as the need arises.

APPENDICES

The last section of the operating manual would contain appendices. The appendices can be used as an effective vehicle to supply any miscellaneous information that managers will need to carry out their mandate. One appendix should contain a list of all the managers participating in the Strategy Management program. This will be a directory or roster of managers with their current titles and telephone numbers. This appendix will identify the management team and produce a sense of cohesion in the organization. This information supports the whole communication undercurrent of the concept.

Another helpful appendix is a glossary of key words or phrases that are used throughout the process. A central source of key word information is a handy reference tool for managers. An index might also be included as an appendix. Managers can use an index to locate any needed Strategy Management information.

The last appendix which an organization may consider including in its operating manual pertains to the discretionary components of the tactical program. It can be used to illustrate the characteristics of a completed departmental recommendation package as described in Chapter Nine of this book. Such an appendix is readily compiled from the earlier sections of the operating manual. Examples of completed forms can be extracted and assembled into a separate presentation. This appendix will provide managers with a precise picture of the end product of the tactical program. It is a concrete objective which they can strive to attain.

Exhibit 13-1 on the following page is an example of a table of contents that could be used to lead off a Strategy Management operating manual. It shows the topics previously discussed in this chapter and includes page numbers to show the volume of material that would likely be contained within each section.

THE ABC ORGANIZATION

STRATEGY MANAGEMENT OPERATING MANUAL

TABLE OF CONTENTS

PAGE

Exhibit 13-1 Example of a possible table of contents to a Strategy Management operating manual.

Post Implementation Review and Maintenance

The implementation of a Strategy Management program, like any other program, can never be perfect. Improvements will always be possible and an organization should not deceive itself by thinking otherwise. It is best to recognize these human limitations while striving to optimize the situation. An organization should anticipate that even with its best efforts mistakes will occur. A wise objective would be to correct these mistakes as soon as possible – normally for the second cycle of operation.

In the early stages of the implementation process, all managers should be made aware that a post implementation review will be made. This will signal that errors on the part of both the project implementation team and the managers themselves are expected. Such an approach is evidence of a flexible and human approach to implementation. It shows that expectations are realistic although the goals call for the highest standards. A commitment to post implementation review presents the picture of a well prepared implementation plan to the managers which will help to win their respect. It is a sound practice for any major undertaking of an organization.

FEEDBACK THROUGH A TROUBLE LOG

A commitment to post implementation review begins with the establishment of a feedback mechanism to evaluate the performance of each component of the Strategy Management process. This mechanism would likely be in the form of a trouble log. A trouble log could be used to record all of the problems and complaints encountered as the process proceeds. Entries in this log would be invited from the members of the implementation team as well as from the managers participating in the program. The managers should be strongly encouraged to contribute so that they will see it as a serious function rather than as a public relations maneuver. An all encompassing invitation stresses the fact that Strategy Management is intended to be the manager's tool. It provides him with an opportunity to mold the system to suit his needs.

Entries in the trouble log should not be limited to negative comments. Managers should be asked to suggest some positive solutions that could be applied to the problems which they uncover. This broadens the scope of participation and results in solutions from those persons best qualified to present them.

Some organizations consciously avoid the use of a formal feedback system as the process is being implemented. Instead, they use an evaluation of Strategy Management by the managers after the program has been completed. Managers are asked to respond to or comment on a series of questions presented to judge the success of the exercise. Information gathered in this manner is usually not reliable. Managers respond the way they think they are expected to respond rather than how they sincerely feel. They perceive that senior management would like to hear that Strategy Management was an unqualified success and answer accordingly. Entries in a trouble log are spontaneous and are more likely to be meaningful. They will permit an organization to improve itself rather than to complement itself.

REACTING TO CHANGING NEEDS OF THE ORGANIZATION

In addition to correcting problems uncovered during the post implementation review, organizations will want to fine tune their

Strategy Management process in accordance with changing needs of their environment. This is maintenance of the program. The original reason for adopting the process, whether it was to solve a problem or to exploit a temporary opportunity, may no longer be present. Hopefully, the problem has been solved or the opportunity has been seized. Some other more pressing need would now occupy the attention of the organization. To optimize the effectiveness of the Strategy Management program, a further tailormaking of the process is now required.

As the most prominent needs of the organization come and go over the years, so too must the Strategy Management program be modified in character. This will permit the process to maintain its high degree of effectiveness as the organization evolves. An organization should always be conscious of the different needs to which it is attempting to respond and the manner in which the management process can be modified to highlight these circumstances. The changing needs will be reflected in the benefits that the organization wishes to derive from the process. Chapter Three presented an extensive portfolio of benefits associated with Strategy Management. As the years go by, an organization can expect that certain individual benefits will become more important than others. This development is caused by the evolution of the organization's needs. Management must be alert to their changing environments and must be anxious to support these changes with improvements to the Strategy Management program. A maintenance program of this sort will allow the process to continue as a healthy vehicle through which management can carry out its responsibilities.

CHANGING THE LEVEL OF THE ACCOUNTING SYSTEM

An organization may come to the conclusion that it is desirable to amend the characteristics of its accounting function. To enhance an organization's ability to exert control, monitor accomplishments and dispense rewards, the level of the accounting system can be lowered to that of expenditure opportunities. Such a development would make the tactical program's expenditure opportunities the centre of focus for both planning and reporting purposes. Modifications of this sort are almost identical

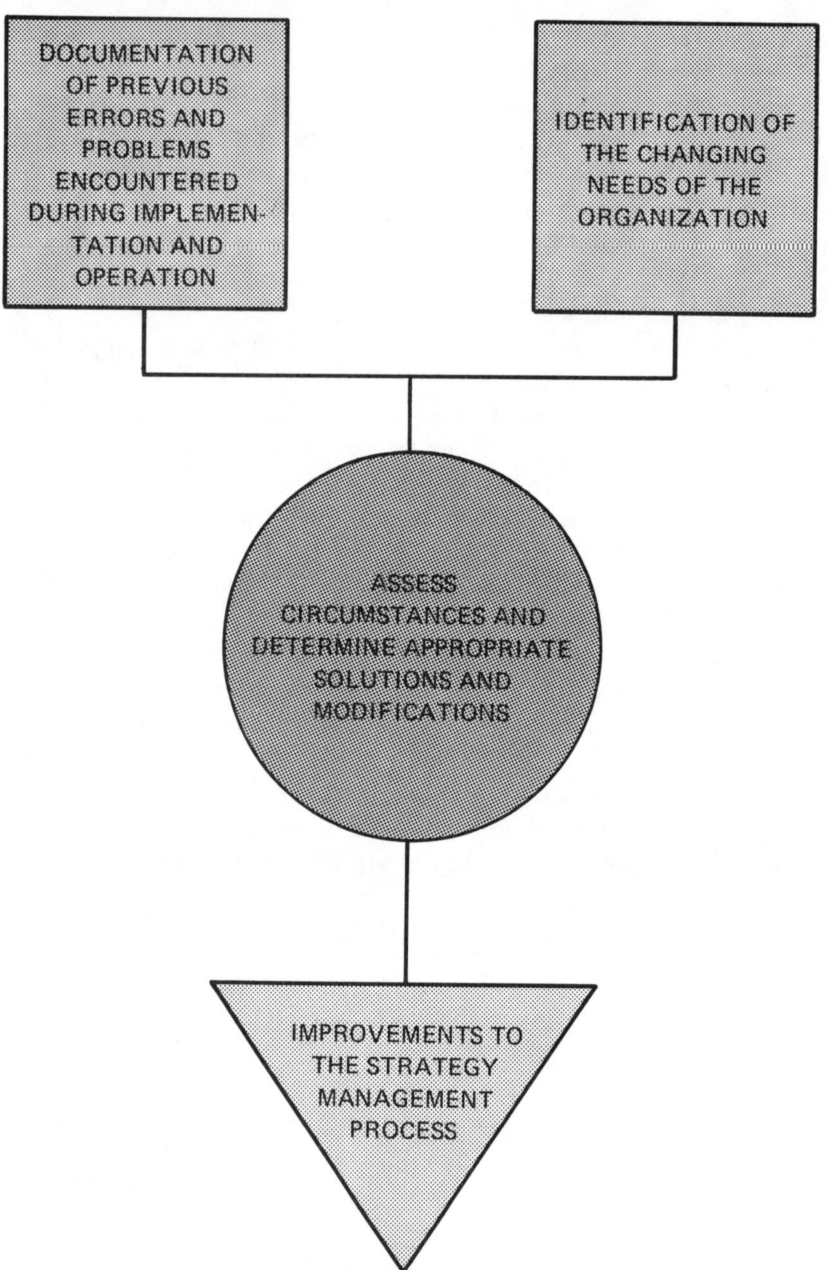

Exhibit 14-1 The post implementation review and maintenance process of Strategy Management.

to the installation of a project accounting system. From the point of view of recording expenses, an expenditure opportunity can be viewed as equivalent to a project. Both are sub-units of the overall department. Expenses can be classified according to these subdivisions in order to align them with specific expenditure opportunities. There would normally be no change in workload to classify these items at a finer level of detail. The effort required to make the expense classification is the same regardless of the coding schemes used. The difficulty arises when modifying the accounting system to cope with these new reporting levels. Depending on the age and flexibility of the accounting system, this task can range in difficulty from a mere changing of consolidation tables to some extensive computer programming adjustments. The training of managers in the use of such new procedures can also be a major chore.

Because of the technical nature of these changes, an organization should be very sure of what it is doing. Modifications to the accounting system need to be well thought out in advance with the benefits to the organization sincerely documented. Changes to the accounting system have a sense of permanence about them and should only be enacted with extreme caution. For this reason, organizations may be advised to wait until the second or third year of operation before attempting to change the level of their accounting system.

COMPUTER APPLICATIONS

Since Strategy Management is primarily a communication tool used by managers within the organization, the opportunity to use computer assistance is rather limited. The clerical functions of the process are the only items which lend themselves to a computer application. These functions would normally be limited to:

1. Summarizing the cross impact analysis exercise beyond the department level. A computer can be used to combine the different cross impact analysis summary matrices prepared by departments participating in the exercise.
2. Tabulating the results of voting exercises used during review meetings. This can be helpful when there is a large group of people analyzing the merits of the expenditure

opportunities as well as when an instantaneous reply is required.

3. Reporting the results of the ranking exercise in an appropriate format. A computer can be quite useful to keep track of how management has ranked certain expenditure opportunities and to display their decisions as required. Modifications to the order of ranking can be easily accepted and reported with the use of computer assistance.

4. Assembling the financial operating plan. A computer can assume many of the clerical chores associated with constructing the financial operating plan. This is especially true when the items of expense used in the expenditure opportunities are the same as those of the accounting system.

The advantages of securing computer assistance for the Strategy Management process are obviously restricted to only very large organizations. The clerical portion of the process in smaller organizations could not justify such an investment in development and operation effort.

A LOOK TO THE FUTURE

In this chapter, we have tried to present the idea of a continuous refinement of the Strategy Management process. This refinement is necessary to eliminate any problems associated with the process and to respond to the evolving culture of the organization. In short, any management process needs constant attention and maintenance if it is to continue operating at peak effectiveness. In closing this book, it is appropriate to emphasize this idea because the long-term vitality of Strategy Management will directly depend upon an appreciation of this principle.

An organization considering the employment of a Strategy Management program will likely be doing so as the result of a distinct behavioural philosophy. Probably, it is an organization that is constantly searching for better management methods and is receptive to new operating ideas. Such an organization possesses an appetite for change when improvement can be made and sees this characteristic as an intrinsic strength and competitive advantage. Nevertheless, the installation of a Strategy Management program should not be seen as the last victory which will forever satisfy this appetite of an organization. It is one step, perhaps large, along a never-ending road. For this reason, it is imperative that all organizations protect and nurture their sense of adventure and continue their exploration for management improvement as well as their search for personal and organizational development.

Glossary

Build Strategy A course of action designed to increase the market share of a business in a particular industry significantly and permanently. This type of strategy usually requires substantial cash expenditure.

Business portfolio matrix A graphic summary of the industry attractiveness, competitive position, market share and market standing of an organization's portfolio of businesses. It is useful in managing and directing strategic business units.

Charter of objectives A formal statement of the fundamental purpose or mission of an organization based upon the needs of society the organization intends to fill. This purpose is expressed as a specific function and includes basic policy statements regarding the categories of objectives important to the corporation.

Competitive position The relationship between a specific business and either the total industry of which it is a part or the key competitors within that industry.

Competitor information bureau The department responsible for the collection and subsequent dissemination of information used to determine the strengths and weaknesses of competitors.

Control A process that assists management in keeping the activities of an organization on plan and that provides information necessary for the determination of rewards. Its function is to ascertain how closely actual events come to planned events with respect to both costs and results.

Corporate strategy That part of the planning process in which an organization determines the appropriate businesses in which it should be participating. Corporate strategy is derived from the charter of objectives.

Cross impact analysis An exercise performed during preparation of the tactical program. It provides a framework for managers to coordinate their receiver/supplier service relationships in accordance with their understanding of the objectives they have developed for the coming year's operations.

Direct costs The cost portion of the variable components of the tactical program. Direct costs are comprised of direct labour and direct material expenditures.

Discretionary components Those parts of the tactical program representing expenditures that do not vary directly in proportion to the volume of business. Discretionary components are the support, service or overhead portions of an organization.

Expenditure opportunity progress report Formal documentation of actual performance compared with planned performance in regard to an individual expenditure opportunity. The report also includes any corrective action which a manager may have planned.

Expenditure opportunity series A small number (from 2 to 5) of comprehensive cost/benefit presentations made by a manager during preparation of the tactical program. Each expenditure opportunity represents an incremental alternative. The series enables management to optimize the organization's resource allocation through a systematic selection of high priority expenditure opportunities.

Financial resource profile Formal documentation of the strengths and weaknesses of a business unit in regard to the key financial issues it faces. The profile includes a similar report for each significant competitor and determines which industry participant is strongest within each financial category.

Goals and objectives Planned positions or results which one strives to attain or realize. They are the highest level in the hierarchy of goals, objectives, strategies and tactics. Goals and objectives can be either open-ended or close-ended.

Harvest strategy That course of action designed to maximize the return on the strategic business unit's existing investment by gradually withdrawing resources. This strategy usually results in a significant generation of cash resources.

Human resource profile Formal documentation of the strengths and weaknesses of a business unit in regard to the key people issues it faces. The profile includes a similar report for each significant competitor and determines which industry participant is strongest within each human resource category.

Industry attractiveness The complementary issue to competitive position. It is also used during corporate strategy formulation. Industry attractiveness is an overall evaluation of the environment of a strategic business unit with respect to the contribution made to an organization's charter of objectives.

Maintain strategy That course of action designed to keep the current competitive position of the strategic business unit while it progresses through the normal stages of industry life cycle. This strategy usually requires a small investment of cash resources since it is used quite frequently in a growing industry.

Organizational resource profile Formal documentation of the strengths and weaknesses of a business unit in regard to the systems, practices and procedures that it has established for itself. It includes a similar report for each significant competitor and determines which industry participant is strongest within each organizational resource category.

Physical resource profile Formal documentation of the strengths and weaknesses of a business unit in regard to fixed assets such as plants, equipment and building. It includes a similar report for each significant competitor and determines which industry participant is strongest within each physical resource category.

Project implementation team The group that is responsible for the design, development and introduction of a Strategy Management program. It is frequently supported by outside management consultants. The majority of team members are operational managers rather than corporate planning staff.

Revenue program The revenue generating activity portion of the variable components of the overall tactical program. The revenue program describes the action plans necessary to realize the strategic intentions of the organization in regard to sales.

Rewards Money as well as other things of value given to employees in recognition of actual performance. Rewards can be either positive or negative (penalties) and are designed to motivate employees to execute the pre-established plans of the organization effectively.

Segmentation analysis Formal documentation of the strengths and weaknesses of a business unit in regard to external market characteristics rather than internal resource characteristics. It includes a similar report for each significant competitor and determines which industry participant is strongest within each market segment.

Stair chart A systematic presentation that compares similar schedules of different strategy recommendations prepared by strategic business units. It concentrates on the financial plan portion of the strategy recommendation, although all other components can be similarly analyzed.

Statement of action plans for the coming year Formal documentation of a first-line manager's perception of what the organization's strategies mean to that manager. This statement represents the conclusion of the organization's efforts to bridge the communication gap between strategies and tactics.

Statement of mission, role or mandate Formal documentation of a first-line manager's perception of the basic role or purpose of the organizational division for which that manager is responsible. This statement is part of the communication bridge between strategies and tactics.

Strategic business unit (SBU) An organizational division, either actual or artificial, representing an independent business mission. Each strategic business unit is a discrete operating entity with its own market jurisdiction; its own unique resource, technology or expertise requirements; and its own set of competitors.

Strategy The major action programs of a medium-to long-term nature employed by an organization to realize its mission, goals and objectives.

Strategy chronicle A formal document prepared by senior management for the benefit of middle or strategic business unit management. It is a communication instrument used to report the results of senior management's efforts in regard to the establishment of the charter of objectives and the formulation of corporate strategy.

Strategy management A unifying approach to managing all the resources of an organization. It effectively integrates the phases planning with both implementation programs and control and measurement of results.

Strategy progress report Formal documentation of the actual strategic performance of an individual strategic business unit in comparison with its planned strategic performance. The report includes any corrective action which may be planned as well as an assessment of the continued validity of the assumptions upon which the strategy was recommended and approved.

Strategy recommendation A presentation made by strategic business unit management to senior management regarding what they want to do, how they plan to do it, what resources will be required and what benefits or results will be produced. The strategy recommendation serves as a request for investment and is made only after a thorough analysis has been performed by the strategic business unit.

Tactical program That part of the planning process which translates the strategies of an organization into day-to-day action plans for employees. It is normally concerned with the coming year.

Tactics The action programs an organization employs to realize its strategies. Tactics are immediate and deal with short-term plans directly before execution.

Selected Readings

Allen, Michael G.: "Diagramming GE's Planning for What's Watt," *Planning Review,* vol. 5, no. 5, September 1977, pp. 3-9.

———: "Strategic Planning with a Competitive Focus," *The McKinsey Quarterly,* Autumn 1978.

Business Week: "Norton Co.: Continuing a Successful Diversification Beyond Abrasives," July 9, 1979, pp. 81-82.

———: "Olin's Shift to Strategy Planning," March 27, 1978, pp. 102-105.

———: "The New Planning," December 18, 1978, pp. 62-67.

———: "Piercing Fog in the Executive Suite," April 28, 1975, pp. 46-54.

———: "Union Carbide: Its Six Business Strategy Is Light on Chemicals," September 24, 1979, pp. 97-100.

———: "Wanted: A Manager to Fit Each Strategy," February 25, 1980, pp. 166-173.

Christopher, William F.: *Management for the 1980's,* AMACOM, New York, 1980.

Cushman, Robert: "Norton's Top-Down, Bottom-Up Planning Process," *Planning Review,* vol. 7, no. 6, November 1979, pp. 3-8, 48.

Drucker, Peter F.: *The Practice of Management,* Harper and Row, New York, 1954.

Gale, Bradley T.: "Planning for Profit," *Planning Review,* vol. 6, no. 1, January 1978, pp. 4-7, 30-32.

Hall, William K.: "SBU's: Hot, New Topic in the Management of Diversification," *Business Horizons,* February 1978.

Hedley, Barry: "Strategy and the Business Portfolio," *Long Range Planning,* vol. 10, no. 1, February 1977, pp. 9-15.

Hofer, Charles W. and Dan Schendel: *Strategy Formulation: Analytical Concepts,* West Publishing Company, St. Paul, 1978.

Hussey, D.E.: "Portfolio Analysis: Practical Experience with the Directional Policy Matrix," *Long Range Planning,* vol. 11, no. 4, August 1978, pp. 2-8.

Keichel, Walter: "Playing by the Rules of the Corporate Strategy Game," *Fortune,* September 24, 1979, pp. 110-115.

Kotler, Philip: "Harvesting Strategies for Weak Products," *Business Horizons,* August 1978.

Lin, Thomas W.: "Corporate Planning and Budgeting: An Integrated Approach," *Managerial Planning,* May-June 1979, pp. 29-33.

Lofthouse, Stephen: "Strategy, Cross-Subsidization and the Business Portfolio," *Long Range Planning,* vol. 11, no. 4, August 1978, p. 58.

Naylor, Thomas H.: "The U.S. Needs Strategic Planning," *Business Week,* December 17, 1979, pp. 18-19.

Palesy, Steven R.: "Motivating Line Management Using the Planning Process," *Planning Review,* vol. 8, no. 2, March 1980.

Pennington, Malcolm W. and Robert J. Allio,: *"Corporate Planning: Techniques and Applications,"* AMACOM, New York, 1979.

Rothschild, William E.: "Competitor Analysis: The Missing Link in Strategy," *Management Review,* July 1979.

———: *Putting It All Together: A Guide to Strategic Thinking,* AMACOM, New York, 1976.

———: *Strategic Alternatives: Selection, Development and Implementation,* AMACOM, New York, 1979.

Seed, Allen H.: "Strategic Planning: The Cutting Edge of Management Accounting," *Management Accounting,* vol. 61, no. 11, May 1980, pp. 10-16.

Thompson, Arthur A. and A.J. Strickland: *Strategy Formulation and Implementation,* Business Publications, Inc., Dallas, 1980.

Index